Praise for Ou

T0029757

"Chris Hedges is the greatest radical writer and journalist of our generation! His courage and consistency are legendary! . . . This magnificent book confirms his grand stature!"

—Cornel West, author of *Race Matters*

"This book could change everything. It could change our minds. It could buttress our hearts. It could make graspable why today's prisons are contemporary slave plantations. I couldn't put it down, and I tried."

—Alice Walker, author of *The Color Purple*

"Chris Hedges opens the door for the long-buried talents of the incarcerated. In turn, they open the door to a new and valuable perspective for us all."

—Tom Fontana, Emmy Award–winning creator of *Oz*

"Raw and intimate. . . . Combining searing, well-informed critiques of the U.S. criminal justice system with sympathetic character profiles and inspirational accounts of intellectual and emotional breakthroughs, this is a powerful look at how creative expression can provide 'a taste of freedom.'"

—*Publishers Weekly*

"Pulitzer-winning journalist Hedges documents the efforts of his drama class students in East Jersey State Prison to write *Caged*, a play consisting of scenes from their lives. . . . Through the men's labor of love, Hedges calls on us to question our view of incarcerated people and our understanding of education's purpose."

—*Booklist*

"Activist and Pulitzer Prize–winning journalist Hedges recounts his time teaching in a New Jersey prison. .... An affecting book in which every page urges more humane treatment of prisoners."

—*Kirkus Reviews*

"A gumbo of genres: personal narratives, plays, songs, poems, and history. There are lurid tales of barbarity and inhumanity, but there is hope in the transformative power of human relationships."

—*Christian Science Monitor*

"*Our Class* will make you angry, but it will also inspire."

—Nathan J. Robinson, *Current Affairs* (podcast)

Also by
Chris Hedges

Our Class

Trauma and
Transformation
in an
American Prison

Chris Hedges

Simon & Schuster Paperbacks
New York   London   Toronto   Sydney   New Delhi

Simon & Schuster Paperbacks
An Imprint of Simon & Schuster, Inc.
1230 Avenue of the Americas
New York, NY 10020

First Simon & Schuster trade paperback edition October 2022

SIMON & SCHUSTER PAPERBACKS and colophon are registered
trademarks of Simon & Schuster, Inc.

For information about special discounts for bulk
purchases, please contact Simon & Schuster Special Sales
at 1-866-506-1949 or business@simonandschuster.com.

The Simon & Schuster Speakers Bureau can bring authors
to your live event. For more information or to book an event,
contact the Simon & Schuster Speakers Bureau at 1-866-248-3049
or visit our website at www.simonspeakers.com.

Interior design by Lewelin Polanco

Manufactured in the United States of America

1 3 5 7 9 10 8 6 4 2

The Library of Congress has cataloged the hardcover edition as follows:

Names: Hedges, Chris, author.
Title: Our class : trauma and transformation
in an American prison / Chris Hedges.
Description: First hardcover edition. | New York : Simon & Schuster, [2021] |
Includes bibliographical references and index.
Identifiers: LCCN 2021018661 | ISBN 9781982154431 (hardcover) | ISBN
9781982154448 (trade paperback) | ISBN 9781982154455 (ebook)
Subjects: LCSH: East Jersey State Prison. | Prisoners—New Jersey—Rahway—
Case studies. | Prisoners—Education—New Jersey—Rahway—Case studies. |
Criminals—Rehabilitation—New Jersey—Rahway—Case studies. | Criminal
justice, Administration of—New Jersey—Rahway—Case studies.
Classification: LCC HV9475.N52 E244 2021 | DDC 365/.60922749—dc23
LC record available at https://lccn.loc.gov/2021018661

ISBN 978-1-9821-5443-1
ISBN 978-1-9281-5444-8 (pbk)
ISBN 978-1-9821-5445-5 (ebook)

For Eunice,
Nunc scio quid sit amor

The play's the thing wherein I'll catch the conscience of the king.[1]

—William Shakespeare, *Hamlet*

Criminals, it turns out, are the one social group in America we have permission to hate. In "colorblind" America, criminals are the new whipping boys. They are entitled to no respect and little moral concern. Like the "colored" in the years following emancipation, criminals today are deemed a characterless and purposeless people, deserving of our collective scorn and contempt. When we say someone was "treated like a criminal," what we mean to say is that he or she was treated as less than human, like a shameful creature. Hundreds of years ago, our nation put those considered less than human in shackles; less than one hundred years ago, we relegated them to the other side of town; today we put them in cages. Once released, they find that a heavy and cruel hand has been laid upon them.[2]

—Michelle Alexander, *The New Jim Crow*

America by the early twenty-first century, had, in disturbing ways, come to resemble America in the late nineteenth century. In 1800 the three-fifths clause gave white voters political power from a black population that was itself barred from voting, and after 2000, prison gerrymandering was doing exactly the same thing in numerous states across the country. After 1865, African American desires for equality and civil rights in the South following the American Civil War led whites to criminalize African American communities in new ways and then sent record numbers of blacks to prison in that region. Similarly, a dramatic spike in black incarceration followed the civil rights movement—a movement that epitomized [the maximum security state prison] Attica. From 1965 onward, black communities were increasingly criminalized, and by 2005, African Americans constituted 40 percent of the US prison population, while remaining less than 13 percent of its overall population. And just as businesses had profited from the increased number of Americans in penal facilities after 1870, so did they seek the labor of a growing captive prison population after 1970. In both centuries, white Americans had responded to black claims for freedom by beefing up, and making more punitive, the nation's criminal justice system. In both centuries, in turn, the American criminal justice system disproportionately criminalized, policed, and forced the labor of incarcerated, disenfranchised African Americans in ways that wrought incalculable damage both in and outside of America's penal institutions.[3]

—Heather Ann Thompson, *Blood in the Water: The Attica Prison Uprising of 1971 and Its Legacy*

Go down, Moses
Way down in Egypt's land
Tell ol' Pharaoh to
Let my people go!

—"Go Down, Moses (Let My People Go!)", African American spiritual

Contents

one

| The Call |

When you try to stand up and look the world in the face
like you had a right to be here, you have attacked the
entire power structure of the Western world.[1]

—James Baldwin

On September 5, 2013, I pulled my old Volvo wagon—a
bumper sticker reading "This is the Rebel Base" stuck on
the back by my wife, a *Star Wars* fan—into the parking lot at
East Jersey State Prison in Rahway, New Jersey. I had taught
college-level courses in New Jersey prisons for the past three
years. But neither my new students nor I had any idea that night
that we were embarking on a journey that would shatter their
protective emotional walls, or that years later our lives would be
deeply intertwined.

I put my wallet and phone in the glove compartment, emptied
my pockets of coins, and dumped them in the console between the
front seats. I made sure I had my driver's license. I gathered up
my books, plays by August Wilson, James Baldwin, John Herbert,
Tarell Alvin McCraney, Miguel Piñero, Amiri Baraka, and a copy
of Michelle Alexander's *The New Jim Crow: Mass Incarceration
in the Age of Colorblindness*. I locked the car and walked toward
the maximum security men's prison, past the telephone poles that
dotted the parking lot, each topped with two square spotlights.

East Jersey State Prison in Rahway was shaped like an X. At its center was a massive gray dome with boarded-up windows, surrounded at its base by a ring of oxidized copper. The wings of the prison stretched out in four directions from the dome. The brick walls of each wing were painted a dull ochre color with off-white patches. There were seventeen oblong windows on each wing with white metal bars. Turrets with what looked like brass spikes on top stood at the far end of these brick wings. The walls were covered with patches of ivy. The dull black roof was peaked and discolored by a patchwork of darker and lighter sections from repairs. Directly over the entrance to the prison, below the dome, was a guard tower constructed of Plexiglas windows. At the base of the guard tower were large yellow letters, EJSP, set against a blue background. The prison complex was ringed with cyclone fencing topped with bright, shiny coils of razor wire. At the front entrance of the prison, on the left, stood a chrome-colored communications tower with antennas.

In the lobby, which led directly into the rotunda covered by the dome, plastic chairs faced a Plexiglas booth. A bulky corrections officer sat at a desk behind the Plexiglas. I pushed my car keys through the small metal slot below the Plexiglas, told him my name, which he checked on an authorization form, and exchanged my driver's license for a plastic visitor's badge. I sat for a half hour and waited to be called.

East Jersey State Prison, originally called New Jersey Reformatory, opened in 1896 as a reformatory for juveniles. It soon became known as Rahway State Prison. There were contact visits every Sunday when the middleweight boxer Rubin "Hurricane" Carter was imprisoned at Rahway from 1967 until his release in 1985. A contact visit, he writes, "was equal to mouth-to-mouth resuscitation for us inmates." There were numerous sports programs, including a boxing program. A drama group called Theater of the Forgotten came in every week to perform plays. Community volunteers ran various programs. The prisoners put on a variety show every year. The prison held an annual Achievement Night when families came to ceremonies where prisoners officially graduated from training and academic programs.[2] There were notorious family days where, out by the back fence, girlfriends and wives would leave pregnant. All of that was gone when I arrived, part of the steady stripping down of programs that have reduced most prisons to warehouses. Rahway State Prison changed its name to East Jersey State Prison in 1988, following complaints from local residents who claimed that naming the prison after the city of Rahway negatively affected property values. Similarly, Trenton State Prison changed its name to New Jersey State Prison. But prisoners continue to refer to the prisons as Rahway and Trenton.

There were riots in 1952, when about 230 prisoners seized a two-story dormitory wing and took nine corrections officers hostage, to protest a rash of beatings. Riots again erupted on Thanksgiving Day 1971, six months after the arrival of a new warden who abolished many recreational and sports programs and imposed a series of harsh and punitive rules. During his short tenure, there were two murders, ten escapes, three prisoners who died from a lack of medical care, a corrections officer stabbed, another hospitalized after being attacked with a pool cue, and a strike by the prison guards.[3] The prisoners took six guards hostage in the 1971 riot, along with the warden, who had foolishly waded into the crowd of prisoners and told them there was no way they could win—that all he had to do was push a button to call in the state police. As Carter recalled in his 1974 memoir *The Sixteenth Round: From Number 1 Contender to Number 45472*, the warden was seized by the enraged mob and "stabbed, kicked, beat over the back with a fire extinguisher, had a chair broken over his head, and ended up the first superintendent in New Jersey prison history to be taken hostage in a riot."[4]

The rioters, many drunk from homemade prison wine, or pruno,[5] eventually issued a list of grievances that included demands for better food, a restoration and expansion of educational and vocational programs, and an end to the chronic shortage of medical supplies, including aspirin. The prisoners in the 1971 uprising dropped bed sheets from prison windows with messages painted on them such as "We are fighting for better food, a new parole system, and no brutality." They held out for 115 hours before negotiations finally resolved the revolt. A year later, three prisoners escaped by sawing through the bars of a third-floor window.

Carter's book galvanized outside support from celebrities, including Muhammad Ali and also Bob Dylan, who opened his 1976 album, *Desire*, with "Hurricane," an eight-and-a-half-minute epic he cowrote to publicize the injustice of Carter's imprisonment.[6] The album sold 2 million copies and spent five weeks at number one. Carter's two murder convictions were eventually overturned, and he was released in 1985. Dwight Muhammad Qawi,[7] a world champion boxer in two weight classes—light heavyweight and cruiserweight—began his boxing career in Rahway Prison's boxing program. He was trained in the prison gym, in part, by another inmate, James Onque Scott Jr., a light heavyweight who was ranked number two by the World Boxing Association (WBA) and who fought in seven sanctioned bouts televised nationally from the prison.

One of the students in my first class at East Jersey State Prison, James Leak, was a New Jersey Golden Gloves champion who had spent three years as an Army Ranger on the US Army boxing team. I boxed for nearly three years as a welterweight for the Greater Boston YMCA boxing team while I was a student at Harvard Divinity School. One time after class, I told Leak I would never have been a great boxer because my hands were not big, nor was I very quick. I held up my right hand with the fingers spread apart. He placed his hand flat against mine. Our hands were the same size. "It's what's in here," he said, tapping his heart, "and what's in here"—he tapped his head—"that counts."

Numerous Hollywood films shot scenes in the prison, including *Crazy Joe*, a film about Joseph Gallo, a member of the Colombo crime family, with Peter Boyle in the title role, and *Lock Up*, starring Sylvester Stallone and Donald Sutherland; as well as *Malcolm X*, directed and cowritten by Spike Lee and starring Denzel Washington; *He Got Game*, written and produced by Spike Lee; *Ocean's Eleven*, with George Clooney and Brad Pitt; *Jersey Boys*; *The Irishman*, which was directed and produced by Martin Scorsese and starred Robert De Niro, Al Pacino, and Joe Pesci; and *The Hurricane*, a 1999 biopic, with the boxer played by Denzel Washington, who was nominated for an Academy Award for Best Actor for his portrayal of Carter.

My students usually lived with a bunkmate, or bunkie, in double cells roughly fifteen feet long, four and a half feet wide, and ten feet high. The cells were grouped together in cell blocks, or wings. If they lived in a single cell on One Wing or Four Wing, the cells were about nine feet long and seven feet high. Most prisoners could hold out their arms and touch each side of the cell wall. Those in single cells could also usually reach up to touch the ceiling. There was a metal toilet, a metal washbasin, one or two bunks, a table, a footlocker, shelves, and a single lightbulb hanging from the ceiling. It was sweltering in the summer, and cold and drafty in the winter.

I stumbled into prison teaching in 2010 after finishing my book *Empire of Illusion: The End of Literacy and the Triumph of Spectacle*. My neighbor Celia Chazelle, a scholar of early medieval history and the head of the History Department at The College of New Jersey, was teaching noncredit courses at the Albert C. Wagner Youth Correctional Facility in Bordentown, New Jersey. She asked me if I would be willing to teach.[8] I had taught before at Columbia University, New York University, Princeton University, and the University of Toronto. It was hard, she said, to recruit college professors who were unpaid, burdened with the cost of buying texts for their students, and required to travel—often over an hour each way—to teach a night class at a prison in a rural part of New Jersey.

Teaching in state prisons returned me to my original calling as a minister working with those who lived in depressed urban enclaves. I had spent two and a half years living in Roxbury, Boston's poorest neighborhood, while in divinity school. I ran a small church, and I preached on Sundays. I oversaw a youth program. I presided at funerals, which entailed helping to carry the casket into the church, opening the lid, and lifting transparent paper placed by the morticians over the face of the dead before conducting the service. The church and manse, where I lived, were across the street from the Mission Main and Mission Extension housing projects, at the time the most violent in the city. I skipped numerous classes to attend juvenile court with mothers and their children from the projects.

I intended to be ordained to serve in an urban church, but I grew increasingly disillusioned with the posturing by the liberal church and my liberal divinity school classmates, who too often talked about empowering people they never met. Too many "liked" the poor but did not like the smell of the poor. I took a leave of absence to study Spanish at the language school run by the Maryknolls, a Catholic missionary society, in Cochabamba, Bolivia. After four months there, I lived in La Paz for two months; then Lima, Peru; and finally Buenos Aires. I worked as a freelance reporter for several newspapers, including for the *Washington Post*, and covered the 1982 Falklands War between England and Argentina from Buenos Aires for National Public Radio. That fall, I returned to Cambridge, Massachusetts, to complete my Master of Divinity degree but had decided that when I graduated I would go to El Salvador as a reporter to cover the war.

The writer James Baldwin, the son of a preacher, as I was—and, for a time, a preacher himself—said that he left the pulpit to preach the Gospel. Baldwin saw how the institutional church was often the enemy of mercy and justice. He saw how it too easily devolved into a sanctimonious club whose members glorified themselves at the expense of others. Baldwin, who was gay and Black, was not interested in subjugating justice and love to the restrictions imposed by any institution, least of all the church. And that is why there is more Gospel—true Gospel—in Baldwin than in the writings of nearly all the theologians and preachers who were his contemporaries. His books and essays are prophetic sermons: among them, *Nobody Knows My Name*, *The Fire Next Time*, and *The Devil Finds Work*. Chapter titles include: "Princes and Power" and "Down at the Cross." His 1953 semi-autobiographical novel, *Go Tell It on the Mountain*, is divided into three chapters: "The Seventh Day," "The Prayers of the Saints," and "The Threshing Floor."

Baldwin deplored the self-love in American society—he counted white churches as being in the vanguard of self-love—and denounced what he called "the lie of their pretended humanism." In his 1963 book-length essay *The Fire Next Time*, he writes: "[T]here was not love in the church. It was a mask for hatred and self-hatred and despair. The transfiguring power of the Holy Ghost ended when the service ended, and salvation stopped at the church door. When we were told to love everybody, I had thought that meant *everybody*. But no. It applied only to those who believed as we did, and it did not apply to white people at all."[9] He goes on: "If the concept of God has any validity or any use, it can only be to make us larger, freer, and more loving. If God cannot do this, then it is time we got rid of Him."[10]

Baldwin, like George Orwell, names truths that few others have the courage to name. He condemns evils that are held up as virtues by the powerful and the pious. He, like Orwell, is relentlessly self-critical and calls out the hypocrisies of the liberal elites and the Left, whose moral posturing is often not accompanied by the courage and self-sacrifice demanded in the fight against radical evil. Baldwin is true to a spirit and power beyond his control. He is, in religious language, possessed. And he knows it.

"The artist and the revolutionary function as they function," Baldwin writes, "and pay whatever dues they must pay behind it because they are both possessed by a vision, and they do not so much follow this vision as find themselves driven by it. Otherwise, they could never endure, much less embrace, the lives they are compelled to lead."[11]

This was a sentiment understood by Orwell, an Englishman who fought against the Fascists in the Spanish Civil War, where at the Aragon Front in May 1937 he was shot through the neck by a sniper. He lived with and wrote about those living on the streets in Paris and London, as well as with impoverished coal miners in the north of England.

"My starting point is always a feeling of partisanship, a sense of injustice," Orwell writes. "When I sit down to write a book, I do not say to myself, 'I am going to produce a work of art.' I write it because there is some lie that I want to expose, some fact to which I want to draw attention, and my initial concern is to get a hearing."[12]

Orwell, like Baldwin, disdained the hypocrisy of the institutional church. He observed that pious Christian capitalists "do not seem to be perceptibly different" from other capitalists. "Religious belief," he writes "is frequently a psychological device to avoid repentance." Moses, the pet raven in the 1945 novel *Animal Farm,* is used to pacify the other animals, telling them they will all go to an animal paradise called Sugarcandy Mountain once their days of labor and suffering come to an end.[13]

"As long as supernatural beliefs persist, men can be exploited by cunning priests and oligarchs, and the technical progress which is the prerequisite of a just society cannot be achieved," Orwell writes.[14]

And yet, like Baldwin, Orwell feared the sanctification of

state power and the rise of the manufactured idols that took the place of God; those who promised an earthly rather than heavenly paradise. Orwell struggled throughout his life to find a belief system strong enough to oppose it. "If our civilization does not regenerate itself, it is likely to perish," he writes shortly before publishing *Animal Farm*. That regeneration, at least in Europe, he said, would have to draw on a moral code "based on Christian principles."[15]

In *The Fire Next Time,* Baldwin writes:

> Life is tragic simply because the earth turns, and the sun inexorably rises and sets, and one day, for each of us, the sun will go down for the last, last time. Perhaps the whole root of our trouble, the human trouble, is that we will sacrifice all the beauty of our lives, will imprison ourselves in totems, taboos, crosses, blood sacrifices, steeples, mosques, races, armies, flags, nations, in order to deny the fact of death, which is the only fact we have. It seems to me that one ought to rejoice in the *fact* of death—ought to decide, indeed, to *earn* one's death by confronting with passion the conundrum of life. One is responsible to life: It is the small beacon in that terrifying darkness from which we come and to which we shall return. One must negotiate this passage as nobly as possible, for the sake of those who are coming after us.[16]

A few weeks before graduation and leaving for El Salvador in the late spring of 1983, I had a final meeting in Albany, New York, with the committee that oversaw my ordination. My father, who had spent three decades as a minister, waited outside the conference room. I had already purchased a one-way ticket to El Salvador, where the military government, backed by the United States, was slaughtering hundreds of people a month. I had already decided, as Baldwin and Orwell did earlier, to use my writing as a weapon. I would stand with the oppressed. I would amplify their voice. I would document their suffering. I would name the injustices being done to them. I would shine a light into the hidden machinery of power. That was, to use religious language, my calling.

I would report on the war in El Salvador for the next five years as a freelance reporter for the *Christian Science Monitor* and National Public Radio, and, later, as the Central America bureau chief for the *Dallas Morning News*. And after leaving Central America, I worked for fifteen years, most of them with the *New York Times*, in war zones in the Middle East, Africa, and the former Yugoslavia. I would experience the worst of human evil. I would taste too much of my own fear. I would imbibe and became addicted to the intoxication and rush of violence. I would witness the randomness of death. And I would learn the bitter fact that we live in a morally neutral universe, that the rain falls on the just and the unjust.

Reporting on the war in El Salvador was not something the Presbyterian Church recognized as a valid ministry. When I informed the committee of my calling, there was a long silence. Then the head of the committee said coldly: "We don't ordain journalists." I left the conference room and met my father outside. I told him I was not to be ordained. It must have been hard for him to see his son come so close to ordination, only to have it slip away, and hard to know that his son was leaving for a conflict in which reporters and photographers had been killed and would be killed. But what the church would not validate, my father did.

"You are ordained to write," he told me.

A few weeks after I started teaching at East Jersey State Prison, I met with the other professors in a restaurant near the prison before our classes. All of us, it turned out, had graduated from seminary, although only one of us served in the church. This vocational synchronicity made sense. Mass incarceration is the civil rights issue of our time. The liberal church, which left the inner city with white flight, had failed to connect its purported concern for the marginalized and the oppressed with meaningful social action. This disconnection had largely neutered its prophetic voice. The church too often became infected by the cult of the self that defines consumer culture. It went down the dead-end path of a narcissistic, self-involved, "How-is-it-with-me?" form of spirituality. Its mission to stand, as the theologian James Cone writes in his 2011 book *The Cross and the Lynching Tree*, with the "crucified" of the earth was lost in all but rhetoric.

The ancient Greeks, like James Cone, understood that we gain a conscience only by building relationships with those who suffer. These relationships place us within the circle of contamination. They force us to confront our own vulnerability, the possibility of our own suffering. They make us ask what we must do. Aristotle understood that virtue always entails action. Those who do not act, Aristotle warns, those who are always asleep, can never be virtuous. It does not matter what they profess.

Most of my students in prison are Muslims. I am not bringing them to Jesus. I speak Arabic, and I spent seven years in the Middle East. I have a deep respect for Islam. I saw in my twenty years outside the United States how men and women of all faiths, or no faith, and in all cultures, exhibited tremendous courage to confront the oppressor in behalf of the oppressed. There is no religious or cultural hierarchy. What people believe, or what language they speak, or where they live, does not determine the ethical life. It is what they do. If there is one constant, it is this, it is that the privileged too often turn their backs on the less privileged.

The point of ministry is to bear witness, not to dream up schemes to grow congregations or engage in religious chauvinism. It is to do the work we are called to do. It is to have faith, as the radical priest Daniel Berrigan—who baptized my youngest daughter—said, to carry out "the good" insofar as we can discern the good. Faith, Berrigan argued, is the belief that the "good draws to it the good." Faith requires us to trust that acts of kindness and empathy, an unequivocal commitment to justice and mercy, and the courage to denounce and defy the crimes of the oppressor, have an unseen, incalculable power that ripples outward and transforms lives. We are called to carry out the good, or at least the good so far as we can determine it, and let it go. The Buddhists call this Karma. But, as Berrigan told me, for us as Christians, we do not know where it goes. We trust, even in spite of empirical evidence to the contrary, that it goes somewhere; that it makes the world a better place.

By 2014, I had been teaching in New Jersey prisons, including the Albert C. Wagner Youth Correctional Facility in Bordentown, State Prison in Trenton, and East Jersey State Prison in Rahway, for four years. That year, I was ordained as a Presbyterian minister for my prison work. The service was presided over by the theologian James Cone, who taught at Union Theological Seminary in the City of New York, and the moral philosopher and Princeton University professor Cornel West. The ordination was held in the depressed section of Elizabeth, New Jersey, in the church of my Harvard Divinity School classmate the Reverend Michael Granzen, who had reopened my ordination process. For music, we hired the New York–based Michael Packer Blues Band. We invited the families of my students. We rewrote the service to focus on the incarcerated and those, especially children, who endure the loss of people they love. My wife, Eunice Wong, who taught poetry in New Jersey State Prison, the men's supermax prison in Trenton, got permission to read two of her students' poems in the opening minutes of the service.

One of the poems, called "Gone," was by Tairahaan Mallard. One morning, when he was in the fifth grade, Mallard woke up to find that his mother had abandoned him and his younger siblings. She never returned.

I awaken on my own.
Strange. Mommy normally wakes me up.
Us, rather. My three brothers and baby sister.
But not today. Today I awake on my own.
Why? Where's mommy.
I'm the only one awake.
Five children, one pull-out bed. In the living room.
Where's mommy?
I walk towards the bathroom.
Cold, wooden floors, squeaking with every step.
Nobody. Nobody's in there.
Where's mommy?
She's got to be in her room. Must be.
No place else she could be.
No one. Nothing but empty beer bottles
And cigarette butts.
Party time's over.
But, where's mommy?
Gone.
Not only is she gone, but where?
Gone is her security.
Gone is my innocence.
Gone is my childhood. Ushering in responsibility.
Prematurely.
Gone is a mother's love for her children.
Gone is her protection.
Gone. But where?
Will she come back? I don't know.
But if she ever does, I will have already been gone.

Eunice also provided two of the highlights of the afternoon, first by appearing in front of the congregation in a black miniskirt, fishnet stockings, combat boots, and a tank top, announcing: "I wore my best Presbyterian minister's wife's outfit today." And at the end of the service, when the blues band began an up-tempo version of "Swing Low, Sweet Chariot." The singer stepped out from behind the microphone and began a soft-shoe shuffle. Eunice leapt up from the pew to join him, her arms swaying back and forth over her long black hair. She beckoned me to follow. It was an unorthodox way to enter the ministry.

I entered into the formal embrace of the church. But in my own mind, and in the mind of my father, who died in 1995, I had been ordained long ago. I was possessed by a vision, a call to tell the truth—which is different from reporting the news—and to stand with those who suffered, from Central America, to Gaza, to Iraq, to Sarajevo, to the United States' vast archipelago of prisons. "You are not really a journalist," my friend and fellow *New York Times* reporter Stephen Kinzer once told me, "you are a minister pretending to be a journalist."

Life is a circle. We return to our origins. We become who we were created to be. My ordination made that circle complete. It was an affirmation of an inner reality, one that Baldwin and Orwell understood.

The profound abandonment that Mallard described in his poem, part of American society's wholesale abandonment of the poor and its endemic racism, was an example of one of the stark social truths that inspired James Cone and his radical, socially liberatory message. In the only ordination sermon James ever gave, he told the congregation:

> The conviction that we are not what the world says about us but rather what God created us to be is what compelled me to respond to the call to become a minister and theologian. The great Black writer James Baldwin wrote about his Harlem junior high school principal who told him that he "didn't have to be

entirely defined by circumstances," that he could rise above them and become the writer he dreamed about becoming. "She was living proof," Baldwin said, "that I was not necessarily what the country said I was."

My mother and father told me the same thing when I was just a child. It did not matter what white people said about us, they told my brothers and me: "Don't believe them. You don't have to be defined by what others say about you or by the limits others try to place on you." I also heard the same message every Sunday at Macedonia A.M.E. Church. "You may be poor," Reverend Hunter proclaimed from the pulpit, "you may be Black, you may be in prison, it doesn't matter, you are still God's child, God's gift to the world. Now go out of this place and show the world that you are just as important and smart as anybody. With God, anything is possible!" That was the message my parents and Black church community gave to me. It was a message I read in the Bible. And I believed it.

Jesus was crucified on a cross as an insurrectionist because he bore witness to the divine truth that no one has to be defined by his or her circumstances. Liberation from oppression is God's gift to the powerless in society. Freedom is Jesus' gift to all who believe. And when one accepts this liberating Gospel and makes the decision to follow Jesus, you must be prepared to go to the cross in service to others—the least of those in society.

Because the Gospel begins and ends with God's solidarity with the poor and weak, ministers who preach that Gospel will inevitably disturb the peace wherever there is injustice. Jesus was a disturber of the peace. A troublemaker. That is why he said, "Do not think that I have come to bring peace to the earth; I have not come to bring peace but a sword. For I have come to

set a man against his father and a daughter against her
mother. . . . Whoever loves father or mother more than
me is not worthy of me; . . . Whoever does not take up
the cross and follow me is not worthy of me. Those who
find their life shall lose it, and those who lose their life
for my sake shall find it" (Matthew 10:34–39). Jesus'
presence creates division and conflict, even in families
and among friends and especially among religious leaders and rulers in government. That was why the Roman
state crucified him, lynched him on Golgotha hill, plac-
ing his exposed, wounded body high and lifted up on
a cross for all to see and learn what would happen to
others who chose to follow the man from Nazareth.

Now, if we Christians today are going to follow this
Jesus and become ordained as one of his ministers, we
too must become disturbers of the peace and run the
risk of being lynched just like Jesus. The great theologian Reinhold Niebuhr said: "If a gospel is preached
without opposition, it is simply not the gospel which
resulted in the cross." It is, in short, not Jesus' gospel.

The love that informs the long struggle for justice, that di-
rects us to stand with the crucified, the love that defines the lives
and words of James Baldwin, George Orwell, James Cone, and
Cornel West, is the most powerful force on earth. It does not
mean we will be spared pain or suffering. It does not mean we
will achieve justice. It does not mean we as distinct individuals
will survive. It does not mean we will escape death. But it gives
us the strength to confront evil, even when it seems certain that
evil will triumph. That love is not a means to an end. It is the
end itself. That is the secret of its omnipotence. That is why it
will never be conquered.

I taught my first prison class in 2010 at Wagner Correctional, which houses men in their teens and early twenties. The course was American history, and I used Howard Zinn's *A People's History of the United States* as my textbook. Wagner, built in the 1930s, had the look and feel of prisons in old black-and-white gangster films. My class met in a small basement room. To get there, I had to pass through a series of descending locked gates. I walked through an open gate that would then close behind me. I would wait fifteen seconds in a holding cell before the next gate opened. I repeated this process several times as I went deeper and deeper into the bowels of the prison. It felt as if I were traveling downward through Dante's circles of hell: limbo, lust, gluttony, greed, anger, heresy, violence, and fraud, and then to the final circle of hell—treachery, where everyone lives frozen in an ice-filled lake. *Lasciate ogni speranza, voi ch'entrate.* Abandon all hope, ye who enter.

We studied Spain's violent decimation of the native inhabitants in the Caribbean and the Americas, the Revolutionary War in the United States, and the genocide of Native Americans. We examined slavery, the Mexican-American War, the Civil War, the occupations of Cuba and the Philippines, President Franklin D. Roosevelt's New Deal, two world wars, and the legacy of racism, capitalist exploitation, and imperialism that continue to infect American society.

We looked at these issues, as Zinn did, through the eyes of Native Americans, immigrants, those who were enslaved, feminists, union leaders, persecuted socialists, anarchists, Communists, abolitionists, antiwar activists, civil rights leaders, and the poor. As I read out loud passages by Sojourner Truth, Chief Joseph, Henry David Thoreau, Frederick Douglass, W. E. B. DuBois, Randolph Bourne, Malcolm X, or Martin Luther King, I would hear students mutter "Damn!" or "We been lied to!" Zinn's work, because it gave primacy to their story rather than to the story of powerful and wealthy white men, captivated them. Zinn elucidated the racial and class structures that, from the inception of the country to the present, perpetuate misery for the poor, and gluttony and privilege for the elite—especially the white elite. A veil was lifted. My students took notes furiously as I plowed through the book in ninety-minute lectures.

Education is not only about knowledge. It is about inspiration. It is about passion. It is about the belief that what we do in life matters. It is about moral choice. It is about taking nothing for granted. It is about challenging assumptions and suppositions. It is about truth and justice. It is about learning how to think. It is about, as Baldwin writes in his essay *The Creative Process*, the ability to drive "to the heart of every matter and expose the question the answer hides."[17] And, as Baldwin notes further, it is about making the world "a more human dwelling place."[18]

Wagner, because it was a youth correctional facility, and the prisoners were young and could be undisciplined, required the imposition of strict rules for classroom behavior. Disagreements could quickly become personal. Homophobia, common in male prisons, generated slurs to belittle others. There were always one or two students that tried to veer the class discussions into tangents, especially since they knew I had lived outside the United States, had covered wars and conflicts, and had been to countries they had only glimpsed on television. In one class, I struggled to redirect the class back to the course material from its insistent questions about the possibility of nuclear war. When I asked why this issue was of such concern to them, a student answered, "Because if there is a nuclear war, the guards will run away and leave us in our cells."

I was unforgiving with those who did not take the class seriously. A student who disrupted the class to mouth off or play the clown, who had little interest in doing the work, sabotaged the chance my students had to learn. An uninterested or unruly student would arrive the next week and find I had crossed his name off the list. My reputation for zero tolerance spread quickly throughout the prison, along with my propensity to be a tough grader. It built a protective wall around my classes for those who had a thirst for education.

The corrections officer rapped on the Plexiglas that first night in Rahway. The three other professors and I were buzzed through the first heavy metal door and into the prison. There were 140 students who had been selected after a rigorous application process from the prison's population of 1,500 to participate in the program known as the New Jersey Scholarship and Transformative Education in Prisons, or NJ-STEP, which allowed them to pursue their college degree. I had twenty-eight of these students in my class.

We walked down a long, drab corridor until we passed through a cavity where a heavy, blue metal door had been electronically opened. I put my shoes, watch, pens, and belt in a plastic bin that rolled through an X-ray machine to an officer at a high wooden desk. I stepped through a metal detector. I lifted my arms to be patted down. The metal door behind us rumbled shut, and an identical door on the other side of the small room rumbled open. I walked into the rotunda. A half circle of metal bars with a gate in the middle separated us from the prison population. The white, throne-like BOSS chair—BOSS stands for Body Orifice Security Scanner, which is used to X-ray the cavities of prisoners for contraband—was on my left.[19] A holding cell with bars on all sides was to my right.

We waited silently. I watched prisoners in khaki uniforms, many carrying meal trays, walk in single file on the other side of the bars. When the corridors were clear, the officer seated by the gate motioned us forward. I went through the gate, passed perhaps a dozen officers, many wearing latex gloves, and another metal detector. On my left, some prisoners, dressed in white to identify them as kitchen workers, were seated on

benches behind another set of bars. As civilians, we were not
allowed into the corridors during movement, when long lines
of prisoners would be walking to and from their cells. I walked
up a flight of metal stairs into an area called the Old School. I
registered with the officer at the desk. He checked the list.

"Your classroom is at the end of the corridor on the left,"
he said.

I entered the room. My twenty-eight students were seated
at desks. Many, given their size, barely fit. I was wearing an
old brown suit. When I had gone to Brooks Brothers to see if
I could replace it, the sales clerk informed me that it was no
longer manufactured because it was not "a power color." Power
colors were probably something Brooks Brothers understood.
The clothing firm got its start buying inexpensive cotton from
slave plantations to make livery and cheap, coarse fabrics called
"Negro cloth," that it sold to slaveholders.

My eyes were immediately drawn to the massive size of one
of my students in the back row. He was, I would learn later, six
foot two and 270 pounds. He had very broad shoulders, a dark,
wide, open face, and short dreadlocks. He was Robert Luma,
known as Kabir, which in Arabic means big. There were other
large men in the room—members of what was referred to as the
400 Club, meaning they bench-pressed more than 400 pounds
in the prison yard—but they appeared dwarfed next to Kabir.

Kabir was a devoted listener of the Pacifica Network radio
station that broadcast from New York City, WBAI. He had
heard me on the air several times and told the other students
they should take the class.[20] Boris Franklin, dark skinned, with a
round, inquisitive face and biceps that rivaled his thighs in size,
was seated next to Kabir. Reading glasses were carefully tucked
in the front pocket of his prison uniform. I assumed, correctly,
that he was a serious reader and a serious student. He eyed me,
however, like much of the class, with skepticism.

"You walked into the room," he told me later. "I thought,

'This little dude is the guy Kabir says is supposed to be so great. Okay. We'll see.'"

I opened the class with my usual imposition of guidelines I had found necessary in the classes I had taught to younger students at Wagner.

"My name is Chris Hedges," I said. "I was a reporter overseas for twenty years, covering conflicts in Central America, the Middle East, Africa, and the war in the former Yugoslavia. Now I write books—a career choice made for me by my former employer, the New York Times, after the paper issued me a formal reprimand for speaking at public forums and on media outlets denouncing George W. Bush's call to invade Iraq. They demanded I cease speaking publicly about the war. I refused. That ended my career at the paper. I was an English major at Colgate University. I have a master of divinity from Harvard. I also spent a year at Harvard studying classics.

"I have taught in colleges before, including at Princeton University. I expect the same decorum and commitment to do the work here that I would in a Princeton classroom. In this class, we will read various plays, along with Michelle Alexander's book The New Jim Crow. But first a few rules: In this class, everyone is treated with respect no matter what their race, ethnicity, religion, politics, or sexual orientation. In this class, we do not interrupt. We challenge ideas, but never integrity or character. I know homophobia runs rampant in men's prisons. But not in my classroom. In my classroom, everyone has a legitimate right to be who they are created to be. In short, I never want to hear any derogatory term used about anyone, and that includes the word *faggot*. Is this clear?"

The class nodded its assent.

East Jersey State Prison was different from Wagner, which did not hold many long-term offenders. My new students were older. They were charged with more serious crimes—often murder. They had usually spent the first few years, even decades, of their time in New Jersey State Prison, the supermax prison in Trenton, where movement is heavily restricted and the prison regime harsh and unforgiving. They rarely went to the prison yard in Trenton, and there were no weights—prisoners call it the pile—which are usually a ubiquitous part of prison life. Those prisoners considered incorrigible by the Department of Corrections are housed in Trenton, often for life.

The atmosphere in Trenton was dark and menacing. The Department of Corrections did not permit college credit courses in Trenton because, as one corrections official said, "They will die in there anyway." I taught noncredit courses there. One summer I taught Shakespeare's *King Lear*. When we discussed Gloucester's aborted suicide, a third of the class admitted they had seriously contemplated or attempted suicide in the prison. My students carried the trauma of Trenton into East Jersey State Prison. In short, the students were adult men, more reserved, more composed, but also hardened in the way the young, often preening men in Wagner were not.

Students got into the college program at East Jersey State Prison by keeping their disciplinary records clean. I would often hear that prisoners "age out of crime," and that is probably the best way to describe my students. They held back emotionally. They watched me carefully. They trusted few people and only after long observation. They had clearly demarcated lines that you crossed at your peril. But they did not have the impulsiveness and immaturity of younger prisoners.

I had more experience with prisons than most of my fellow professors. I had been inside numerous prisons in Latin America, the Middle East, India, and the Balkans as a foreign correspondent and had been locked up for brief periods in cells myself—including in Iran, where I managed to get through 180 pages of Fyodor Dostoyevsky's *The Idiot* before being released. I was also, as a war correspondent, accustomed to being around violence and those who perpetrated violence.

In my class in East Jersey State Prison, we would have a long discussion that semester about prisoners who murder other prisoners.

"Don't they take into consideration that they will almost certainly get caught and add a life bid to their sentence?" I asked.

The class assured me that the high cost of the murder was known and accepted by the assailant. It was part of the price to pay for a killing that was often seen as an act of justifiable revenge, they insisted. As the students filed out that night, one of them came up to me and whispered, "Everything you heard is bullshit. I shanked a dude in Wagner. I didn't think about any of that. All I wanted was to take the motherfucker out."

The next week, a student said he had watched my face as his classmate confessed to a killing and was surprised by my composure.

"Well," I said laughing, "in the world I come from, the killers in here are amateurs."

"The most powerful prisoners are not the gangsters," Boris Franklin wrote later. "They are those who have earned the respect of the other prisoners and the guards. There is less violence in a well-run prison than many on the outside assume, since it is the word and stature of these prison leaders that creates social cohesion. These leaders ward off conflicts between prisoners, raise issues of concern with the administrators, and intercede with the guards. They intuitively understand how to navigate the narrow parameters set by prison authorities, giving them something that resembles freedom. Prison is a lot like the outside world. There is a stratum of people you try to avoid. There are the majority who spend most of their free time slack-jawed in front of a television set, and then there are those who have recovered their integrity and even, to an extent, their moral autonomy. They have risen above prison to become better people. Yet even they can be arbitrarily disappeared into solitary confinement or shipped to another prison by the administration. Everyone in prison is disposable.[21]

"It was this last group . . . that Professor Chris Hedges met when he walked into a prison classroom in Rahway, New Jersey, in September 2013," he continued. "These were some of the 140 men who comprised what we called Rahway University; those of us who dedicated all our free time to studying to earn our college degree. We would be in the yard working the pile talking about Plato or Augustine. We exchanged ideas about the readings from our bunks or in the mess hall. And we tutored those who were falling behind. We had converted our cells into libraries. Our books were our most precious possessions, especially since we had to scrape together the money to buy them. We did not lend them unless we were sure they would be read and even surer they would be returned. And if you read one of our books, you had better be prepared to give an intelligent commentary on its contents. We were a dedicated fraternity of prison scholars."[22]

My class contained highly literate men. None of this was apparent from looking at most of them, but their passions and mine were identical. I was not, I would soon find out, the only writer in the room.

two

The Antenna

The years passed, and I lay on the same bunks, marched
in the same formations, and worked in the same work
brigades with hundreds of others. And always that secret sensor relay, for whose creation I deserved not the
least bit of credit, worked even before I remembered it
was there, worked at the first sight of a human face and
eyes, at the first sound of a voice—so that I opened my
heart to that person either fully or just the width of
a crack, or else shut myself off from him completely.
This was so consistently unfailing that all the efforts
of the State Security officers to employ stool pigeons
began to seem to me as insignificant as being pestered
by gnats: after all, a person who has undertaken to
be a traitor always betrays the fact in his face and in
his voice, and even though some were more skilled
in pretense, there was always something fishy about
them. On the other hand, the sensor relay helped me
distinguish those to whom I could from the very beginning of our acquaintance completely disclose my
most precious depths and secrets—secrets for which
heads roll. Thus it was that I got through eight years
of imprisonment, three years of exile, and another six
years of underground authorship, which were in no
wise less dangerous. During all those seventeen years,

I recklessly revealed myself to dozens of people—and didn't misstep even once.[1]

—Aleksandr Solzhenitsyn,
The Gulag Archipelago, vol. 1

My first three classes did not go well. The students were wary and distant. They were nearly always silent when I asked questions about *The New Jim Crow*. I often waited uncomfortably until finally answering my own question. If someone did volunteer an answer, it was terse and neutral, nothing that I, or any informant or snitch assigned to monitor the class, could report back to prison authorities. They watched carefully to assess who I was and what I was about. There is a natural and understandable mistrust of do-gooders: those who come into a prison to burnish their own credentials as social progressives, who seek an unattainable bond of solidarity with the incarcerated and revel in the exoticism of prison, like visiting wild animals in a zoo. I knew the protocol by then. I didn't pretend to be hip—my collection of button-down shirts, round Harry Potter glasses, and Brooks Brothers suits precluded that. I did not pretend I knew who they were or what their lives were like, despite experiences in war zones that overlapped their own. I did not ask a student why he was incarcerated. I had learned that important prohibition from my neighbor Celia, who first approached me to teach in a prison. Indeed, I rarely looked up their sentences, which I could do on the Department of Corrections search engine. I knew their crime, if they committed a crime, was used by the penal system, and the wider society, to freeze them in time as a criminal, even decades later. They were acutely aware of this branding, and when you peeled back their defensive layers, you would find this wound.

Kabir, from the start, was talkative, in part because he had listened to interviews and lectures I had done on WBAI, but also because he was Kabir—bighearted, open, and giving in a closed world. He was, from the start, my greatest ally in the class, determined to bolster my credibility and help build the trust I would need to reach the other students. The majority had learned the danger of exposing their inner selves to all but a tiny circle of trusted friends. I was from the outside. I was not poor. I was white. I was educated. These were not assets.

"I watched you," Boris Franklin, who always sat in the back row with his glasses case tucked in the front shirt pocket of his prison uniform, would tell me later. "I was worried. You were willing to care about people who did not know how to care about themselves. In prison, that's dangerous."

The class was filled with powerful personalities.

Steph Williams, not physically imposing though athletic, had a full beard and the mark on his forehead that comes from kneeling to pray five times a day. He and Boris, I could see from their interactions with the other students, commanded great respect. The class deferred to them. Steph spoke softly and rarely. His attitude toward me was distrustful, almost antagonistic. Only when these two spoke openly and candidly would everyone speak openly and candidly. Kabir, I noticed, sat next to one of them or between them in class.

While some, like Kabir, were of a size and strength that made challenging them a foolish proposition, what protected most of my students was the finely honed ability to read those around them. Life on the streets and, later, prison meant that survival often depended on this emotional intelligence; knowing whom to trust, who was fake, who could keep quiet, who talked too much, who was real, who told the truth and who did not, who would sell you out, who would stand by you, who had courage and who didn't.

This ability to read others quickly was also one of the most important skills in war zones, where one false step, one

misplaced trust in heavily armed militia leaders or command-
ers, one misjudgment about a potential source who lured you
to a remote location, could lead to disaster. I did not, after a
couple of years covering the war in El Salvador, go into combat
with green, inexperienced reporters or photographers. Those
who panicked in a firefight could get everyone killed. There was
also, much like the military, an iron understanding among war
correspondents that no matter how dangerous it became, you
never left anyone behind. Fear might be ripping out your guts,
but you waited every excruciating second until you left together.
You earned your way into the tight fraternity of war correspondents, just as you earned your way into the tight hierarchy of the
prison. Your schooling, gender, race, nationality, and religion
were irrelevant. I had that antenna. I recognized it instantly in
the men around me. The Soviet dissident Aleksandr Solzhenitsyn never had to censor his speech during his eight years of imprisonment in the gulags, three years in exile, and six years of
underground authorship because he knew whom he could trust
and who would betray him.

I had previously taught *The New Jim Crow* in prison. I had
brought in dozens more copies for distribution. It is an important book. The class was focused. They took careful notes, flipped
to whatever page I was discussing, and marked the passages. Alexander, a civil rights attorney, lays bare the inner workings of
judicial machinery; the interlocking pieces that keep the poor
poor. She explains that militarized police who are empowered
to strip citizens of their most basic rights, along with mass incarceration, are primarily forms not of justice but of racialized social control. On average a thousand people are killed every year
in the United States by police.[2] The official police reports state
that the vast majority of those they kill, about half of whom are
white, are armed.[3] "The racial violence once associated with brutal slave masters or the Ku Klux Klan has been replaced, to some
extent, by violence perpetrated by the state,"[4] Alexander notes.

As Alexander points out, the court system would collapse if everyone had a jury trial. It is built around the necessity of coerced pleas, which is why 97 percent of federal cases and 94 percent of states' cases end in plea deals.[5] It is also why those who come into prison with the harshest sentences are often those who insisted on a trial, believing that because they were innocent, they would be found innocent. They expected justice. They trusted the system. Instead, they were handed sentences, often decades longer than what they would have gotten with a plea deal, as a warning to anyone foolish enough not to plead guilty. This is one of the bitterest ironies of the American court system. The students with the longest sentences are often those who did not commit the crime.

"How many had a trial?" I asked my students. Three or four hands went up. I could see from several of the looks I received that I had trespassed. The majority of the class, coerced to take a plea, I would learn later, were ashamed they had failed to stand up to power.

I went back to the text.

"Every police reform going back decades, including due process, Miranda rights and protocols for filing charges, has only resulted in increased police power and resources," I said. "Has our national conversation on race and crime, which refuses to confront the economic, social, and political systems of exploitation and white supremacy, been a whitewash?"

The class had heard me, but no one was ready to venture into that discussion. I let them think about the question.

"Are the vast pools of the unemployed and underemployed, especially among people of color, the inevitable result of predatory corporate capitalism?" I asked. "Is the primary task of state institutions, especially the police, the courts, the jails, and the prisons, justice, or is it the social control of those cast aside?

"After decades of more training, body cameras, community policing, the hiring of more minority members as police officers, an expanded probation service, equitable fines, and special units to investigate police abuse, have things improved for poor people of color?"

Lawrence Bell, seated in the front row, light skinned with a short afro and wearing heavy framed glasses, shook his head from side to side.

"No," he muttered in his raspy voice.

"You slash taxes for corporations and the rich, and what happens in poor communities?" I asked.

They waited for me to answer my own question.

"Police departments are used to make up lost revenue through the seizure of assets for drug offenses, constant imposition of fines on the poor, often for manufactured crimes such as blocking pedestrian traffic—which means standing on a sidewalk—drinking from an open container, or selling tax-free cigarettes," I said. "These are called quality-of-life actions. This war on the poor has been a bipartisan project. No one was executed in the United States between 1968 and 1976,[6] but drastic changes in laws occurred in the 1990s. Mandatory minimum sentences were imposed by Ronald Reagan's war on drugs and the Violent Crime Control and Law Enforcement Act of 1994 passed by Bill Clinton. Mandatory minimums were made law—in New Jersey, they were put into force on September 1, 1979—and over the next few decades, the length of sentences and range of crimes that required mandatory minimums were steadily increased by 'law-and-order' politicians from the two ruling parties.

"During the administration of President Bill Clinton, Democrats and Republicans passed a series of law-and-order bills that saw the number of crimes punishable by death leap to sixty-six in 1994.[7] In 1974 there had been only one such crime identified in federal law.[8] The two parties, in the words of Naomi Murakawa, the author of *The First Civil Right: How Liberals Built Prison America*, engaged in 'a death penalty bidding war.'[9] Senator Joe Biden was one of the leading proponents of expanding the death penalty. Biden boasted that he had 'added back to the federal statutes over fifty death penalties.'[10] The Clinton crime bill provided funding for tens of thousands of community police officers and drug courts. It banned some assault weapons. It mandated life sentences for anyone convicted of a violent felony after two or more prior convictions, including for drug crimes. The mandated life sentences were known as three-strikes provisions.[11] Three decades ago, there were only three hundred thousand people in our prison system.[12] Now there are 2.3 million. The United States, as Alexander points out, imprisons a larger percentage of its Black population than did apartheid South Africa.

"The Thirteenth Amendment abolished slavery, but not for those being punished for a crime. This is why you do not earn minimum wage in prison. It is why in many prisons, especially in the South, prisoners are forced to work for no pay. The population in state and federal prisons during the Clinton administration rose by 673,000—235,000 more than during Ronald Reagan's presidency.[13] The courts became a conveyor belt transporting the poor into the nation's jails and prisons.

"How is success determined in policing?" I asked. "Is it measured by combating or investigating crime or by generating arrests and handing out summonses? Do police care about real crime in your communities?"

The class knew the answer to this. Several answered "No."

I had largely lectured, moving through the chapters: "The Rebirth of Caste," "The Lockdown," "The Color of Justice," "The Cruel Hand," "The New Jim Crow," and "The Fire This Time." I read passages out loud, including this one toward the end of the book:

> The process of marking black youth *as* black criminals is essential to the functioning of mass incarceration as a racial caste system. For the system to succeed— that is, for it to achieve the political goals described

in chapter 1—black people must be labeled criminals before they are formally subject to control. The criminal label is essential, for forms of explicit racial exclusion are not only prohibited but widely condemned. Thus black youth must be made—labeled—criminals. This process of being made a criminal is, to a large extent, the process of "becoming" black. As [the novelist] John Wideman explains, when "to be a man of color of a certain economic class and milieu is equivalent in the public eye to being a criminal," being processed by the criminal judicial system is tantamount to being made black, and "doing time" behind bars is at the same time "marking race." At its core, then, mass incarceration, like Jim Crow, is a "race-making institution." It serves to define the meaning and significance of race in America.[14]

"That's right," Kabir piped up from the back row. "But you wake up to this and you find you can't talk to people on the outside that don't see it; that still believe in the system, even if the system has never done anything for them. It is like you and they don't speak the same language. That's the problem with education. You figure out how the system works, and you don't have anyone to talk to."

"How does blaming Black crime on crack addiction feed this narrative?" I asked.

The class was silent.

I returned to carrying the discussion alone.

"If crack is seen as the root cause of Black crime, then joblessness, failed schools, poverty, white supremacy, urban violence are not the primary causes," I said. "The war becomes waged against a drug, against drug dealers and drug users, as if once crack is eradicated, the problems of urban poverty and urban violence will be solved. Crack makes it socially acceptable to label Black people as savages, predators. Think about all the sensational news stories about crack, how they made white people afraid, how they justified all the new laws to lock people up, even for nonviolent crimes, often for life, and how they were used to expand the prison system."

I waited for the class to respond. They were listening. Most were bent over their notebooks, taking copious notes or flipping open the book to mark passages. But no one was going to say anything risky.

"The war on drugs is the latest way for white people to be racist without sounding racist," said Kabir, who again struggled valiantly to keep my class alive.

"How has the system changed?" I asked once we had finished the book. "How does our society finally acknowledge the long continuum of racism and move toward reparations and its eradication? How do we build a world where we no longer rely on the police and prisons to carry out social control? How do we create a society where people who are mentally ill or suffering from long-term addiction or homelessness are not thrown into jails and prisons? How do we reform a court system that punishes the poor and absolves those with the wealth to hire armies of private attorneys?"

Silence again. These were questions that would take a long time to answer.

It was the last class on *The New Jim Crow*. In the final minutes, I turned to the plays we would read during the remainder of the semester. I planned to introduce my students to drama, which most of them had not been taught. I wanted to open them up to a new art form and to use the plays to help them articulate and reflect on their own experiences. I wanted them to experience the musicality of language.

"We will start with *Fortune and Men's Eyes* by John Herbert," I said. "It is an autobiographical play about a gay man, Queenie, who, as a teenager, is sent to Canadian reformatory, where he is raped and beaten. Herbert, who later became a well-known drag performer and theater director in Toronto, served a six-month sentence in a reformatory after he was mugged. His assailants had told the judge that he had been trying to solicit sex. So, Herbert, rather than his attackers, was incarcerated. The play chronicles the life of gay incarcerated men.

"How many of you have seen a play?" I asked the class.

Three or four students raised their hands.

"How many of you have read a play?"

No one moved.

"Why is theater, music, poetry, literature, and art important in our lives?" I asked.

Nothing.

We listened to the noisy air-conditioning unit in the barred window.

"The role of art is transcendence, creating the capacity for empathy, especially for those who appear strange, foreign, different," I said. "Art is not about entertainment, or at least not solely about entertainment. It goes deeper than that. It's about dealing with what we call the nonrational forces in human life. These forces are not irrational. They are nonrational. They are absolutely essential to being whole as a human being. They are not quantifiable. They cannot be measured empirically. Yet they are real—maybe more real than those things we can see and touch and count. Grief, beauty, truth, justice, a life of meaning, the struggle with our own mortality, love. These nonrational forces are honored by the artist. The origins of all religions are fused with art, poetry, music. This is because religion, like art, deals with transcendence, with empathy, with justice, with love—realities we experience viscerally but that are often beyond articulation. Religion, like art, allows us to hear and heed the voices of our ancestors.

"The Buddhists say you can memorize as many sutras, which are their religious rules, as you want. That will never make you wise. How did African Americans endure and find the power to resist the nightmare of enslavement, lynching, Jim and Jane Crow, segregation, discrimination, police terror, and mass incarceration? How did they find the capacity to remain human in a world that was inhuman? How did they find the strength not to be consumed by hate? It was through art, poetry, chants, spirituals, and music, celebrated in the Black church, but also in the blues and jazz and hip-hop. I have spent enough time teaching in prison to know the importance of Tupac Shakur. It's what, as the novelist Ralph Ellison said, Blacks had in place of freedom. It's a paradox. When you sink to that level of powerlessness, you find power. I would call it the power of the sacred, or, if you want, God. And it is that power we will explore in this class. The great theologians, the great philosophers, the great artists, the great novelists, the great musicians, the great playwrights, the great dancers, the great painters, and the great sculptors struggle to honor, to sustain, to impart to us the sacred, not only within ourselves but within others. We need these transcendent forces to remind us of who we are, of our capacity for the sacred, of why we're struggling, of what life finally is about. That's why James Baldwin, August Wilson, Amiri Baraka, and Lorraine Hansberry, the first Black female playwright to have a show on Broadway, *A Raisin in the Sun*, are so important."

This was new territory for most in the room. They bent over their notebooks, writing furiously, trying to capture as much of my explanation as possible.

I usually demand term papers in my classes. I expected, until that moment, to do the same this time. But it occurred to me that if I was going to get my students invested in the plays we were reading, they would also have to become familiar with dramatic form. The best way to do that, I thought, would be to get them to write dramatic dialogue.

"What is dramatic dialogue?" I asked the class. "To write

effective dramatic dialogue, you have to understand your characters. What do they want? What are they able to see and understand? What are they *unable* to see and understand? Who they speak with determines how they speak. Do you speak the same way to a white person as you do to a Black person? Do you speak the same way to a corrections officer as you do to another prisoner? How do you speak to someone you love? How do you speak to someone you fear? How do you speak to someone you detest? How do you speak to someone who bores you? How do you speak when you are grieving? How do you speak to someone who is grieving? How do you speak to someone you want something from? And how do people in these emotional states or situations speak to you?

"Your aim is to use dialogue to build a story. You need, first of all, to listen carefully to how people speak and capture this in your writing. You need the reader and the audience to empathize with the character. This requires the character to have all the complexity, ambiguity, and nuance that define us all as human beings. And you need to remember you are traveling somewhere in your story. Dramatic dialogue is not empty chatter. As August Wilson said, 'The simpler you say it, the more eloquent it is.' Words, in the hands of great writers like Wilson, are a form of music. His characters speak in the cadence and in the harshness and truth of the blues, leaping lyrically from one evocative image or emotion to the next. Line after line in Wilson's plays hit you in the gut.

"In his play *The Piano Lesson,* Wilson looks at the power of ghosts, how we communicate with our ancestors. The voices and spirits of our ancestors are our legacy, what informs and defines us. They are our invisible witnesses; those we must not betray. Theater brings our ancestors to life—those who speak to us from beyond the grave—and, in this sense, theater is a religious experience. Winning Boy in Wilson's play goes down to the railroad tracks to speak to the Ghosts of the Yellow Dog, the ghosts of four Black men burned to death in 1911 by whites in a railroad car. He finds strength, purpose, and good fortune by reaching out to these martyred spirits."

I began to read:

> **WINNING BOY.** Nineteen thirty. July of nineteen thirty. I stood right there on that spot. It didn't look like nothing was going right in my life. I said everything can't go wrong all the time . . . let me go down there and call on the Ghosts of Yellow Dog; see if they can help me. I went down there, and right there where them two railroads cross each other . . . I stood right there on that spot and called out their names. They talk back to you, too.
>
> **LYMON.** People say you can ask them questions. They talk to you like that?
>
> **WINNING BOY.** A lot of things you got to find out on your own. I can't say how they talked to nobody else. But to me, it just filled me up in a strange sort of way to be standing there on that spot. I didn't want to leave. It felt like the longer I stood there, the bigger I got. I seen the train coming, and it seem like I was bigger than the train. I started not to move. But something told me to go ahead and get on out the way. The train passed, and I started to go back up there and stand some more. But something told me not to do it. I walked away from there feeling like a king. Went on and had a stroke of luck that run on for three years. So, I don't care if Berniece believe it or not. Berniece ain't got to believe. I know 'cause I been there.[15]

Wilson's words moved them. The men were silent again, but the distance and reserve had melted from their faces. Wilson had taken them, for a moment, to a place outside the prison walls.

"Your writing does not have to be sensational," I said. "It can be something ordinary. A conversation you remember with a friend or a family member. An important moment from your memory. It does not have to be long. Three or four pages is enough."

The bell sounded. The students quickly gathered up their books and left the room. Those who are late to line up in the hall can get a charge, so classrooms empty swiftly. I walked past my students, now standing single file in the hallway, to the library, where I and the other teachers were required to wait until the prisoners were escorted out and the halls were empty.

three

Mama Herc

QUEENIE (*sigh of despair*). See, Smitty! I try to sharpen
the girls I like, and she don't listen to a screwin'
word I say. I coulda got her a real good old man,
but she told him she liked her "independence," if
you can picture it.

SMITTY. I can understand that.

QUEENIE. Yeah? So what happens? One day in the gym,
a bunch of hippos con her into the storeroom to
get something for the game, and teach her another
one instead. They make up the team, but she's the
only basket. They all took a whack, now she's public property. You can't say no around here unless
you got somebody behind you. Take it from your
mother . . . I know the score.

SMITTY. I'll have to think about it.

QUEENIE. Well, don't wait until they give you a gang
splash in the storeroom. Mona had to hold on to the
wall to walk, for a week.

—*Fortune and Men's Eyes*, John Herbert[1]

I was sitting on a bench outside St. Joseph Social Service Center in Elizabeth, New Jersey, with three men who volunteered in the center, sorting donated clothes and handing out
meals. They were known as Big Frankie because of his massive

size—well over three hundred pounds—Little Frankie, who was over two hundred pounds but looked small next to Big Frankie, and Al. All had spent time in prison. We were eating donated Entenmann's danishes that were past the expiration date. The centers of the pastries were filled with bright red goo, approximating fruit, and the surrounding pastry was drizzled with lines of white frosting. Men and women inside the hall were poring over old clothes. Screaming children darted around the tables. The chaos was overseen by the Catholic nun Jacinita Fernandes and Edie Cheney, who founded St. Joseph Social Service Center in 1986. Fernandes and Cheney, and others like them, rescue the good name of the church.

A man in a tattered coat approached. Big Frankie offered him a danish. The stranger, in his fifties, with flecks of gray in his curly black hair, took it and sat down wearily. It was usual for transients—those who lived elsewhere or nowhere—to pass through Elizabeth for a day or two, getting something to eat or wear at St. Joseph, and then disappear. Big Frankie told me later he was sure the stranger was from New York, although there was nothing the man said that tied him to any location.

Big Frankie, who liked to eat, was telling us that when he did time, the food inside wasn't bad.

"We did the cooking, an' we had some good cooks," he said of the prisoners who ran the kitchen.

"That's all changed now," said Al. "Food ain't fit for dogs."

"The food gives everybody in the jail diarrhea," added Big Frankie, who had just come out of two weeks in Union County Jail and previously spent two years there. "There was never enough food. People were hungry all the time."

"When I was in there, everyone came down with food poisoning from tacos," Al said. "It was awful. All the prisoners, except the ones who were vegetarian and didn't eat the meat in the tacos, had diarrhea for three days. Whenever we tried to eat anything for those three days, we threw it back up. We were all sweating and felt dizzy."

Al had a job in the jail's kitchen. He prepared the food under the supervision of two civilian employees from the private food contractor Aramark. Corporations such as Aramark, which provides the food to some five hundred correctional institutions across the United States,[2] are billion-dollar-a-year industries[3]

"You have to check the sizes and weigh the food," he said. "They even made us weigh the garbage. Mostly we served soy, rice, potatoes, and pasta. There was mice running around and mice shit everywhere. The spoons for cooking were dirty. Some of them making food would use the can and not wash their hands or wear gloves. Hair would fall in the food. The bread was hard, and the portions we gave were real small. You could eat six meals like the ones we served and still be hungry. If we put more than the amount they said on the tray, the Aramark dudes would make us take it off. It wasn't civilized. I lost thirty pounds. I'd wake up in the middle of the night and put toothpaste in my mouth jus' so I could stop feelin' hungry, man. The only way anyone survived was to have money on the books that they could use in the canteen, but I didn't have no money. It was real bad for the diabetics, an' there's lots of diabetics inside."[4]

"We used to get some good eats in the ol' days," Big Frankie said.

"We didn't get no good eats where I was," the stranger, who had remained silent until then, said with a growl.

"Where was that?" Big Frankie asked.

"Florida," the stranger said. "That was a bad time."

"Yeah," said Al. "I hear Florida's rough."

"Open pods," the man said. "Everything be goin' on: shankin', rapin'. I was in with the notorious Mama Herc."

"Mama Herc?" I asked.

"Yeah, Mama Hercules: biggest, baddest booty bandit in the Florida prison system. He owned the weight pile. Put it all up. Had shaved legs, plucked eyebrows, and wore little strings of colored plastic beads 'round his neck. Had a soft, sweet voice, but he wait with the other faggots pickin' out the new fish, specially the scared little white boys, gettin' processed when they come into the prison to rape 'em. He take 'em to the pod and do it under the blanket in front of everyone. He got his, though."

"How?" I asked.

"One of those skinny white kids he raped come into the yard and shanked him in the chest while he on the pile," the stranger said. "I seen it. Mama Herc was a giant. He threw those weights off like they was nothin', stood up, that shank stickin' straight out of his chest, an' died right there."

Mama Herc, it turned out, was a legend within the prison system. His size, strength, and ravenous sexual appetite—it was said he preferred white boys—struck fear in cells across the country. The legend of Mama Herc is colored by various versions of his story, especially how he died. There are some who claim he died living on the streets of Saint Petersburg, Florida, from AIDS or was murdered. Others insist he was shanked, as the stranger said, in the prison yard. Still others say one of his victims pushed the bar of the prison yard bench press, loaded with hundreds of pounds of weights, onto his neck, crushing his windpipe and killing him.

Charles P. Norman, who was imprisoned with Mama Herc, wrote an essay, "Fighting the Ninja," that was published in 2008 by PEN America, a nonprofit organization formed to defend and promote free speech. The ninja is prison slang for AIDS. Norman writes of Mama Herc:

> Mama Herc was a genuine prison legend, infamous beyond his razor wire boundary. When I was in the county jail for a couple of years, fighting my case through the courts, recidivists shared chain gang horror stories about what would happen to the scared newcocks upon

their arrival in prison. All that was missing in those jail cells to make it any scarier was crackling campfires and hooting owls.

"When you get to prison, boys," one scrawny, toothless thirty-year-old six-time loser, his toothpick arms stained blue with crude, self-inflicted tattoos crisscrossed with white razor blade scars intoned, "you're gonna run into Mama Herc." He smiled, revealing gums, and smacked his lips.

"Who's Mama Herc?" some frightened teen burglar or car thief would always ask.

"Boy, Mama Herc is a sweet young white boy's worst nightmare," he'd say, warming up. "She, or he, whatever you wanna call it, is the biggest, meanest, strongest damn queer in the prison system. He's a monster, can lift all the iron in the weight pile, gets his strength and his protein from eatin' up young boys like you, and you, and you, every day."

"What?"

"Yep. Mama Herc's a black giant with plucked eyebrows and shaved legs, arms pumped up like Virginia hams. When I came into prison, sweet sixteen, all clean, not like I am now, I heard these footsteps behind me, turned around, and there was Mama Herc, the black Goliath, Frankenstein, Sasquatch, and Medusa rolled into one."

"What happened?"

"Mama Herc grabbed me by the throat with one hand, picked me up in the air, pulled me toward him, kissed me right dead on the lips, and grinned at me."

Groans and yechs resound.

"You should have smelled that breath. It'd make a vulture puke. Least he didn't stick his tongue in my mouth."

More groans and gags.

"Mama Herc looked me right in the eye and said, 'White boy, I'm gonna suck your dick.' And he did. What was I supposed to do?

"When he got done, he squeezed my neck a little bit, just to let me know he could pinch off my head if he wanted to, and told me, 'Now you're gonna suck mine.'"

Louder gasps and groans.

"Mama Herc's still up there waiting for you boys to show up. When the bus pulls in, he'll be standing on the side with the other faggots and booty bandits picking out the fish and the fresh meat. Welcome to prison."

But later in the essay, Norman writes that "the reality was quite different."

Months later, Herc signed up for a prisoner self-help program where men spend days sitting in a circle and telling their life stories, among other activities. Herc opened up, and I learned the terrible truth behind his chain gang legend.

He'd gone to the state reform school not much more than a scrawny child, and had been brutally raped, abused, and passed around by the older teens. He was too small to fight them off. His life was a living hell for weeks and months. He turned to the weight pile, desperate to add size and become strong, and in a couple of years, he'd spurted upward, at fifteen, bigger and stronger than most fully grown men. By then, he'd developed a taste for homosexuality, and the weak prey of years past morphed into a predator.

Now he was a grown man, having spent most of his life in captivity, turning into that which he'd feared and hated most as a helpless youth. He denied the

veracity of the chain gang stories about his attacking
fresh young prisoners in years past, and beneath that
frightening exterior a little boy still hid.

I developed a respect for Herc, for his sheer determination as a survivor. I'd been a grown man when I
came to prison. I couldn't imagine how damaging and
horrifying it might have been had I come to prison as
a child. Might I have developed into something like
Mama Herc? I shuddered to think about it. I would
rather have died. Many did.

We became friends, as odd as that may seem. He
had a childlike innocence of many things. He'd never
had a life in society, never had a job, never drove a car.
He was scared to death of women. He was insecure
and uneducated, and had no skills but one. He was the
strongest man in prison. He owned the weight pile. He
was truly institutionalized, a product of his environ-
ment, and life in a "free society" was as alien to him as
life on Mars or Jupiter.[5]

I handed out Norman's essay before we began the discussion of
Fortune and Men's Eyes. Herbert's play takes place in a cell and
the corridor outside. The play opens with Smitty, a first-time of-
fender, being placed on his first day in a cell with three older prisoners. His bunkmates are Queenie, a flamboyant drag queen who
is serving time for male prostitution; Rocky, a young tough who
insists he is straight but had a wealthy male lover on the outside;
and Mona, a bookish and sensitive gay man who was arrested
for allegedly making a pass at a police officer. Rocky pressures
Smitty to accept him as his "old man," forcing him into a sexual
relationship and turning Smitty, who is not gay, into his "bitch."
The repeated rapes and demeaning subservience demanded by
Rocky gradually numbs and hardens Smitty, transforming him
into a thug and sexual predator who eventually takes down

Rocky. The fifth character in the play is a cynical and corrupt corrections officer, nicknamed Holy Face, who is plagued by ulcers and biding his time until he can retire to Florida.

"How does the cruelty of prison foster cruelty among the incarcerated in the play?" I asked.

"It's about survival," said the student Reggie "Sincere" Jackson, who would later legally change his name to Sincere U Allah, always seated on my left against the wall, with his long dreadlocks and glasses. "You have to adapt. If you can't stand up for yourself, if you stay soft, you get eaten."

"But aren't there people who physically are so overpowering that fighting them is useless?" I asked.

"You can't think like that in prison," said Sincere, who was a little over six feet and about 230 pounds. "First of all, you'd be surprised, but a lot of those queers can fight. And there are always ways of getting back. Put your lock in a sock and bring it into the shower. You got to push back, even if you lose, or you get stomped all over."

Herbert examines the loss of heterosexual identity in prison. Most male prisoners turn to contraband porn for self-relief, although in the late 1980s and early 1990s, the guards that manned the third shift at Rahway operated a prostitution ring inside the prison with female officers. Roughly 10 percent of a prison population engages in male-on-male sex. Sometimes these sexual relationships are consensual. Sometimes they are not. Sometimes they are sporadic and rare. Sometimes they are frequent and sustained. Sexual activity is not limited to the prisoners—especially in women's prisons, where male guards engage in rape or routinely grant privileges or give contraband items to female prisoners in exchange for sex. When I taught in the Edna Mahan Correctional Facility for Women, New Jersey's only prison for women, the students never referred to corrections officers as COs or guards but always as "pigs," in a tone dripping with contempt and hatred.

The US Department of Justice, in a 2020 report investigating Edna Mahan, found that corrections officers routinely coerced prisoners into sexual acts, groped them during strip searches, and called them "bitches," "dykes," and other slurs. A single male officer, the report said, was often assigned to patrol a building holding fifty women. Camera coverage was, in the words of the federal report, "spotty" in the building's remote areas and nonexistent in its storage room. The investigators found a mattress on the floor of the storage closet. The report said that corrections officers "make efforts to watch prisoners as they shower, undress, or use restrooms."[6] While I was teaching there, seven staff members were convicted of sexually abusing prisoners, and there were ongoing investigations into abuses by other members of the prison staff.

In every prison, male and female, there are older sexual predators who force young, new prisoners to be their sex slaves. The guilt and shame of sexual encounters with another prisoner, or of rape, feeds homophobia, with prisoners lashing out, sometimes violently, at gay men or women.

The sexual promiscuity among male prisoners stunned the boxer Rubin "Hurricane" Carter when he first entered Trenton State Prison, now New Jersey State Prison. In quick succession, he saw "two hard-looking, dewy-eyed sissies straining against each other, kissing passionately in a hidden nook of the jail; a bald-headed, muscular black man withdrawing his oversized swipe from the flushed anus of a skinny, freckled white boy in a shower stall; two convicts sitting together in the movies, one of them with his hand in the cut-out pockets of the other one's pants, jerking him off; a black hardcore tough guy titillating the nasty ass of a Confederate-flag-tattooed cracker in the Catholic chaplain's office with his nasty tongue; a jailhouse pimp sucking his fag's dick in the officers' locker room during mess."[7]

I began with Herbert's play not because I wanted to explore

the shame of male-on-male sex, which I knew no one in the class was going to speak about openly, but to make it clear that it was not gay prisoners who took from them their identities as straight men.

"Remember," I said, "gay prisoners don't prohibit relationships with women; the prison system does. And yet the anger and sexual frustration often get taken out on homosexuals. They become the scapegoats; the victims of misplaced anger. You see this in the play in Rocky, and later with Smitty, who ends the play by looking out at the audience with what Herbert calls 'a slight, twisted smile that is somehow cold, sadistic, and menacing,' saying, 'I'll pay you all back.' Herbert's play also makes clear what you know: that prison mirrors the power dynamics of the outside world, one where the ruthlessly ambitious seek status and power, no matter what it takes to achieve it or who gets crushed in the process."

I posed a question to the class: "Who is the one character in the play who retains his humanity and why?"

"Mona," answered Sincere, his dreadlocks falling around his face. "'Cause he won't be anyone's bitch, even if it means going without protection and getting raped. He stays sensitive. I mean, he expresses himself through poetry. Like when Smitty wants to make Mona his bitch, Mona refuses and tells Smitty he's afraid of his own feelings. So Smitty gets pissed and calls Mona things like filthy fairy and cocksucker. But then Mona gives Smitty a Shakespeare sonnet, 'Fortune in Men's Eyes,' and makes Smitty read it, and that humanizes Smitty—brings him back to a world where he can feel. Prison is designed to make you numb, you know, to cut you off from feeling. But Mona fights this; he stays vulnerable, stays human."

Toward the end of the play, Mona reads a passage from the courtroom scene in Shakespeare's play *The Merchant of Venice*, in which Portia, a beautiful, young heiress, appeals for mercy from the Jewish moneylender Shylock. I read it to the class:

The quality of mercy is not strained.
It droppeth as the gentle rain from heaven
Upon the place beneath. It is twice blest:
It blesseth him that gives and him that takes.
'Tis mightiest in the mightiest; it becomes
The thronèd monarch better than his crown.
His scepter shows the force of temporal power,
The attribute to awe and majesty
Wherein doth sit the dread and fear of kings;
But mercy is above this sceptered sway.
It is enthronèd in the hearts of kings;
It is an attribute to God Himself;
And earthly power doth then show likest God's
When mercy seasons justice.[8]

"What is Shakespeare saying about mercy, about compassion?" I asked.

"It's how we come closest to God, by showing mercy, being gentle and kind," Lawrence said hesitantly. "The person who gives it, the person who receives it, both get humanized. Mercy is even stronger than force and authority, 'cause it's not trying to make people obey you—what it does is transform them. But, I have to say, you gotta know who you can reach with mercy and who you can't, hear me? 'Cause if you show mercy to those who can't feel, who are determined to destroy you, you put yourself at risk."

"True," I said. "There are those incapable of being merciful. There are those incapable of being swayed by mercy—many would argue in the play that this is Shylock's failing—but they ultimately destroy themselves, consuming themselves with hatred and rage. Mercy, as Herbert says in the play, is that quality that saves us from the darkness within ourselves.

"How does the play portray the judicial process?" I asked. "How does it portray rehabilitation?"

"The judicial system in the play, like in real life, is a joke," Kabir said from the back of the classroom. "Prisons take boys and turn them vicious, hard, which they were not when they came in. That's Smitty's story."

I read a passage spoken by Mona.

> No real defense. A deal. Magistrate's court is like trial
> in a police station—all pals, lawyers and cops together!
> Threw me on the mercy of the court. Oh, Christ: that
> judge, with his hurry-up face, heard the neat police
> evidence and my lawyer's silly, sugar-sweet plea. So
> halfhearted—I wanted to shout, "Let me speak; leave
> me some damn dignity!" The fat, white-haired frown
> looked down at me—"Go to jail for six months!"—like
> I'd dirtied his hands, and that would wipe them clean.[9]

"I knew a guy who got a life sentence," said Boris, who, seated next to Kabir, looked up from the book, his reading glasses perched on his nose. "As soon as the judge sentenced him, the defense lawyer and prosecutor turned to each other and starting talkin' 'bout where they would have lunch. I mean, this guy's life was just destroyed. He was sitting right between 'em. And all they could think about was where they were gonna go to eat. He bolted, tried to throw himself out of the courtroom window to kill himself."

I closed the class with the Shakespeare sonnet that gave the play its title:

> *When, in disgrace with fortune and men's eyes,*
> *I all alone beweep my outcast state,*
> *And trouble deaf heaven with my bootless cries,*
> *And look upon myself and curse my fate,*
> *Wishing me like to one more rich in hope,*
> *Featured like him, like him with friends possessed,*

Desiring this man's art and that man's scope,
With what I most enjoy contented least;
Yet in these thoughts myself almost despising,
Haply I think on thee, and then my state,
(Like to the lark at break of day arising
From sullen earth) sings hymns at heaven's gate;
For thy sweet love remembered such wealth brings
That then I scorn to change my state with kings. [10]

"Okay," I said, "leave your scenes on my desk. Next week we will discuss *Dutchman* by LeRoi Jones, who later changed his name to Amiri Baraka. I also want you to write up a scene with your mother, or someone close to you."

The students put their handwritten scenes on my desk. They were three or four pages long, all written out on lined paper. The pile of paper gave off the familiar musty, pungent smell of the prison. I was anxious to read them. I was curious about what the class had chosen to write about and how open they would be about their lives.

Timmy, a tall, gangly student who had not yet spoken, waited until the rest of the class was outside in the corridor.

"What if we are a product of rape?" he whispered.

I was momentarily thrown.

"Then that's what you have to write," I said.

four

Rage and Terror

The root of the black man's hatred is rage, and he does not so much hate white men as simply wants them out of his way, and more than that, out of his children's way. The root of the white man's hatred is terror, a bottomless and nameless terror, which focuses on this dread figure, an entity which lives only in his mind.[1]

—James Baldwin

The scenes submitted by the class were mixed. There were three or four powerful scenes, written with great pathos and skill. There were several scenes, composed of short, staccato moments that leapt from location to location, which does not usually work in theater. There were scenes that used the tired, hypermasculine clichés that glorify the lives of thugs, hustlers, killers, and drug dealers. There were also scenes that went nowhere. But I was intrigued by the good ones. They were written by students with strong writing skills and an ear for the cadences of speech. I did not understand at the time why Sincere, one of the brightest and most gifted students in the class, and who I could sense was a talented writer, handed in dramatic passages that read like bad television scripts. Subsequently, I learned that he had been framed for his crime, had little experience on the streets, and based his portrayal of violent thugs on popular culture and prison lore, which invariably romanticizes gangsters. He wrote, in all capital letters at the bottom of each of his papers, "I am innocent."

Sincere's submissions centered around one of the most notorious mobsters and serial killers in the New Jersey prison system: Richard Kuklinski, known as "the Iceman," a nickname he was given after it was discovered that he had stuffed the body of one of his victims into a freezer to mask the time of the murder.[2]

I have taught two, perhaps three psychopaths, including a hitman for the Russian mob in Atlantic City, New Jersey, who dispatched his victims by strangling them. They were intelligent and articulate, adept at flattery and manipulation, emotionally dead, and very creepy. One insisted, in a class I taught a few years later, on sitting next to me every time, often pulling his desk close to mine. He showered me with obsequious compliments. I, and everyone else in the room, suspected he was working as a prison snitch to report anything a student or I might say, which could be reported and used against us. I assigned the class Bruno Bettelheim's essay "Individual and Mass Behavior in Extreme Situations." The essay examines how prisoners coped psychologically in Germany's Dachau and Buchenwald concentration camps, where the Austrian-born Bettelheim was interned by the Nazis. Bettelheim, who later emigrated to the United States and became a world-renowned psychologist, writes about prisoners who identified with their Nazi SS guards:[3]

"Old prisoners who identified themselves with the SS did so not only in respect to aggressive behavior. They would try and acquire old pieces of SS uniforms. If that was not possible, they tried to sew and mend their uniforms so that they would resemble those of the guards. The length to which prisoners would go in these efforts seemed unbelievable, particularly since the SS punished them for their efforts to copy SS uniforms. When asked why they did it, the old prisoners admitted that they loved to look like the guards."[4]

"We have people like that in here," said a student from the back laconically.

The class glared at the student seated next to me.[5]

Prisoners, even those who may have committed murder, give these psychopaths a wide berth, especially those who touched and manipulated dead bodies, whether that meant killing with their hands or handling or mutilating the corpse.[6] I have met few prisoners who advocated the total abolition of prisons, with most conceding that there were psychopaths and killers who would always be dangerous. But they also stressed that this was primarily a mental health issue rather than a criminal justice issue. These prisoners made up only 5 percent, or less, of most prison populations.

Kuklinski, who worked as a hitman for the Gambino crime family and who died in March 2006 at the age of seventy, specialized in the desecration of his victim's corpses. On February 1, 1980, he shot a business associate, George Malliband, with a .38 revolver five times in the left side of his chest, killing him. Kuklinski crammed Malliband's three-hundred-pound bulk into a fifty-five-gallon oil drum, slicing Malliband's tendons on one leg to snap his knee to close the lid. He rolled the barrel off a cliff in Jersey City, where the decayed corpse was discovered a few days later.[7]

In Sincere's hands, Kuklinski became a violent drug dealer named Push. *Push* is slang for being killed, or pushed to the other world. Sincere dramatized Kuklinski's murders, including thrusting a body into a fifty-five-gallon oil drum, but little of the dialogue rang true—even to me, who had no experience in what my students called "the game." Once Sincere wrote about what he knew—and it was not the criminal underworld—he was brilliant. And there were writers in the class, such as Steph, taciturn and acutely perceptive, and Boris, a lyrical writer, who clearly did know the game and produced gritty scripts that brought to life the sordid world of police, hustlers, drug dealers, addicts, hookers, and street thugs.

Timmy, whom I had told the previous week to write about

being the product of rape, had written a dialogue, using his legal name of Terrance, about chopping yams in the kitchen with his mother and half brother. I handed him the scene and asked him to read it to the class. He lifted his six-foot-three, 180-pound frame from his seat and began to read:

MOTHER. I hope you don't love dem yams like dat bird you begged me for a couple of years ago. You loved it fer what? Two weeks? Poor little thing starved to death. What was the name of that bird?

TERRANCE. Tweety.

BROTHER. 'Member da day he brought that mangy street dog home?

MOTHER. Oh, Lord. I wanted to choke that dog an' Terrance. An' he let dat dirty thing up on my sofa. Took me two weeks to get the smell outta da house. An' he smelled as bad as dat dog by the time I got dat creature outta here.

TERRANCE. Y'all styling. Wasn't that bad.

MOTHER. Now, boy, hand me dat knife, and let me finish dem yams. Neither of you gonna find no woman take care of you like your ma. So you better learn to do fer yerself 'cause you don't learn how to cook, you ain't gonna eat.

BROTHER. I be cookin' for Terrance when he grown, Ma, fer sure.

TERRANCE. This from the dude nearly burned down the house tryin to make us French toast.

MOTHER. Now look how thin I cut deez yams. Jus' like my mama taught me.

TERRANCE. Grandma, she live fer Jesus. All I know is the truth . . .

ALL THREE IN UNISON. Before I lie to you, I'll say bye to you.

MOTHER. She was a Christian woman. She always tryin'
to beat the black off yer uncle Robert.

TERRANCE. That wouldn't be hard, yella as Uncle Robert was.

MOTHER. That's why he so yella. He used to be black
as daddy.

"These little moments are what I am looking for," I told the
class when Timmy finished. "Intimate glimpses of life conveyed
through dialogue in dramatic form."

In this class, we discussed the 1964 play *Dutchman*, written
by Amiri Baraka, known at the time as LeRoi Jones. It was also
the class when the supervisor of the prison education program,
Toby Sanders, sat in. Toby was a graduate of Morehouse College and had a master of divinity degree from Princeton Theological Seminary. Teaching *Dutchman* in his presence was a bit
unnerving, because his knowledge of Black literature, culture,
and history was vastly superior to my own. I would glance in his
direction throughout the class to try to read his facial expres-
sions to make sure I wasn't too off the mark. Fortunately, Toby
was as generous as he was erudite.

I handed out Baraka's manifesto "The Revolutionary Theater," which had been commissioned by the *New York Times* in
1965 but rejected for publication, along with Robert Crumb's
controversial comic "When the Niggers Take Over America."
Crumb, a founder of the first underground comix publication,
Zap Comix, had also done a comic called "When the Goddamn
Jews Take Over America." He expressed in savage satire the
same white hatred and terror of the Black male that lay at the
heart of *Dutchman*. This terror is a reflexive feeling among
many whites—even white liberals who cannot shake it and yet,
often unconsciously, are ashamed of it. Not long before the
class, there had been a food drive in Princeton, New Jersey, for
the food pantry in Trenton, which was running low on stock. As

I handed over some supplies to the woman collecting the donations in downtown Princeton, she thanked me and said: "We have to keep the pantry in Trenton full, or they'll be coming here." That was, at least, an honest expression of the motivation for the pitiful acts of charity by those with white privilege.

"Coming here?" I replied. "That would be the best news I heard in a long time."

Black rage, along with white hatred and terror of Black men, are the central themes of *Dutchman*. They define the impasse of race relations in the United States, one masked by rhetoric about equality, tolerance, affirmative action, desegregation, and a postracial America. As James Baldwin writes, because this terror and hatred of Black men is unexamined by white society, because it is a product not of reality but of depraved racial fantasies, it festers like a moral cancer, impoverishing and degrading the souls of the white majority and marginalizing and endangering the lives of the Black minority. When the *New York Times* theater critic Howard Taubman reviewed *Dutchman* in March 1964, he dismissed it as "an explosion of hatred rather than a play."[8]

"LeRoi Jones, as he was then known, feverishly pounded out the play in a couple of days," I said to the class. "Why does he set the play underground on a subway?"

The class thought for a moment.

"Because a Black man is always in some sense trapped underground?" Lawrence asked in his guttural, raspy voice. "Because once the doors shut, he can't get off? Because the subway car is like a prison?"

"Exactly," I said.

There are two main characters: a white woman, Lula, who is thirty, and a well-dressed, twenty-year-old Black man, Clay, who is a poet. Lula is the temptress, seeking to ignite Clay's sexual passions and lure him into the taboo of miscegenation. Lula flirts outrageously. She repeatedly asks him to invite her to a party.

"Now, you say to me, 'Lula, Lula, why don't you go to this

party with me tonight?' It's your turn, and let those be your lines," she says.[9]

The temptation—Lula is constantly eating an apple, evoking the biblical Eve's fatal flirtation with evil—begins from the moment the play opens, when Clay sees Lula eyeing him from the subway station platform.

I asked two students to read the parts.

LULA. Weren't you staring at me through the window?

CLAY. [*Wheeling around and very much stiffened*] What?

LULA. Weren't you staring at me through the window? At the last stop?

CLAY. Staring at you? What do you mean?

LULA. Don't you know what staring means?

CLAY. I saw you through the window . . . if that's what it means. I don't know if I was staring. Seems to me you were staring through the window at me.

LULA. I was. But only after I'd turned around and saw you staring through that window down in the vicinity of my ass and legs.

CLAY. Really?

LULA. Really. I guess you were just taking those idle potshots. Nothing else to do. Run your mind over people's flesh.

CLAY. Oh, boy. Wow, now I admit I was looking in your direction. But the rest of that weight is yours.

LULA. I suppose.

CLAY. Staring through train windows is weird business. Much weirder than staring very sedately at abstract asses.

LULA. That's why I came looking through the window . . . so you'd have more than that to go on. I even smiled at you.

CLAY. That's right.

LULA. I even got into this train, going some other way than mine. Walked down the aisle . . . searching you out.

CLAY. Really? That's pretty funny.

LULA. That's pretty funny . . . God, you're dull.

CLAY. Well, I'm sorry, lady, but I really wasn't prepared for party talk.

LULA. No, you're not. What are you prepared for? [*Wrapping the apple core in a Kleenex and dropping it on the floor.*]

CLAY. [*Takes her conversation as pure sex talk. He turns to confront her squarely with this idea.*] I'm prepared for anything. How about you?

LULA. [*Laughing loudly and cutting it off abruptly.*] What do you think you're doing?

CLAY. What?

LULA. You think I want to pick you up, get you to take me somewhere and screw me, huh?

CLAY. Is that the way I look?

LULA. You look like you been trying to grow a beard. That's exactly what you look like. You look like you live in New Jersey with your parents and are trying to grow a beard. That's what. You look like you've been reading Chinese poetry and drinking lukewarm sugarless tea. [*Laughs, uncrossing and recrossing her legs.*] You look like death eating a soda cracker.[10]

"Why is Clay so frightened?" I asked.

"White society justifies violence against Black men on the supposed sexual desires they have for white women," Boris answered immediately. "Clay's being set up. His survival depends on him assuming the humiliating role of a second-class citizen assigned to him by whites."

"Right," I said. "And so, what is the power dynamic here?"

"Lula wants to get him to express lust for her," Sincere said. "It gives her the power over him of life and death."

"Who can tell me the story of Emmett Till?" I asked.

Steph, who spoke rarely, raised his hand from his seat in the last row.

"Nineteen fifty-five," he said. "Emmett Till was a fourteen-year-old kid from Chicago visiting family in Mississippi. A white woman said he whistled at her and said lewd things to her. Till gets abducted, badly beaten, shot in the head, and his body gets tossed in a river. Till's mama took the body back to Chicago. She holds a funeral with an open casket and invites the public to see the body. Tens of thousands of people show up. Black newspapers print photographs of Till's mutilated face. Blacks see they will never get justice waiting for white people to give it to them. They have to organize. Rosa Parks was at a rally for Till held by Martin Luther King. After that rally, she refuses to give up her seat on a bus to a white person. Rosa Parks says that the whole time she's bein' told to get to the back of the bus, she kept thinking 'bout Till and couldn't go back there. That started the Montgomery, Alabama, bus boycott. Black boys and men were always lynched to supposedly protect the purity of white women. That's always the excuse."

As I was writing this chapter, a story about a white woman named Amy Cooper was being widely reported. While walking her cocker spaniel unleashed in New York City's Central Park, a Black man, Christian Cooper (no relation), asked her to please follow park rules and leash her dog. The woman responded by calling 911 on her cell phone. She told the police, her voice breathless and hysterical, that "an African American man" was "threatening my life."[11] The call immediately put Christian Cooper's life in jeopardy. Christian, who'd come to the park to bird-watch, captured their exchange and her call on *his* cell phone.

Columnist Ginia Bellafante of the *New York Times* writes: "The moment provided a bracing tutorial in what bigotry among the urbane looks like—the raw, virulent prejudice that can exist beneath the varnish of the right credentials, pets, accessories, social affiliations, the coinage absorbed from HBO documentaries and corporate sensitivity seminars."[12]

Christian Cooper, who graduated from Harvard University, could easily have become another grim statistic linking him to the more than one hundred Black people massacred in Ellenton, South Carolina, when Mrs. Lucky Harley claimed she had been assaulted by two Black men in 1876;[13] or to the Blacks murdered in the 1921 Tulsa massacre when seventeen-year-old Sarah Page alleged that a young Black man had assaulted her;[14] or to the 1923 massacre in the all-Black community of Rosewood, Florida, also triggered by claims that a Black man tried to sexually assault a white woman named Fanny Taylor.[15] Cooper could have become Joe Coe, Emmett Till, the Scottsboro Boys, or the five teenagers wrongly charged and imprisoned in the Central Park jogger case. White women suffered, and continue to suffer, discrimination in patriarchal America, but they have always had the power to weaponize white hatred toward Black men.

Lula knows that by provoking Clay's lust, she lures him to his own destruction. She stabs him to death at the end of the play. She and the other whites on the subway car toss his body onto the tracks when the doors open. The play ends with Lula approaching another young, naïve Black man reading a book.

But there is also another death Jones explores: the death of consciousness and identity by Black people who attempt to placate white society by becoming—in dress, mannerisms, and behavior—like whites. Lula is determined to push Clay into the box of a racial stereotype, mocking him repeatedly for his education, literacy, and dress.

"What right do you have to be wearing a three-button suit and a striped tie?" she asks. "Your grandfather was a slave;

he didn't go to Harvard."[16] A few lines later, she says, "I bet you never once thought you were a black nigger."[17] It is only at the end of the play, when Clay understands he is cornered and doomed—that he has always been cornered and doomed—that he lashes out in rage at Lula and the other whites on the subway car.

Clay shouts:

> I'll rip your lousy breasts off! Let me be who I feel like being. Uncle Tom. Thomas. Whoever. It's none of your business. You don't know anything except what's there for you to see. An act. Lies. Device. Not the pure heart, the pumping black heart. You don't ever know that. And I sit here, in this buttoned-up suit, to keep myself from cutting all your throats. I mean wantonly. You great liberated whore! You fuck some black man, and right away you're an expert on black people. What a lotta shit that is. The only thing you know is that you come if he bangs you hard enough. And that's all. The belly rub? You wanted to do the belly rub? Shit, you don't even know how. You don't know how. That ol' dipty-dip shit you do, rolling your ass like an elephant.[18]

"Why is the play called *Dutchman*?" Lawrence asked.

That was a question I should have been able to answer. I looked at Toby.

"It comes from Samuel Coleridge's *The Rime of the Ancient Mariner,*" Toby explained. "The *Flying Dutchman* was a ghost ship, doomed to remain at sea on an eternal voyage of death. The Dutch were also the first owners of the slave ships between Africa and America. Clay is trapped in America inside the modern incarnation of a slave ship—a death ship for Black people."

When Toby had finished, I announced, "We will discuss August Wilson's play *Joe Turner's Come and Gone* next week, which was Wilson's favorite of his plays. Wilson wrote a series of ten plays that chronicled the African American experience in the twentieth century. *Joe Turner's Come and Gone* is part of this cycle."

The class filed out, dropping their scenes on my desk.

"Drive home safe," they said, as they did each night. No student I taught at a university outside prison ever expressed concern about my getting home safely.

I read Timmy's dialogue about being the product of rape when I got back to Princeton. Timmy, who used his legal name Terrance in his dialogues, had served nineteen years of his thirty-year sentence. His scene was set in the county jail where he was awaiting trial. It was a phone dialogue between him and his mother. He tells her that he has sacrificed himself to keep his half brother—the only son his mother loves—out of prison.

TERRANCE. You don't understand, Ma.

(*Pause.*)

TERRANCE. You're right. Never mind.

(*Pause.*)

TERRANCE. What you want me to say, Ma?

(*Pause.*)

TERRANCE. Ma, they were going to lock up Bruce. The chrome [the gun] was in the car. Everyone in the car would be charged with murder if no one copped to it—

(*Pause.*)

TERRANCE. I didn't kill anyone. Ma. . . . Oh yeah, I forgot, whenever someone says I did, I did it.

(*Pause.*)

TERRANCE. I told 'em what they wanted to hear. That's what niggas supposed to do in Newark. I told them what they wanted to hear to keep Bruce out of it. Did they tell you who got killed? Did they say it was my father?

(*Pause.*)

TERRANCE. Then you should know I didn't do it. If I ever went to jail for anything, it would be killin' him . . . an' he ain't dead yet. Rape done brought me into the world. Prison gonna take me out. An' that's the way it is, Ma.

(*Pause.*)

TERRANCE. Come on, Ma, if Bruce went to jail, you would've never forgiven me. Me, on the other hand, I wasn't ever supposed to be here.

(*Pause.*)

TERRANCE. I'm sorry, Ma . . . I'm sorry. Don't be cryin'. You got Bruce. You got him home. He's your baby. Bye, Ma. I call you later.

I showed the scene to my wife, Eunice, a graduate of the Juilliard School, and a professional actor.

"Wow," she said after she read it. "Amazing."

I had asked the class to write scenes to help them become familiar with dramatic dialogue and the mechanics of plays. The power of their writing, however, made my goal for the class more ambitious.

"They should write a play," I said.

five

The Song

It grieved him to see me in the world carrying other people's songs and not having one of my own. Told me he was gonna show me how to find my song.

—August Wilson, *Joe Turner's Come and Gone*[1]

I would need the outline of a story to hang a play on. I had heard while in Elizabeth about Emmanuel Mervilus who managed to get his sentence overturned, which happens very rarely. I took him to lunch at the El Salvadoreño restaurant in Elizabeth. I spent the afternoon writing down his story. Afterward, I typed out the interview. The twenty-eight printed copies of the transcript sat on the beige passenger seat next to me.

Mervilus was six feet tall, with long, thick dreadlocks. He was never in a gang. He was not a drug dealer. He had a job. He came from a close and loving family. But there are cops in poor communities who hunt Black boys and men as if they are prey. To them, it is a sport. These cops are not always white, although they often are. But they are always sadists. Intoxicated by the power to instill fear, use lethal force indiscriminately, and destroy lives—and allowed to do so by a judicial system that does not protect the most basic rights of the poor, including due process, adequate legal representation, and the right to a jury trial—they circle around their victims like vultures. If we were to use the strict dictionary definition, these police officers are criminals.

"There is a cop who used to tell me when I was a boy he was going to give me my first adult charge," Mervilus told me. Mervilus said he did not want to name the officer, now a detective, for fear of retribution. This cop made good on his threat when Mervilus turned eighteen and was a senior in high school. The cop saw Mervilus on the street smoking a joint. Mervilus ran. The cop chased him. Mervilus turned, put his arms up, and shouted, "I give up! I give up!" The cop threw him on the hood of a police car.

"I don't remember anything after that," he said. "I saw a flash. Next thing, I'm in the back of the police car. There are scratches on my face.

"I'm not a saint," Mervilus said to me. "I did things. But everything I did, I owned up to."

When he got to the police station, he was charged with having a dozen bags of marijuana. That was a lie.

"They need more than simple possession to lock you up, so they plant drugs," he said. "It makes the charge stick."

The teenager was in the county jail for two weeks and was assigned a public defender who told him to plead guilty. "The public defender told me, 'How are you going to prove this [your innocence]?'" he recalled.

"No one wants to believe cops lie," Mervilus continued. "Why would a cop lie? Lots of reasons. Promotion. Quotas. And I don't look like a regular citizen. I'm Black. I got dreads. I fit the description. I figured I ran. I didn't know much of anything at that time, you feel me? So, I said, 'I'll take it.' I thought that probation could be expunged if I did good. But I was wrong. From that day on, I said I would never, ever, plead guilty to something I didn't do."

Mervilus went back to high school, repeated senior year, and graduated. He got a minimum-wage job in the kitchen of a nursing home in Linden, New Jersey. It was 2005. He was twenty-one. He was living at home. One afternoon a cop stopped him randomly on the street. The officer ran his name in the system.

"He says there is a warrant for my arrest," Mervilus said of the police officer. "He says I just jumped two fences and put something under a rock. It was a total lie. I am arrested with another guy for manufacturing and distribution. I spent a month in Union County Jail. And when you spend a month in Union County Jail, it makes you want to plead guilty. You're confined to a little area. You don't get out.

"I was first put in a holding tank with someone else; some type of drug dealer going through withdrawal," he recalled. "It was nasty. Throwing up. Diarrhea. Two steel bunks. One steel toilet. No windows.

"They put my bail at seventy-five thousand dollars. I paid seventy-five hundred—ten percent—and bailed out. I tried to get my old job back. They refused to let me back; said 'abandonment of work.' I didn't *want* to hustle. When your back is against the wall, you can't find a job, and you have to pay a lawyer, often all you can do is hustle. But if I hustled, I'd probably catch another charge and go to prison."

Eventually his girlfriend's stepfather helped him get a job at the port in Newark. Mervilus was making $12 an hour. But the Elizabeth police were not done with him. In October 2006 Mervilus and a friend had just left a Dunkin' Donuts and were walking down the street, when cops stopped them. There had just been a stabbing and robbery. The shaken victim, there with the police, said that Mervilus and his friend had attacked him.

"Why would he point a finger at me?" Mervilus said to me. "I look the part: a Black man with dreads. But there was no evidence to corroborate his story. I didn't have any blood on me. He said we stole his book bag."

The cops rushed him and his friend. They shouted, "Put

your hands on the wall!" He complied. He was put in jail, and his bail was set at $100,000.

The loss of his job while he was in jail meant that Mervilus could no longer support his mother, who was dying of breast cancer, his sister, and two brothers. His father had left the family.

"Rent has to be paid, everything has to go on as if I'm there," he said. So, he told his family not to use their paltry resources to bail him out. "My younger brother was sixteen. I played the father role. The system failed me. It failed him. He lost me."

His family believed the cops. That hurt the most.

"I'm Haitian," he said. "My family is looking at me like, 'What? This guy's robbing people? He stabbed someone who almost died?' I get blackballed. No one comes to see me, not even my mom. My mom raised me better than that. All these Haitian people were saying, 'Well, why is he locked up if he didn't do it?' I was hurt and depressed."

One night after he had been in jail for seven months, Mervilus was jolted awake in his cell. "It felt like there were claws digging into my stomach," he said. "The pain was horrible."

As he found out later when his brother visited, his mother had died that night. She was fifty-two. After the visit, feeling enraged and frustrated, he provoked another prisoner into a fight. "It didn't fill the void," he said.

Mervilus finally got out on bail. His family had taken his mother's body to Haiti for burial. He flew there to visit her grave. It was made out of cement blocks painted white and surrounded by a small gate. He brought flowers.

"I told my mom I was sorry I wasn't there when she died," he recalled. "I told her I was innocent. I wasn't going to plead guilty. I told her I had let her down by not watching over my little brother. I was sitting talking to her for two or three hours. It was very emotional. It was the first time I cried. Her dying was my biggest fear. My mom would be asleep, and I would stand at the door looking in to make sure she was breathing. I was a momma's boy. Serious. Every day when I came home from work, I brought her a chicken sandwich with mayo and pickles from Wendy's."

The prosecutor offered him a deal of five years in prison if he would plead guilty to the crime in which the man was stabbed and robbed. Mervilus refused. Though he was facing twenty years, he went to trial. The victim changed his story several times. At one point, when asked if his assailant was in the courtroom, the man pointed to someone other than Mervilus. It did not matter. Mervilus was sentenced to eleven years for first-degree robbery.

His younger brother, who had been sheltered and protected by Mervilus and his mom, took to the streets to earn money for a lawyer for his older brother. He raised the $12,000 needed to retain an attorney, who took the cash from the boy as a "down payment." Mervilus was able to file an appeal. The lawyer exposed a series of discrepancies and inconsistencies in the testimony of the stabbing victim. Mervilus was retried, acquitted, and freed. He had been in prison for four years. The process cost his brother a total of $32,000. His lawyer called the acquittal "a Halley's Comet occurrence."

It was cold and rainy on the hourlong drive to the prison. I had only two modes of heat in my twenty-three-year-old Volvo wagon. Full blast or none. I decided to run the heat for a few minutes to get the chill out of the car.

The windshield wipers struggled noisily back and forth in arcs on the foggy glass. The blurry lights of oncoming traffic grew closer and closer and then disappeared, replaced by small, diminishing red taillights in my rearview mirror. Finally, the looming dome of the prison appeared through the sheets of rain. I turned right and then right again until I came to the parking lot. I emptied my pockets and darted through the downpour to the prison lobby.

East Jersey State Prison had a heating system like that of my Volvo. In the middle of winter, the old steam pipes would roar with heat, forcing us to open the windows and let the cold air come in through the bars. It was always too hot or too cold. The prison, that rainy night, had turned on the heat. We could barely breathe. Marvin Spears, an army veteran who, like James Leak, the former boxer; Sincere; and Mervilus, should never have been in prison, had pushed up the window and turned on the floor fan, which helped a little. I handed out the interview with Mervilus.

"I've read through your scenes," I told the class. "Many of them are very powerful, moving, and well written. They capture your lives, your reality, which few people outside your communities and prison understand. Look, I'm not a playwright. And just because I'm a journalist and have written books doesn't mean I can write a play. But if you would like to try and hammer these scenes into a coherent narrative, into a play, I will help you do it. My wife is an actor. She said she will read it and critique it. That will help."

The offer provoked a flash of audible excitement.

"Yes!"

"Great idea."

"We should do this!"

"Definitely."

"Okay," I said. "Then we will read plays, always looking closely at how the masters do it, and write our own."

I gave the class a summary of Mervilus's story.

"We need a narrative, and it seems like this one might work," I said of Mervilus's experience. "Of course, you will make the story your own. But it gives us a rough outline. What do you think?"

The class accepted the proposal.

"We will need two teams of writers," I said. "One team will write about life outside the prison. The other will write about life inside the prison. We will flesh out two parallel narratives and then put them together.

"How many parts should we have?" I asked. "Who would like a part?"

Seven hands went up, including Boris, Kabir, Marvin, Timmy, and Sincere.

"Okay," I said. "The play will have seven main characters. We will need a mother, her two sons, a powerful drug dealer in the neighborhood—that's four—and then I guess three people inside the prison; maybe a corrections officer."

"Don't make him white," Steph, taciturn and laconic as usual, said abruptly.

The class murmured its approval.

"Make him Black, middle-aged, sick of his job, all worn out by the prison," Steph went on. "It's too easy to make him white. There's plenty of Black police showing out for [trying to impress] white cops, willing to serve the system harder. They could be the worst at times."

In that moment, there was a change in the classroom. The men became more than students. They would create. They would give expression to their experiences, their pain and suffering, their hope, their grief, and their loss. They would do this not as individual students but as a collective. They would validate their lives, if only to one another. They would be able to hold this play in their hands when the class was over. They would be able to look at it months and years later. They became, in that instant, playwrights and actors, identities none had ever thought to assume. This would be their song, for as James Baldwin writes, "the subdued and the subduer do not speak the same language."[2] The emotion of the moment, which I had unleashed unwittingly, swelled up inside me. As Boris would tell me later, "This became the class we hoped would never end."

"You must only write out of your own experience, what you know, what you have seen and felt," I said. "Don't copy the images and stories on movies or television, or even in popular books. What is produced for mass culture is almost always sentimental, stereotypical, and idealized drivel. The images and stories of mass culture will corrupt and destroy the integrity of your work. Amiri Baraka said the Black artist's role in America is to aid in the destruction of America as he or she knows it. The Black artist should tell the truth about American society, and about him or herself, in that society. This rarely spoken truth, lifted up by the Black artist, empowers those whose voices are demonized and silenced. It forces, Baraka says, the dominant white ruling class to confront the 'filth of their own evil.'[3] Baraka, like Baldwin, said that artists are perhaps the only people who speak the truth about us.

"And that is the key: Truth. Truth. A relentless, unsentimental truth that you are not afraid to speak about the society around you and, most importantly, about yourselves, even if that truth can, at times, be unflattering and damning. Honesty—and this takes deep and sometimes painful reflection—will give your work depth and power and make it resonate. August Wilson got it right: 'Confront the dark parts of yourself and banish them with illumination and forgiveness. Your willingness to wrestle with your demons will cause your angels to sing.'"

I opened my copy of James Baldwin's *Collected Essays* and began to read from "The Creative Process":

> The artist is distinguished from all other responsible actors in society—the politicians, legislators, educators, and scientists—by the fact that he is his own test tube, his own laboratory, working according to very rigorous rules, however unstated these may be, and cannot allow any consideration to supersede his responsibility to reveal all that he can possibly discover

concerning the mystery of the human being. Society must accept some things as real; but he must always know that visible reality hides a deeper one, and that all our action and achievement rest on things unseen. A society must assume that it is stable, but the artist must know, and he must let us know, that there is nothing stable under heaven. One cannot possibly build a school, teach a child, or drive a car without taking some things for granted. The artist cannot and must not take anything for granted but must drive to the heart of every answer and expose the question the answer hides.[4]

"Okay," I said, "let's look at August Wilson's *Joe Turner's Come and Gone*, then we'll look at the scenes for our play."

Joe Turner's Come and Gone is set in 1911 in a boarding-house in Pittsburgh's Hill District. The play's title comes from the blues song "Joe Turner's Blues," written in 1915 by the composer and musician W. C. Handy. The song refers to a man named Joe Turney, the brother of Peter Turney who was the governor of Tennessee from 1893 to 1897. Joe Turney trans-ported Black prisoners, chained together in what is called a coffle, along the roads from Memphis to the Tennessee State Penitentiary in Nashville. While en route he used to hand over some of the convicts, for a commission, to white farmers. The prisoners he leased to the farmers worked for years in a system of convict leasing—slavery by another name.

In Wilson's play, Herald Loomis worked as a convict on Turner's farm. He arrives in Pittsburgh with his eleven-year-old daughter, Zonia, in search of his wife. He is haunted by the trauma of his bondage. At a boardinghouse, he meets a conjurer named Bynum Walker, who tells him that to face and overcome the demons that torment him, he must find his song.

"Bynum Walker, the conjurer, talks about the importance

of our song," I said. "What is this song? Why is it important? Why can't we be whole until we find our song?"

"Is our song like prayer?" asked Sammy, who had entered the prison illiterate and, through grit and intelligence, made it into the college program. Before class began, he would ask me if I would like a coffee. He would disappear down the hall and return with instant coffee in a white Styrofoam cup. Sammy was a devout Christian. As we wrote the play, he would sometimes object to the use of curse words, a squeamishness that never sat well with Sincere, whom I was glad was seated on the opposite side of the room.

"Yes," I said. "That's good. Like prayer. And what else?"

"Is it like memory?" Lawrence asked.

"Yes, prayer and memory, exactly."

I waited. Finally, I asked, "Whose history were you taught in school?"

"The white man's version of history," the good-natured Kabir answered, laughing. "How George Washington was a great dude, and America was a great country, the land of liberty—that kind of stuff."

"That's right," I said. "The American historian Carl Becker says that history is the artificial extension of social memory, and what he means is that those with the power to shape history and social memory choose what we remember and what and who we forget."

"Like Confederate monuments," commented Sincere.

"Yes, almost all put up in the 1890s and early twentieth century at the height of lynching and segregation," I said "A validation and celebration of white supremacy."

"The white man's version of history," Kabir said.

"The dominant history is an expression of power—not power in the past but power in the present," I said. "Those with power decide what we remember and honor from our past and what we do not. So, if you remember, in the play, Bynum

Walker keeps talking about how there are forces trying to steal your song; this is what he is referring to. Your song functions, as Sammy said, like prayer, and, as Lawrence said, like memory. It connects you to where you came from. It connects you with your ancestors. It connects you with your own history; your own story. It validates and lifts up your suffering, your dignity, your humanity, and your resistance. It tells you that you will not be defeated by the troubles of this world. It affirms you and your people. The white power structure seeks to erase and deny your song—to steal it from you, to leave you voiceless. Loomis, if you notice, reacts angrily to all the songs in the play. These songs remind him of slavery, of Joe Turner, of God and the Holy Ghost, which for him are malevolent forces of authority.

"Blacks after the Civil War were routinely arrested on minor or invented charges and provided for a fee as convict laborers to white plantation owners," I went on. "It was a perpetuation of slavery, although far more dangerous. The constitutional basis for convict leasing was the Thirteenth Amendment, which was passed right after the Civil War in 1865. The Thirteenth Amendment, still in force, prohibits involuntary servitude unless it is punishment for crime. This is why prisoners do not have to get paid for their labor. Enslaved people were considered property by slaveholders. They were expensive. Slaveholders had a vested interest in at least keeping them alive. But convict laborers cost little. They were often worked to death because they could be replaced easily. Convict laborers worked up to fourteen hours a day, usually in chains, in cotton fields, clearing malaria-infested swamplands, laying railroad tracks, building levees, working in coal and iron mines, in sawmills, and in turpentine camps. Tens of thousands died."

I read the class a passage in historian Leon Litwack's book *Trouble in Mind: Black Southerners in the Age of Jim Crow*, which I had taught the year before at the Wagner Correctional Facility. Litwack writes about Joe Turney, the historical model for Joe Turner:

Most of the prisoners had been rounded up for minor infractions, often when police raided a craps game set up by an informer. After a perfunctory court appearance, the blacks were removed, usually the same day, and turned over to Turney. He was reputed to have handcuffed eighty prisoners to forty links of chain. When a man turned up missing that night in the community, the word spread quickly, "They tell me Joe Turner's come and gone." Family members were left to mourn the missing.[5]

I read the lines from Handy's blues song:

They tell me Joe Turner's come and gone.
Ohhh Lordy.
They tell me Joe Turner's come and gone.
Ohhh Lordy.
Got my man and gone.
Come with forty links of chain.
Ohhh Lordy.
Come with forty links of chain.

"And how does Herald Loomis react when he first hears Bynum sing the song, with its refrain 'Joe Turner's come and gone'?" I asked.

"He's furious," said Timmy, his lean frame rising from his desk like a beanpole. "He says he doesn't like hearing Bynum sing about Joe Turner. Wants him to stop."

"Why?" I asked.

"Because it hurts."

Sincere spoke up: "Bynum sings this song later, and Loomis admits he was enslaved by Turner. He was taken away in chains when his girl was a baby. He got back after seven years, and he found his little girl living with his wife's mama and his wife gone up north. He left with his girl and went north and spent the next four years tryin' to find his wife, just to see her face, so he can start again in the world, because he had been living in somebody else's world. He needed to make his own world."

I asked three students to read the parts of Bynum, Loomis, and Seth from the scene where Bynum confronts Loomis about his trauma.

BYNUM. You a farming man, Herald Loomis? You look like you done some farming.

LOOMIS. Same as everybody. I done farmed some, yeah.

BYNUM. I used to work at farming . . . picking cotton. I reckon on everybody done picked some cotton.

SETH. I ain't! I ain't never picked no cotton. I was born up here in the North. My daddy was a freedman. I ain't never even seen no cotton!

BYNUM. Mr. Loomis done picked some cotton. Ain't you, Herald Loomis? You done picked a bunch of cotton.

LOOMIS. How you know so much about me? How you know what I done? How much cotton I picked?

BYNUM. I can tell from looking at you. My daddy taught me how to do that. Say when you look at a fellow, if you taught yourself to look for it, you can see his song written on him. Tell you what kind of a man he is in the world. Now, I can look at you, Mr. Loomis, and see you a man who done forgot his song. Forgot how to sing it. A fellow forget that, and he forget who he is. Forget how he's supposed to mark down life. Now, I used to travel all up and down, this road and that. . . looking here and there. Searching. Just like you, Mr. Loomis. I didn't know what I was searching for. The only thing I knew was something was keeping me dissatisfied.

Something wasn't making my heart smooth and easy. Then one day, my daddy gave me a song. That song had a weight to it that was hard to handle. That song was hard to carry. I fought against it. Didn't want to accept that song. I tried to find my daddy to give him back the song. But I found out it wasn't his song. It was my song. It had come from way deep inside me. I looked long back in memory and gathered up pieces and snatches of things to make that song. I was making it up out of myself. And that song helped me on the road. Made it smooth to where my footsteps didn't bite back at me. All the time, that song getting bigger and bigger. That song growing with each step of the road. It got so I used all of myself up in the making of that song. Then I was the song in search of itself. That song rattling in my throat, and I'm looking for it. See, Mr. Loomis, when a man forgets his song, he goes off in search of it . . . till he find out he's got it with him all the time. That's why I can tell you one of Joe Turner's niggers. 'Cause you forgot how to sing your song.[6]

"He's got his past written on his face," Boris said. "A lot of us feel like that."

"And," I asked, "at the end of the scene where Loomis admits he was held in bondage for seven years by Joe Turner, what does he say to Bynum?"

Marvin: "He says that Bynum is one of them bones people."

"And what are bones people?" I asked.

"Loomis said he saw bones rise up out of the water once," Lawrence explained, "and walk across the water. And the water was bigger than the whole world. Then a big wave came, and they weren't bones anymore: they had flesh on them, and they were Black people. Were these the bones of those who died in slave ships and were thrown into the sea? Like, our ancestors?"

"They're denied their humanity," Sincere said. "They are not seen by white people as fully human. They are only bones. They have to do the work themselves to put on their flesh and blood and become human. After he tells that story, Loomis tries to stand up, but he can't stand up 'cause he still all bones. He only stands up at the end of the play, when he finds his song, when he's resurrected as a free man, when he is able to shout out his song, when he can say who he is and where he came from."

"All that," I said. "And why is this song, this truth that Wilson says is so vital, so difficult to sing?"

"Because of the pain," Boris said. "Because it's about loss, about suffering and death, about families ripped apart, about people not being treated as if they were real human beings, because that's the story then, and it's still the story. Like, look at us. Nothing changes. Nothing has ever changed. So, it hurts to sing it. Herald Loomis is trying to find his wife and his little girl who was taken from him from when he was imprisoned, enslaved on Joe Turner's plantation for seven years, like all of us lost our women and children once we got locked up too. And when he finds her, she says she waited for him for five years and then left 'cause she thought he's dead, and that's about right: five years, that's when the visits and the phone calls stopped here too. And then you wonder where they went, who they are with, do they remember you, and all that kind of shit. That's hard to sing."

We read out loud the passage Boris had referenced at the end of the play:

MARTHA. Herald. I didn't know if you was ever coming back. They told me Joe Turner had you, and my

whole world split half in two. My whole life shattered. It was like I had poured it in a cracked jar, and
it all leaked out the bottom. When it go like that,
there ain't nothing you can do put it back together.
You talking about Henry Thompson's place like I'm
still gonna be working that land by myself. How I'm
gonna do that? You wasn't gone but two months,
and Henry Thompson kicked me off his land, and I
ain't had no place to go but to my mama's. I stayed
and waited there for five years before I woke up one
morning and decided that you was dead. Even if you
weren't, you was dead to me. I wasn't gonna carry
you with me no more. So I killed you in my heart.
I buried you. I mourned you. And then I picked
up what was left and went on to make life without
you. I was a young woman with life at my beckon. I
couldn't drag you behind me like a sack of cotton.[7]

"I want to look at how Wilson writes moments of emotional intensity," I said. "These moments can easily become sentimental
and mawkish, and once that happens, the emotional power is
lost. You have to keep your writing tight when you write about
intense emotional experiences, as Timmy did. You have to think
carefully about every word. You have to push the reader to an
emotional height and then pull back, push again and then pull
back, until the final line or action lands like a punch in your
gut. Wilson does this at several moments in the play, when Seth
is used to deflate the emotional tension between Loomis and
Bynum, letting the intensity build slowly, like a kind of dance.
You see it at the end of the play when Martha recites a verse
from the Twenty-Third Psalm, and Loomis answers each verse
with derision. She recites the line about the shadow of death,
and Loomis tells her that's just where he has been. Or the line
about dwelling in the house of the Lord, and he answers, 'Great

big old white man . . . your Mr. Jesus Christ,' until the scene cul-
minates with him slashing himself across his chest and rubbing
the blood over his face."

I passed out a front-page story I'd written for the *New York
Times* in 1991 during the first Gulf War.

"This is a story about a sergeant who goes to make his last
phone call home to his wife before the invasion of Kuwait," I
said. "The conversation is emotionally charged, but if you look
closely, you will see that I try to do what Wilson does. I coun-
tered each of the emotional highs with an image or interrup-
tions that were emotionally neutral to bring us back down, so
that the emotions never become too overwhelming. I tried to
build the emotional pitch in the same back-and-forth Wilson
uses so effectively—until the emotional climax at the end of the
article, where his wife asks him where he wants to be buried if
he gets killed, has a punch."

I read the story to the class:

> After buying $156 worth of candy bars, King Edward
> cigars, and Pepsi for his platoon, Sergeant Ted L.
> Smith walked through the shallow puddles that filled
> the streets of a northern Saudi border town toward a
> clothing store.
>
> He entered the store, which had a painted sign out
> front that read, in shaky English: "Atantion: Here is
> Atelphone Service."
>
> "This is what I came into town to do," he said as
> he unclipped his mud-covered web belt and cartridge
> cases and let them fall on the floor. "I have been think-
> ing about this for a while."
>
> The thirty-year-old squad leader braced himself
> for what has become a painful ritual for troops who
> soon expect to go into combat: the final call home.
>
> Soldiers now wait for hours outside the roadside

telephone booths marked "International Telephone" or stores that have phones with international lines.

They use credit card numbers to call their loved ones, usually collect. By dialing 1-800-100, they can speak with an operator in the United States.

But the conversations that had dwelled on mundane affairs—financial worries, family problems, weather, and loneliness—have now taken on a dark air as the soldiers verbalize, many for the first time, about where they want to be buried and what kind of life they want for children they may never see again.

"Hey, what's up?" the sergeant said to his sleepy wife, Wendy, in Panama, where he is based. "Wake up."

"How's the baby?" he asked about his sixteen-month-old daughter, Amber Elise.

"Are you hanging in there?" he asked.

Outside the store, small children, now accustomed to the sight of heavily armed American troops, smiled and flashed V signs to soldiers driving by.

Several yelled "*Akel! Akel!*," the Arabic word for food, and held up an empty brown plastic pouch that had once held an American meal ration.

Sergeant Smith, his face and hands dark brown from six months in the desert, had not spoken to his wife since the first week in January.

"This is probably the last call," he said, his voice dipping almost to a whisper.

"It is good to hear your voice," he said. "Get a grip, get a grip, Wendy. You know me better than that."

"Take it one day at a time," he said softly. "That's what I'm doing. Everything passes. This will pass."

"I love you too, honey," he said, a phrase he would repeat innumerable times throughout the conversation.

"Don't do that now," he said to his distraught wife. "You have got to be hard. I get tired of this too."

"I read an article about President and Mrs. Bush in that *People* magazine last night," he said. "Don't show weakness. You've got to stand your ground like President Bush."

The sergeant, who took part in the assault on the army command headquarters in Panama in December 1989 as part of the airborne branch of the 193nd Infantry, assured his wife that the battle would closely mirror the attack in Panama.

"I don't underestimate any armed man," he told his wife, "but I am not impressed with the Iraqis. They remind me of the Panama Defense Forces. They just have a lot more guns."

His twenty-four-year-old wife, apart from her husband for the last half year, went into the litany of problems of trying to run a house and raise a child alone.

"Family problems," he said, cupping his hand over the receiver.

Then it came time to deal with the issues that had gone unmentioned in previous letters and calls.

"Whatever happens, keep your chin up, no matter what," he said. "If I get waxed, I'm going to heaven, and I'll be waiting for you. I'm not afraid, but I don't want to lose you and Amber."

"Fifty or sixty years, that sounds good to me," he said, responding to his wife's question about how long he wanted to be with her.

"When Amber gets up in the morning, give her a big hug and tell her that Daddy loves her," he said.

The sergeant, leaning forward on his chair, folded and unfolded a strap on his web belt with his left hand, his fingernails black with dirt. He listened quietly. His wife was asking him where he wanted to be buried.

"Some place close to you," he said, "so you can come with Amber to see me."

"Hey," he said. "I want Amber to go to college."

"Have faith, honey," the sergeant said, "but sometimes things happen that we don't understand. You just have to go on."

"Wendy," he said imploringly. "Wendy."

He waited silently on the line as trucks and jeeps splashed through the puddles outside.

And then the clouds broke as his twenty-four-year-old wife remembered to tell him the latest news, her piercing of their daughter's ears.

"I bet she is pretty," he said. "Send me a picture with her earrings in."

The shopkeeper came over to tell the sergeant in broken English that he must close his store for noon prayers.

"When it is all said and done, it's just us," he said. "That's what it is all about."

"I love you," he said.[8]

I turned to the pile of scenes in front of me. Timmy's was on top.

"This is very powerful," I said to Timmy. "Can you read it?"

He shook his head no.

"Could I read it to the class?" I asked.

He agreed. I read it slowly. It was greeted with a stunned silence. It was the first time anyone in the room was aware that Timmy was a product of rape, how much that stigma hurt, and how he had sacrificed himself for his half brother. I held in my hands another scene, equally as powerful, by an older student, a father, who wrote of the last visit with his wife and six-year-old son. The boy started speaking about "Uncle Jimmy," and he realized that his wife was seeing another man.

I asked him if he would read it. His eyes welled up with tears. In a hoarse voice, he said no.

"Would you rather not have me read it?" I asked.

"You can read it," he said.

When I finished, I asked him if he was able to stay in touch with his boy.

"I never saw him again," he said mournfully.

"And how old is he now?" I asked.

"Twenty."

Another student wrote a scene about being found dead in his cell. The guards talked nonchalantly over his body as they clamped shackles on his corpse, as required by prison regulations, before lifting him onto a stretcher and wheeling him out.

Steph wrote a scene about being locked in Ad Seg—administrative segregation—in Trenton. He was sent to Ad Seg for 365 days in 2009 after being found in possession of a contraband cell phone he had bought from a guard for $200 while he was in Newark's Northern State Prison. There are guards willing to sell prisoners contraband items from cell phones to drugs, including heroin.

Nearly every student in the class had spent some time in solitary confinement—what are known euphemistically as control units. Those accused of committing an infraction are first sent to "the hole," a prehearing control unit, until they are found guilty or innocent, which is almost always determined by the statements submitted by the corrections officers. Prisoners in the hole are not permitted to have any personal property or phone privileges. They are held there for between five and thirty days before being returned to the general population, or, if found guilty, transferred to Ad Seg. Prisoners can remain there for many years.

The prolonged isolation is psychologically damaging, fostering aggressive and self-destructive behavior. Prisoners can receive up to ninety days in Ad Seg for even minor infractions. It is not uncommon to spend a year, sometimes longer, in Ad Seg, especially since a single infraction—say, a fight—can cause prisoners to be charged with numerous infractions such as an assault charge, a fighting charge, and a disruption of the institutional movement charge. Prisoners who engage in only one fight can violate in that one instance so many infractions that they spend as long as three to five years in Ad Seg. It was banned by a law on Isolated Confinement in New Jersey in August 2020, but it has been resurrected in the New Jersey prison system under a new name, Restorative Housing Unit.

Ad Seg cells are six feet by eight feet. They include a bed, sink, and two small shelves. There are no windows. In the summer, it is so hot the metal walls sweat, and temperatures can rise to ninety-five degrees. Steph had a small fan in Ad Seg. He could purchase a small bag of ice for seventy-five cents. He would rub the ice on his face as it melted quickly. In the back wall was a depression that was three feet tall, two feet wide, and eighteen inches deep. That was his toilet. It did not flush. It was cleaned out every few days. The stench of feces and urine filled the tiny cell. He was locked in for twenty-three hours a day. The noise of the voices reverberating off the walls and down the corridors was deafening and constant. The cell was infested with mice. The meals were often rancid, and all portions were so small that he was constantly hungry. Another prisoner kept a mouse on a string as a pet, a detail that Steph wrote into the play. Steph was strip-searched every time he left the cell, forced not only to stand naked but also to open his mouth, run his fingers through his mouth, lift up his genitals, and bend over and cough. Guards, to belittle him, often forced him to repeat the process from the beginning so that he would be putting his fingers in his mouth after having handled his genitals.

"I saw inmates losing their grip on reality while in Ad Seg and how it damaged their mental health," reflected Steph, who would go on to graduate summa cum laude from Rutgers University. "They would play with their own feces, and even tried to kill themselves. The psychiatrist would walk through a tier once a week, slow down without stopping by each cell, and ask through the bars: 'Are you okay in there? Do you feel like harming yourself?' Inmates would never answer affirmatively. This was because one's neighbors could hear this inquiry, and not being able to deal with Ad Seg was a sign of weakness, which one should not display in prison.

"I became antisocial. I felt uncomfortable around people once I got out. I became more callous and had difficulty holding a conversation for some time. It made me angrier. I hated those in authority by the time I got out of solitary. To me, any person who could live with subjecting a human being to such dehumanizing conditions was evil. Ad Seg was the most savage moment of my life."

It was eleven o'clock at night, and everyone was locked in their tiny cells in the Ad Seg in the scene Steph wrote. The prisoners were yelling up and down the hall for things they needed. Steph shouted out that he wanted a newspaper.

Items were passed up and down the corridor by "fishing," in which seven or eight narrow strips of cloth, ripped from a sheet down its length, were tied together in a line. A bar of soap was tied to the end of the line. The prisoner wrapped the end without the soap around his left hand and lay down on the floor facing the bars. Then he reached between the narrow opening in the bars and began tossing the long cloth line out of the cell. Once it was out, he grabbed the end with the soap. Lying on his stomach, with his right arm reaching out of his cell through the bars, he lifted his left arm in the air. He let the soap dangle on about ten inches of line. He twirled the line in a lasso motion, with the soap swinging in midair, and tossed it down the hall until the soap slid as far as the line allowed. Steph had attached a laundry bag to the end of the line. When the line was returned and the laundry bag came back, he took out the newspaper and read a story about an eighteen-year-old named Amir, the same age and name of his son, being shot dead in Newark. But even then, it did not fully register. "It's a common name. It's a common name," he desperately repeated to himself. He called home the next morning.

"I was readin' the paper . . ." he said to his daughter.

"Yeah, that was him," she said.

"That must have been hard," I said to Steph after he had read the scene.

"It was a trying time," he conceded.

Steph did not attend the viewing for his son. The cost was prohibitive. Prisoners get fifteen minutes to visit a dying family member or a deceased family member in a funeral home. No one else, other than the corrections officers, is allowed to be present. The prisoners are charged the overtime pay for the corrections officers that accompany them, which costs hundreds of dollars.

Clandestine forms of communication between prisoners are probably as old as prisons themselves. The German playwright and left-wing revolutionary Ernst Toller finished the first draft of his play *Masses Man* while incarcerated in Eichstätt prison in 1919. In his 1933 autobiography, *I Was a German,* he writes about male prisoners tapping on the ceilings of their cells to communicate with the women imprisoned on the floor above them. Toller's clandestine communication with female prisoners was one that most of my students had replicated a century later in county jails, where many were held for months, even years, before going to trial and being sentenced.

"They sent notes by the lavatory pipes, rolled up paper tied with string," Toller writes. "They started love affairs in which mistress and lover had never seen each other; in clumsy words, they tried to describe their appearance to each other. They exchanged keepsakes, locks of hair, little pieces of cloth that had lain against their breasts at night."[9]

The women worked during the day in a washhouse in the prison yard. One day the matron assigned to watch the female prisoners left the yard, leaving one woman alone in the washhouse.

"She gazed out of the window trying to make out the cell of the man with whom she had been corresponding for weeks," Toller writes of the young woman. "She loved him, she wanted to see him; but how should she recognize him? But the man had already seen and recognized her, and was waving to her to show that it was he who was her lover. She shook her head incredulously. He pointed to his brown, curly hair, his hooked nose, the scar by his ear. At last, she was convinced; she smiled at him and stretched out her arms to touch him just once, to embrace him just once. But the heavy bars of prison stood between them. Then, in a moment of overwhelming emotion, she jumped back from the window, unbuttoned her coarse gray linen dress and showed him her body—her firm little breasts; her sturdy, round legs. She laughed and wept for joy; at last, she had been able to do something for him, to show him how much she loved him."[10]

A few weeks earlier, I had been drinking coffee and eating doughnuts in the backroom of the Second Presbyterian Church of Elizabeth with three women: Gloria Blount, who has been in and out of Union County Jail over the years; Irene Pabey, who spent about four months there; and Alveda Torrado, who had been imprisoned in the jail for eighteen months. The women were part of a weekly support group I ran at the church for the formerly incarcerated. They explained the details behind setting up and operating what in county jails is known as the bowl phone.

The bowl phone crudely replicates the speaking tubes on ships that sailors once shouted through. Drained metal toilets

are used as megaphones to build friendships, carry out court-
ship, fall in love—although the lovers may never meet—have
phone sex, pray, pass news about court cases and families, and
exchange gossip. The bowl phone was a ubiquitous part of my
students' lives while they awaited trial in county jail cells.

Elizabeth was devastated by the 1982 closure of its Singer
Company plant, which had been built in 1873 and at one time
employed ten thousand workers.[11] The thousand or so African Americans at the plant worked mostly in a foundry that
made cast-iron parts for the sewing machines. The foundry
work paid poorly and was dangerous. White workers, many
of them German, Italian, Irish, Jewish, Polish, or Lithuanian
immigrants, dominated the safer and higher-paying positions
on the factory floor. The city was built around the sprawling
plant. Generations of residents organized their lives and their
families on the basis of Singer jobs.[12] And then, after a long decline, the factory was gone. The year Singer closed its flagship
factory in Elizabeth, there were 2,696 plant shutdowns across
the United States, resulting in nearly 1.3 million job losses.
Singer workers in Elizabeth under the age of fifty-five lost all
retirement benefits, even if they had worked for the company
for decades.

The closure was not only an economic blow, leaving workers
without a steady income, health benefits, and a pension, but also
brought with it a loss of identity. Daily routines disintegrated.
Social bonds ruptured. Many of the laid-off employees fell into
despair. Marriages crumbled under the weight of domestic violence, alcoholism, and drug use. Crime skyrocketed. Enraged,
dispossessed white workers scapegoated the city's Blacks and
Latinos. Today Latinos, many of them from Central America,[13]
make up roughly two-thirds of its population. Elizabeth, like
many other US cities in decline, now provides the bodies for
low-wage jobs and mass incarceration.

The church, located downtown, was founded in 1820. It

was once the church of the city's white professional and business elites. In the 1950s, the building, with its brick façade and
white steeple, drew 1,200 people to Sunday services and had 600
students enrolled in the Sunday school. Its numbers, however,
had been in free fall since the early 1960s, as whites abandoned
Elizabeth for the suburbs, and new immigrants, who were never
welcomed by the dwindling white congregation, changed the
city's demographics.

My divinity school classmate Michael Granzen had been
the pastor at the church for two decades. He used the facilities,
which included an indoor basketball court he had built with the
insurance money from a fire that destroyed the Fellowship Hall,
to run basketball leagues, soccer camps, tutoring and youth programs, as well as a homeless shelter. The congregation hovered
at around 120 people. The church was in disrepair, and there
weren't any funds to fix it. The failure by the liberal church to
adapt as the city changed was a fatal mistake. "Whiteness pre-
vailed over Christianity," Michael observed.

Union County Jail was a thirteen-story facility with about
eight hundred prisoners. Female prisoners, at the time, were
housed on the top floor, men on the floors below. The prisoners
were forced to spend twenty-three hours a day in their cells.
There was little structured activity and no educational classes.
Prisoners with good disciplinary records—they are referred to
as trusties and wear green as opposed to khaki uniforms—were
allowed to work in the kitchen or clean the jail. They were not
paid.

Pabey, a thirty-year-old Latina who had black, short, curly
hair with raspberry streaks, told me about the bowl phone prisoners created in Union County Jail. First, she explained, "You
have to plunge the phone."

"You take a piece of cloth," said Blount, a small, wispy African American in her forties. "You take the water out of the
bowl. You keep pumpin' the water out until it get lower. Then

you take the little cup or somethin'. You take a little sock or a little cloth or somethin'. You pump it out with the cloth, the water out. And as you're doin' that, it's the water's going out. It's goin', it's goin'. It don't take but like about a minute."

"But like three seconds," Pabey interjected.

"Yeah, it don't take that long," Blount said. "You scoop the rest of the water."

Next, said Pabey, "You make a mic," using empty toilet paper rolls. Some prisoners prefer to curl up the book of jail regulations and stuff that into the drained toilet.

To send or receive a call, a male prisoner one or two floors below must similarly prepare a bowl phone. It is difficult for the parties to hear each other if they are separated by more than two floors.

To keep the lines of communication open, bowl phones are seldom used as toilets and rarely flushed. Cells with bowl phones become, in essence, public phone booths, identified by their cell numbers.

Pabey said that to start a conversation, "You do the knock." With her knuckles, she rapped out on the table a distinct series of taps that in the jail identified her to other prisoners. "Everybody has a different page," she said. "It's called a pager. Like, it's, the knock is the page."

"It's like a code," Blount clarified.

Pabey and Torrado imitated the start of a bowl phone conversation. "*Heyyy,* baby!" they chorused.

"I be like, 'Papi, you there?'" said Torrado, Pabey's aunt, a Latina in her forties who had long, streaked blonde hair pulled back behind her head and was wearing a low-cut emerald blouse.

"'Yeah, baby, I'm there, baby,'" she went on. "'Hi, baby,' I go. 'Hi, Papi, I miss you.'"

"We be talkin' like that all night," Torrado said. "So then when I see it's daylight, 'Baby, I'm going to bed.' 'Me, too, baby. I'll see you in the morning.'"

I was sitting next to Todd Clayton, a student at Union Theological Seminary in New York City, who was working with me at the church. I asked the women how Todd, if he were a new prisoner in the jail, would get hooked into the bowl phone system.

"They be like, 'Fresh meat in the building,'" Pabey said.

"So you'll be like, 'Okay. Hold on. We got a girl in such and such room that's lookin' for a guy,'" she explained. "Everybody ends up hookin' up."

"Girls come and be like, 'You talkin' to my man on the bowl?'" Torrado said. "I be like, 'Girl, that ain't your man! Next time I hear you talkin' to my man, it's gonna be a problem.'"

"Eventually a woman literally sticks to the person that she's dealin' with," Pabey explained.

"That's where the complications come from," Blount said. "'Cause you fall in love with that person."

"I did it over there," Torrado said. "I met my boyfriend through the toilet bowl. We been together nine years."

"Toilet bowl love," Blount muttered.

"This one girl used to be loud, but I done used to let her talk for a long time," Blount said. "She was a bowl ho, 'cause she stayed up—I mean day and night—and be, 'Hey, blah blah blah,' 'cause you be on, yeah, you be talkin' to different people, you a whore. You a ho, on the bowl."

Pabey offered an example of jailhouse romance: "Say I'm datin' Todd. We're on the mic. I'm like, 'Hey, baby, whatchu doin',' you know what I mean? 'How was your day?' Whatever. And then, without knowing, Todd gets released."

Blount let out a gasp of empathy.

"That hurts," Blount said. "That can be heartbreaking. I seen a girl cry. She like, 'I know he goin' come to the window.' They used to pray and stuff before they go to sleep. And, all of a sudden he got released. So, she was at the window waiting for him to come by the window and say hi or whatever. She say, 'I know my baby comin' to the window.' I know she came to the window looking for him. She be cryin'. I said, 'You ain't think that man really goin' come to the window? He goin' home.'"

"Ah, he goin' get him some pussy," Pabey said. "'Scuse my language, but it's the truth. He goin' go get him some poontang."

"He went out," Blount said. "He was gone. You know what I'm sayin'? She was cryin', her heart breaking. People get hurt. People fight."

I asked what most of the prisoners liked to talk about.

"Sex," Pabey and Blount answered together.

Most "bowl sex" takes place at night, when, as Pabey said, "the freaks come out."

"Now, mind you, if it's my aunt and her dude talkin' on the bowl, you've got to let the other female know," Pabey said. "Courtesy. So it's you and your dude on his bowl, and he's tellin' his roommate, 'Yo, you gotta go.' You feel me? So you have to give that person courtesy. And, you get it on."

"He be like, 'Baby, how big is your boobs?'" Torrado said. "'How big is your butt?' 'Thirty-two.' 'Wow, baby. Keep telling, keep talkin'.'

"And they be like, 'Baby,' they be like, 'Open up, baby, talk nasty to me,'" she said. "'Baby, what do you want me to say?' 'Anything, baby, say anything, to . . .' 'Okay, baby, come here, baby. Let's do this.'"

"Imagine me lickin' on your . . ." Pabey offered.

"He be like, 'Oh, baby, I'm startin' feelin' hot already down here, baby,'" Blount said.

"They be like, 'Hold up, I'm about to bust a nut off-a this fool,'" Pabey said, adding, "I be on my bed readin' a book."

"Me too!" Blount said. "I be laughin'."

"And I'll be like, 'Yo, this bitch is crazy,'" Pabey said. "She's like, 'Baby, yeah, stroke it harder, stroke it harder.' And I be like, 'What the fuck?' And he's like, 'Baby, I'm about to bust. I'm about to come.'"

She mimicked the moans of an orgasm.

"And I be like, 'Ah, shit,'" she said. "And then we'll bust out laughin'. 'Oh, you're a two minute. Uhhh.' She be like, 'Leave my baby alone. Leave my boo alone.'"

"A girl could be sittin' there talkin' to a guy through the toilet bowl but still gettin' her coochie licked by another girl," Pabey threw in.

"I've seen, like, the guy tell the girl, 'Oh, baby, climb on top of the bowl and smack your coochie,'" Pabey said. "Literally sit there and be smackin'—so the guy can hear it."

The only opportunity to see a bowl phone partner occurs when both put in requests to go to the medical department on the same day. Male and female prisoners are not permitted to speak to each other there, but some bowl phone lovers manage to communicate through surreptitious hand signals in the medical waiting area.

The bowl phone is prohibited by the jail, but the punishment for those caught using it is mild: most often a one or two-day loss of his or her hour of recreational time outside the cell.

"Whoopidee-freakin'-doo," Pabey said, smirking. "You're already locked down twenty-three hours, so what the fuck? Like, 'scuse my language, but you can't do shit. That's the only excitement you get. You still be in the bowl, 'Baaah. Oh, well, you punish me for how long?' 'Two hours.' 'I'll go on the bowl.'"

Arguments were terminated with a flush.

"And they be stressin', bangin' the wall," Torrado said in describing male partners' reaction to a flush.

"Yeah, that's the flush, that's it," Blount said.

"They be bangin'," Pabey said as she knocked furiously on the table. "They'll send another guy to another bowl and be like, 'Yo, tell my fuckin' girl that she better get on the phone!'"

She banged again on the table.

"'I want her right now!'" Torrado shouted. "And then you be in the bowl, 'What, baby? Baby, I didn't mean to hurt you, baby. I'm sorry, baby.'"

Scenes like the one Steph wrote set the gold standard for the class. They were sensitive portraits of the world of pain, loss, and suffering that all my students endured. They gave the class permission to speak what was unspoken. With scenes like these, we could build a play that would at least be authentic and real, whatever their shortcomings as pieces of drama.

I instructed the class, "Make sure you read the play *Short Eyes* by the Puerto Rican playwright Miguel Piñero for next week. He was imprisoned when he was twenty-five for armed robbery. He began writing the play in a prison playwriting workshop. The title comes from 'short heist,' prison slang at the time for child molestation. In Spanish, the *h* is silent, so Spanish speakers pronounce *short heist* as 'short eyes.' It is about Black, white, and Latino prisoners, all separated into competing, antagonistic clans, and a white pedophile who is imprisoned with them. The play eventually ended up at the Public Theater, where it won an Obie Award for the best play of the year. It later moved to Broadway."

I collected the scenes.

"One more thing," I said. "I can add an additional class each week for those who need remedial help. I signed the entire class up for Friday evening. We won't be able to write this play unless we add another class every week."

There was some audible grumbling, but no one protested. I was writing a book that fall, but knew I would have to drop it for the next three months to work full-time on the play, merging scenes, shaping the narrative, editing copy, and identifying holes for the students to fill.

"Those who are writing about life on the street should give us scenes from the outside, and those writing about life inside should give us prison scenes," I reminded them.

After class, Sincere had some questions about the scene he wanted to write. I was late getting into the corridor. The prison requires professors to gather in the prison library before prisoners are moved in single file from the school area back to their cells. The corrections officers don't react well to civilians disrupting movement or the highly regimented schedule of the prison. I hurried down the hall to the library.

"We got a bunk for you," Steph joked as I rushed past my class lined up against the wall.

"I don't know if I could handle prison," I said.

"You'd be a'right," he said kindly, "'cause we'd watch out for you."

six

Rebels

People who treat other people as less than human must
not be surprised when the bread they have cast on the
waters comes floating back to them, poisoned.

—James Baldwin[1]

We had, after three weeks of work, the outline of the play.
It centered around a poor Black family in Newark, home
to many in the class. The twenty-eight students, who cumula-
tively had spent 515 years in prison, settled on the title *Caged*.
Omar McNeil, quiet, reserved, was incarcerated at eighteen.
He wrote scenes about his younger brother, Quan, and himself.
Omar and Quan became the names of the brothers in our play.
Omar supports the family by selling drugs after he loses his job.
The mother is dying of cancer. Omar, who is fiercely protective
of his mother and Quan, is determined to keep the younger boy
off the streets and in school.

But Omar ends up in prison for a crime he did not commit. The family's finances collapse. They are evicted. Quan is
forced onto the streets to hustle to raise money for a lawyer
to get Omar out. The class was insistent that Quan, who grew
up sheltered from the streets, would be unable to cope with its
harshness and brutality.

"If you don't come into these streets by the time you're

sixteen years old, you're late," Boris said. "You'd be a complete victim. You're too naïve. You'll be taken advantage of. I got on the streets at about thirteen. There's a lifetime in three years that you could learn in the streets, from thirteen to sixteen. Me, first getting into these streets, I got taken advantage of. I come up to a guy, I'm looking to sell drugs. So, I see a guy that I know from the community, I told him, 'Well, you know, I need to buy some cocaine, I want to sell cocaine.' And he said, 'All right, I'll take care of you.' He actually knew my older brother. My brother might have been in jail or something. He took me to a house right behind a little chicken shack. I bought two hundred dollars' worth of cocaine from him to sell at a street value of about five hundred, six hundred. And then he left running. Well, I give the cocaine to somebody else to sell, and then they come back, and the guy says, 'This isn't cocaine.' He ran off with my money, you know? If Quan gets in the street at sixteen years old, he'd be at a complete disadvantage.

"When you get into the streets, you open yourself up to everything because most of the people that you're selling the drugs to are adults," Boris continued. "So, this is where the juvenile and adult world collide. A guy could come up, he's jonesing, and he's trying to get high, and you've got this little kid, he's about, what, eighty, ninety pounds, he got coke on him, you need it. Get in the car with an adult, they put a knife to you, tell you to get out, take all your stuff. It happened to my brother. 'Listen, if you don't go in your house and get that stuff and bring it back out, we comin' in there,' this guy told my brother. My brother was so scared, he went in and got the drugs and brought it back out.

"But it's not like we had much of a choice," Boris said of his time as a drug dealer. "There was times when my mother would say 'Well, eat whatever you see in there,' with her head down because she realized there was actually nothing in there. You knew guys that went to school. And they were starving.

You knew guys that graduated school; my sister's generation graduated school. A lot of them were starving. Some of them were riding ten-speed bicycles. They were janitors, at best. They were starving. You go to school, for what? Then what? Nobody's going anywhere. Nobody's doin' anything. You're still not going to have any money. It still doesn't solve your problems; your hierarchy of needs. Going to school becomes an obstacle. Because when I started, when I became a full-time drug dealer, a lot of guys who had left school and needed money lined up for work. I started feeling like I'd wasted a lot of good hours at school when I could have been somewhere, you know, trying to make some money to change my situation. Things so horrible you don't even know the difference between heaven and hell no more. You know, because when you're doing extreme poverty, that's hell. So, when a person says, 'Here's over two hundred dollars' worth of cocaine,' you go out in the dangerous streets, and it looks like hell, but soon as I get that two hundred dollars, this shit turned to heaven for me. You know? I'll stay here."

But the life on the streets comes with a high emotional cost.

"Chronologically, everybody is growing up, and some of us are intellectually growing up, but emotionally everyone is just like they're still in fucking eighth grade, man," Boris said. "The only difference is between a little baby and a big baby. A little baby throws a tantrum and hits you in the head with a bottle. A big baby has a tantrum and puts a bullet in you."

In the play, Quan does not get his brother out. He is unable to navigate the streets and is murdered by a rival drug dealer. The killer ends up in the prison with Omar. Should Omar shank his brother's killer, as demanded by the prison code, or let him live? This question evoked a passionate debate in the class.

Around this rough outline, students wrote scenes, drawn from their experiences, about drug dealing, absent or abusive fathers, conversations between brothers and sisters, relationships with mothers, encounters with the police, being in courtrooms, and life in prison. The students took great pride in what they had written. Each one walked to the front of the class to read his scene. When he finished, often highly charged with emotion, the class applauded. On days when not every scene could be read, there was a palpable disappointment. I had to promise we would read them next time. I struggled to balance the classes around the assigned reading and our work on the play the class was writing, which for the students took on a momentous importance.

Boris, Sincere, and Lawrence were the script doctors. During class, I would send them down the hall to the law library to mold several scenes into one or to write a new scene to fill a gap in the play. Marvin put together one of the most chilling scenes: the strip-search that is a frequent part of prison life. When the play was performed five years later at the Passage Theatre in Trenton, many in the audience, including former prisoners, said it was the hardest to watch.

The scene takes place in the admissions and departures unit, or intake unit, of Central Reception and Assignment Facility, or CRAFT, in Trenton, where prisoners go before being assigned to a prison. The prisoners are brought in, shackled hand and foot to anywhere from five to ten other prisoners, and placed into a noisy room. There they are met by a corrections officer: in the play, named Officer Watkins, a large Black man.

WATKINS. My name is Officer Watkins. This is Officer Watkins's prison. What Officer Watkins say in Officer Watkins's prison goes. Officer Watkins don't care why you here. Officer Watkins don't care who you are. Officer Watkins sure don't care who you *think* you are. As long as you here, you do what Officer Watkins say. Is that clear? Do y'all hear Officer Watkins?

(*Pause.*)

WATKINS. Are you motherfuckers deaf? Officer Watkins said, *Do you all hear Officer Watkins?*

THREE PRISONERS IN UNISON. Yes!

WATKINS. When Officer Watkins call you up to the bench, you step up. You state your full name and date of birth. On Officer Watkins's command, you remove your clothing one article at a time in the following order: shirt, pants, T-shirt, underwear, socks, and shoes. Do you follow so far?

THREE PRISONERS IN UNISON. Yes!

WATKINS. Next, Officer Watkins will do a visible inspection of your complete person. When Officer Watkins tells you to spread your ass and cough, you damn well better get it right the first time. Officer Watkins don't want to be lookin' up your hairy ass any more than you want Officer Watkins lookin' up your hairy ass. Are we clear?

THREE PRISONERS IN UNISON. Yes!

WATKINS. If you fail to comply with Officer Watkins's instructions, you will receive your first blue sheet from Officer Watkins. And then you can look forward to spending the next six months all by your lonesome in Ad Seg! Are we clear?

THREE PRISONERS IN UNISON. Yes!

WATKINS. First man in line. Step up and state your name and date of birth.

OMAR. Omar Moore. August 17, 1980.

(*Omar complies with this and all of Watkins's instructions.*)

WATKINS. Give Officer James your coat and hat. Hand Officer Watkins your shirt. Slowly take off your

T-shirt and hand it to Officer Watkins. Hand Officer Watkins your boots. Bang 'em together and hand 'em to me. Take off your socks. Turn 'em inside out. Hand 'em to me. Don't shake 'em. Take off your pants. Hand 'em to me. Take off your boxers. Turn 'em inside out. Hand 'em to me. Stretch out your arms. Let me see your palms. Are you wearing dentures?

OMAR. No.

WATKINS. Open your mouth wide. Stick out your tongue. Lift up your top lip. Pull your bottom lip down. Lift your arms straight in the air so I can see your armpits. Bend your right ear. Bend your left ear. Fingers through your hair. Lift your piece. Lift your nut sack. Turn around. Lift your right foot. Lift your left foot. Bend over. Spread your cheeks. Cough. Okay. Get dressed. Walk to the end of the hallway. Face the wall. Don't talk.

(*Stage goes dark.*)

The part of Officer Watkins was read by Marvin Spears, one of the most thoughtful and dedicated students in the college program. He was forty-eight, stood five foot three, and weighed about 160 pounds. He had been in prison since 1994. He had a daughter, Ta'nazia, who was two when he was arrested. His daughter was his life. Until his arrest, he doted on her, cooking her meals, playing with her, making sure she took her baths. He scrimped and saved from his prison job all year to send her $100 for her birthday. He drew pictures of Ta'nazia and other family members and sent them to her in the mail. Marvin had spent four years in the army, stationed in Germany. When he got out, he worked in a Ralph Lauren warehouse. He later drove one of his father's ice cream trucks in Irvington, New Jersey, often bringing Ta'nazia along with him on his route. He, his fiancée, Cheyonne, and his daughter lived on the first floor of his parents' house.

Police arrived at his door one night and arrested him for a robbery that resulted in a murder. He insisted he did not commit the crimes. Witnesses said the suspect was over six feet tall, had a beard, which Marvin did not, and drove a blue car, while Marvin's car was red. The prosecutor offered him a ten-year sentence as part of a plea deal. Marvin refused, saying he was not going to serve time for something he did not do. So, he went to trial and got a thirty-year sentence based largely on the testimony of a man with a criminal record who had robbed Marvin a few weeks earlier. The murder weapon was never found. Marvin did not own a gun. Cheyonne started dating a year after he was imprisoned, which at first made Marvin angry, but then he agreed that she should not wait for him, although they have remained in frequent communication.

The script doctors would return to the class to read the scenes for approval. There were some writers, especially Timmy, Boris, Steph, Lawrence, and Sincere, who turned in scenes that went straight into the play. But most scenes were a compilation of everyone's work. The energy in the room was radically different from the first day. The excitement was contagious.

"We don't have to limit our play to seven parts," I told the class. "Does anyone else want a part? We can write more parts in."

Twenty-one hands rose in the air. Everyone in the class wanted a part. The nearly impenetrable emotional walls my students had erected over decades were crumbling. I was momentarily speechless. The class had agreed to become what one rarely dares to become in prison: vulnerable.

"Well," I said to the class, "that's called courage."

The class insisted that the prison in the play be modeled on New Jersey State Prison in Trenton, where most had spent time, because of its harshness and reputation for violence and cruelty. A prisoner with many years inside, known as an "Old Head," who in the final version of the play would be named Ojore, gives a tour of the yard to a newly arrived Omar, the principal character.

> GUARD. Yard out! Yard out! Yard out! Prepare for the yard!
>
> OMAR. Whose dat?
>
> OLD HEAD. C.O. Yard time.
>
> OMAR. You goin'?
>
> OLD HEAD. Yeah . . . every chance I get, barrin' rain.
>
> OMAR. What do you do? Walk around?
>
> OLD HEAD. There are people and places in the yard you want to stay clear of. Get ready. They'll bust the gate soon.
>
> OMAR. What?
>
> OLD HEAD. They hit the brake and unlock the door. You have to move quick. When they close the brake, you miss out and be locked in. Get what you need. Bring a towel and a water bottle. You might have time to work out.
>
> (*The Old Head and Omar enter the yard. It is a large stone box filled with about two hundred prisoners.*)
>
> OLD HEAD. See these faded lines? They run in a loop around the yard. This is the track. Make sure you stay out of the runners' way. They run on the inside. You walk on the outside. Block a runner, and you got a problem. Now, over there is the weight pile. The guys work out in groups. If you ain't in a group, you probably not gonna work out. Try and

barge in on a group, and you could get a weight
dropped on you or get a beat down. Get permission
to join first.

OMAR. Why everything in prison got to be 'bout shankin'
somebody?

OLD HEAD. You shank somebody before they shank
you. See that patch of new cement? That used to
be dirt. The COs would run metal detectors over
it regular 'cause guys would bury so many shanks.
Then they cemented it over. See that corner, under
the tower?

OMAR. Where the white boys are?

OLD HEAD. That's their spot. That's their pull-up bar.
That's their blue handballs. See where the wall is
higher? That's for the Muslim brothers. Has more
shade. That corner is for the Five Percenters. The
Latins mass near the handball wall, next to those
two tables. That's the gamblin' an' playin' area.
Trenton's little casino. If you gamble, pay your debts
on the spot. Try and pay later, and you get drama.

OMAR. So the shanks are gone?

OLD HEAD. There still shanks. An' you can always get
smashed with a weight bar. The Latins let you play
handball if you good. But if you ain't, they won't invite you back. The basketball leagues have the courts,
and ya got to get in the league to play. But those
games get hot. The man who was the ref got shanked
a couple of days ago when some Latin didn't like his
calls. One or two more things. Don't mess with the
fags. No matta what. Don't mess with 'em.

OMAR. I got a girlfriend.

OLD HEAD. You got a *friend*. You ain't got no girlfriend
with your sentence. Think that way, an' it'll save you
a lot of pain.

Short Eyes, the play by Miguel Piñero, opens with the Black and
Puerto Rican prisoners, along with a handful of white prisoners,
camped out in their respective territories in a prison dayroom.
Prisons, and especially prison yards, are carved up into spaces
reserved for racial, gang, or religious groups, or for activities
such as gambling or lifting weights. These boundaries are sac-
rosanct, and a prisoner violates them at great risk. The play has
many of the archetypes found in a prison: an older man, the
"old head," who plays the moderating role of the father con-
fessor, sage, and conciliator; an angry Black nationalist preach-
ing death to "whitey" but unable to kill whitey when given the
chance at the end of the play; a small group of white prisoners
who, because they are a minority in the prison, are often the
most aggressive fighters.

The cast of characters also includes effeminate homosexuals and a pretty young man, nicknamed Cupcakes, who several
prisoners, gay and straight, want to turn into their bitch. There
are also the cynical and callous guards. All these divisions dis-
solve when a white pedophile is placed on the tier. The warring
tribes, including the corrections officers and the prisoners, unite
in disgust and hate, spitting in his face, calling him a freak, shov-
ing his head in the toilet, and ostracizing him. He is ignored or
tormented. In the end, he is murdered.

Sincere, who was seated on my left, said of the murder of
the pedophile: "The outside world sees us as savages. It's too
often how we see ourselves. We aspire to be the gangster the
wider society wants us to be, fulfilling the role the white man
placed on us to keep us down. You see it in here. The stories
people tell about how bad they were on the outside, most of
which are exaggerated or not true. This is how you make a slave
want to be slave. The society tells Black men this is what it means
to be Black. They tell us this on television, on the news, in the
movies, in the newspapers, in entertainment, in the courts, in
prison. And not knowing any better, young Black men start to

believe the lie about themselves. They want to achieve the identity forced upon them. They want street credentials. It's a trap."

"Five Percenter," someone muttered.

A slight grimace rippled across Sincere's face.

"Five percenter?" I asked.

"Five Percenters believe ten percent of the people in the world know the truth about existence," volunteered a student at the back of the class. "This ten percent uses its knowledge to keep eighty-five percent of the world locked in ignorance. The other five percent, who don't have power but are enlightened, also know the truth. This five percent tries to wake up the eighty-five percent trapped in darkness and free them. It comes out of Harlem and Malcolm X."

"Let the Five Percenters talk about the Five Percenters," Sincere, flicking back his dreadlocks, said with annoyance.

New Jersey State Prison in Trenton housed, and still houses, Jesse K. Timmendequas, who in 1994 raped and murdered Megan Kanka, a seven-year-old girl, in Hamilton Township, New Jersey. Thirty-three at the time of the crime, he had previously been convicted of sexual assaults on five and seven-year-old girls.[2] The case resulted in what became known as Megan's Law, a federal law that requires law enforcement officials to disclose to the public the location of registered sex offenders. Timmendequas was sentenced to death by lethal injection, a punishment commuted to life without parole in 2007 when the state of New Jersey abolished the death penalty. His pariah status in Trenton, and the abuse he endures by the prisoners and, often, corrections officers, mirrors that of the pedophile in *Short Eyes*.

"Rapists are despised," Boris explained, "but a pedophile is lower than the lowest of the low."

Piñero's play evoked a passionate discussion in the class about whether the code in a prison is real or part of the macho hype of prison culture. In the play, which takes place over a day, the various clans debate what to do to the pedophile, Clark Davis. It is certain that the prison administrators will rule Davis's murder a suicide, especially as the corrections officer on the tier is vocal about wanting him killed.

The white corrections officer in *Short Eyes* makes it clear the moment Clark Davis enters the prison that there will be no racial solidarity.

I assigned the parts to students to read out loud. In the first scene, Officer Nett and a white prisoner, Longshoe, insult and taunt Clark.

> NETT. On the gate [slang for "open the door"]. (*Nett opens gate, enters with Clark's belongings, leaves gate open.*)
>
> NETT. Come here . . . come here . . . white trash . . . filth . . . Let me tell you something, and you better listen good, 'cause I'm only going to say it one time . . . and one time only. This is a nice floor . . . a quiet floor . . . There has never been too much trouble on this floor . . . With you, I smell trouble . . . I don't question the warden's or the captain's motive for putting you on this floor . . . But for once, I'm gonna ask why they put a sick fucking degenerate like you on my floor . . . If you just talk out the side of your mouth one time . . . If you just look at me sideways one time . . . if you mispronounce my name once, if you pick up more food than you can eat . . . if you call me for something I think is unnecessary . . . if you oversleep, undersleep—if, if, if—you give me just one little reason . . . I'm gonna break your face up so bad your own mother won't know you.
>
> LONGSHOE. Mr. Nett is being kinda hard—
>
> NETT. Shut up! . . . I got a eight-year-old daughter who

was molested by one of those bastards . . . stinking sons of bitches, and I just as well pretend that he was you, Davis, do you understand that?

PACO. Short eyes.

LONGSHOE. Short eyes? Short eyes . . . Clark, are you one of those short-eyes freaks? Are you a short-eyes freak?

NETT. Sit down, Murphy . . . I'm talking to this . . . this scumbag . . . yeah, he's a child rapist . . . a baby rapist. How old was she? How old? Eight? . . . Seven? . . . Disgusting bastard. Stay out of my sight . . . 'cause if you get in my face just one time, don't forget what I told you: I'll take a nightstick and ram it clean up your asshole . . . I hope to God that they take you off this floor, or send you to Sing Sing . . . The men up there know what to do with degenerates like you.[3]

The tormenting of Clark mocks the racial solidarity in the prison.

LONGSHOE. Kick . . . hey, let me see that chain . . . gold . . .

CLARK. Yes.

LONGSHOE. How many carats?

CLARK. Fourteen.

ICE. Damn, Shoe . . . If you gonna take the chain, take the chain.

LONGSHOE. I . . me . . . take . . . Who said anything about taking anything? That would be stealing, and that's dishonest, ain't it, Clarky baby? . . . You wanna give that chain, don't you: after all, we're both white, and we got to look out for one another. Ain't that true, Clarky baby? . . . You gonna be real white about the whole thing, aren't you, Clarky baby?

CLARK. It's a gift from my mother.

ALL. Ohhh.

LONGSHOE. I didn't know you had a mother . . . I didn't think human beings gave birth to dogs, too.

OMAR. Looks like the freak ain't upping the chain, Shoe.

LONGSHOE. Oh, man, Clarky baby, how you gonna show in front of these people? You want them to think we're that untogether? What are you trying to say, man? You mean to stand there in your nice cheap summer suit looking very white and deny my whiteness by refusing to share a gift with me? That totally uncool . . . You're insulting me, man.

OMAR. Man's trying to say that you're not white enough.

LONGSHOE. You're trying to put a wire on me, creep?

OMAR. Man saying you're a nigger lover.

LONGSHOE. You saying that I'm a quadroon?[4]

EL RAHEEM. What? Freak, did you say that devil has some royal Congo blood in his veins?

ICE. I ain't got nothin' to do with it, Shoe, but I swore I heard the freak say that you were passing, Shoe.

CLARK. I didn't say that. I didn't say anything.

ICE. You calling me a liar.

CLARK. No, no . . . no.

LONGSHOE. Then you did say it?

(*They all push Clark around.*)

CLARK. Please, please, here, take this chain, leave me alone.

ICE. (*Yanks chain from around neck.*) Pick the mother-fucking chain up, freak.[5]

Open defiance in prison cannot be made impulsively. It must be warranted. It must be carried out only after an egregious and usually sustained injustice, because everyone pays for acts of insubordination. Those who capriciously and thoughtlessly destroy what the sociologist Gresham M. Sykes calls the "delicate system of compromise and corruption which prisoners have established with their guards" end up sacrificing "the well-being of the inmate population as a whole for the sake of a childish, emotional outburst, and his fellow inmates view him with contempt."[6]

In short, all acts of defiance are not equal. Prisoners who lose control and carry out impulsive acts of defiance are despised. It is usually, Sykes writes, those who have the patience and fortitude to endure oppression without flinching, with dignity and composure, who command the most respect. But there are men and women, although endowed with patience, fortitude, dignity, and composure, who can be pushed only so far. They refuse to endure sustained, sadistic abuse that makes even prison intolerable. And they are willing to pay for their resistance with their lives.

The stories of these rebels and their exploits are repeated and embellished. During a class I taught in New Jersey State Prison in Trenton, students spoke with profound admiration and gratitude about a prisoner who beat unconscious a sadistic guard whose daily torments made life on the tier a nightmare. They said that when the guard was attacked by this prisoner, whose power and size were intimidating, the other guards initially fled the tier. Following the attack, the prisoner disappeared from the prison population and no doubt endured many months, if not years, in isolation. But the guard, once he recovered and returned to work, was broken and chastened. He no longer swaggered down the corridor "like Rambo." This prisoner sacrificed himself for everyone else. The story of the beating was told endlessly, with what I suspected was the embellishment of other guards fleeing in fear, even to people who had heard it many times.

My students spoke in this way about the Black revolutionary Ojore Nuru Lutalo. His first name, he says, means "man of war," his middle name means "born in daylight," and his last name means "warrior." He is a former member of the Black Liberation Army (BLA), an armed insurrectionist movement of the 1970s that grew out of the Black Panthers. He lived for many years underground. In 1975, at the age of twenty-nine, he was imprisoned for a bank robbery, which he calls "an expropriation from a capitalist bank" and for engaging in a shoot-out with Trenton police.

Ojore, who was sent to Trenton State Prison in 1982, was placed in isolation in 1986 in the Management Control Unit, or MCU, a special housing unit designed to isolate prison leaders. He refused to wear his prison uniform. He ended the practice of runners—that is, having prisoners deliver and collect things for the corrections officers. "Let the pigs do it themselves," he told his fellow prisoners. A rash of fires were set in cells on his tier that belonged to those suspected of being snitches until there were no snitches on the tier. He insisted the prisoners refer to the corrections officers as guards, a term that many corrections officials dislike. Whenever they objected to his using the word, he would sneer, "What's your function? All you do is count us like sheep. You're a security *guard*. You don't have no power."

The revolutionary encouraged the prisoners around him to read and study. "Physically, they can undermine anyone, kill you, beat you down, put the dogs on you, shoot gas through the porthole," Ojore told them. "If you're a thinker, particularly if you're a political thinker, that worries them. They understand what could happen. Mao Tse-tung said, 'A single spark could start a prairie fire.' That's what they didn't want." Prison lore claims that when Ojore was released in 2003, a large black limousine was waiting for him at the prison gate, and inside was the well-known prisoner rights advocate Bonnie Kerness, her pleats of blonde hair curled up into a bun. This did not happen.

Ojore spent twenty-two years of his twenty-eight-year sentence in the MCU, a prison within a prison. He was not banished to the unit for breaking any prison rules but because he was a revolutionary. The contagion of revolution, along with a leader to direct it, terrified prison authorities. Ojore was allowed out of his cage for two hours every other day.

"The guys singled out for the MCU were viewed as potential troublemakers or political leaders who needed to be segregated to keep them from influencing the rest of the population," admitted the corrections officer Harry Camisa in his book *Inside Out: Fifty Years Behind the Walls of New Jersey's Trenton State Prison.* "This was a new and controversial concept in New Jersey."[7]

Police killings of Black youth and Black radicals were rampant then, as now. In Chicago, twenty-one-year-old Black Panther leader Fred Hampton was shot dead by the FBI and other law enforcement units during a predawn raid on December 4, 1969, as he lay in bed in his first-floor apartment. Another member of the Black Panther Party, twenty-two-year-old Mark Clark, was also killed in the raid.[8,9]

City police chiefs such as Philadelphia's Frank Rizzo boasted openly about the macho brutality of their cops, especially toward Black people. In 1979 the US Department of Justice filed a civil rights lawsuit against the Philadelphia Police Department for shooting nonviolent suspects, beating people while they were handcuffed, and using a "purposely fragmented system" for internal investigations that effectively nullified civilian complaints.[10] Between 1970 and 1978, Philadelphia police shot and killed at least 162 people.[11] In 1978 alone, the police shot 17 unarmed people, killing 8. In one incident, a police officer shot and killed a man who was naked and clutching a tree limb. Another time, police shot dead a nineteen-year-old man, charged with a traffic violation, while he was handcuffed. But the fact was, most city police departments did not keep detailed records of police shootings.[12] White radicals, often from the middle class, were largely spared, although on May 4, 1970, the National Guard fired on unarmed student antiwar protestors at

Kent State University, in Kent, Ohio, killing four and wounding nine others.

The FBI's covert program COINTELPRO targeted radical movements, especially Black revolutionary organizations. Under COINTELPRO, law enforcement fabricated or withheld evidence to wrongfully imprison activists, fomented conflict within groups, hired armies of informants, carried out witness harassment, engaged in perjury, planted fabricated stories in the press to discredit political dissidents, and used violence, including assassination, to kill movement leaders.[13] "The alleged murder of a police officer took the place of the mythical rape of a white woman to justify the lynching of Blacks," a former Black Panther leader named Eddie Conway once told me. Conway, framed for the killing of a police officer in Baltimore, spent forty-four years in prison, from 1970 until 2014.

The Black Liberation Army carried out its first armed attacks, killing two New York City Police officers, in May 1971 to mark the anniversary of Malcolm X's birth. The group insisted its violence was in response to state violence; a result of the indiscriminate targeting and killing of Black men, especially radicals, by police and the FBI in cities across the country. Unlike their white counterparts in the radical Weather Underground organization, who talked about "offing the pigs" but largely refrained from confronting the police, the BLA meant it. The communique it issued that day read:

> The armed goons of this racist government will again meet the guns of oppressed Third World People as long as they occupy our community and murder our brothers and sisters in the name of American law and order; just as the fascist Marines and Army occupy Vietnam in the name of democracy and murder Vietnamese people in the name of American imperialism are confronted with the guns of the Vietnamese Liberation Army, the

domestic armed forces of raciscm [sic] and oppression will be confronted with the guns of the Black Liberation Army, who will mete out in the tradition of Malcolm and all true revolutionaries, real justice.[14]

It is estimated that from 1970 through 1976, more than a dozen law enforcement officials were killed and perhaps two dozen wounded by the BLA, which also attacked government buildings, bombed police vehicles, robbed armored vehicles and banks, and carried out prison breaks. At its height, the BLA probably numbered no more than a few dozen people. This history, and an old revolutionary such as Ojore, had to be integrated into the play to give the play context and roots.

Ojore now lives in Elizabeth, New Jersey, but I met him in the cramped office of the American Friends Service Committee Prison Watch office in Newark, run by Bonnie Kerness. He had a shaved head and wore thick, dark-framed glasses and an open-collared short-sleeve shirt. He was diffident and wary, but because of Bonnie Kerness, who has long fought for prisoner rights, he agreed to speak. In 1961, at the age of nineteen, Kerness left New York and spent a decade in Tennessee in the civil rights movement, including time at Tennessee's Highlander Research and Education Center, which trained Rosa Parks and other civil rights leaders. She later led housing campaigns for the poor in New Jersey and eventually founded Prison Watch with the American Friends Service Committee, which advocates for prisoner rights and investigates the abuse and mistreatment of incarcerated men and women.

"Guards are fascists, racists," Ojore said when I asked about the corrections officers that oversaw the MCU in Trenton. "Lots of times, you get better treatment from white guards than Black guards. Black guards think, 'You're making us look bad.' They got that house slave mentality."

"Are they sadists?" I asked.

"There's so many of them," he said. "They beat prisoners down. Once they get you handcuffed, they hog-tie you and beat you, and beat you, and beat you, and beat you. Then they brag about it. You can see the murder in their eyes. They start losing it. A guard comes up to me and knocks on the door with a stick. 'Lutalo, you got a pass.' I get up, take my clothes off. Turn around. Get handcuffed. Each guard has a stick. They're called 'Nigger Beaters.' Sometimes a camera is watching. Most of the time, it's two guards for one prisoner. Even though you are handcuffed, and you have shackles on, they'll beat you. You have to judge them individually. Some guards surprised us. One guard came to me and said, 'Damn, Lutalo, I've been watching you for a while. What they tell me about you is not true, that all you want to do is escape and you're a troublemaker.' They programmed the guards to be against us. And they believe it."

"How common was suicide?" I asked.

"This one guy was on eight different types of psychotropic drugs," he recalled. "He couldn't cope no more. He climbed up on the sink with a cloth rope around his neck, jumped off and hanged himself. One guy cut himself up, painted his cell red. It's common. They can't cope. They give up, lose all hope. The control unit is a never-ending cycle. We try to talk guys out of using psychotropic drugs. Some guys did. Some guys didn't. You see the look in their eyes. The medication causes them to do smack mouth. They start shuffling side to side on their feet. They're gone. Next thing you know, you see them in the special needs unit. These are young prisoners. They should be full of rebellion. But they aren't. That's how the administration wants it. The drugs destroy your central nervous system. That way you get smack mouth. Your hands lock up. Your central nervous system, there's no coming back from it. They just want to be in another time zone when they're on psychotropic drugs. It's pitiful. It's sad. You see these people waiting for you to self-destruct psychologically. They get a kick out of it."

"Is it ever necessary to shank someone in prison?" I asked.

"Oh, sure," he said. "In prison, you have to take all threats seriously. It's best to resolve it through dialogue. He's got his boys. You've got yours. But let's say someone tries to take advantage of you sexually. You have to set an example. You have to stab them up. So other people will say, 'Hold on, hold on. This is how I'll do.' If someone snitches on you, it's best to get that individual."

"By shanking them?"

"Shanking him," he said matter-of-factly. "Setting a cell on fire while he's in the cell. Pedophiles, sexual predators, catch a real bad deal in prison. Everybody disrespects them. Then you got guys in prison who are waiting for a chance to rape a nurse or a guard. One guy, he tried to rape a schoolteacher. She knew martial arts, so she body slammed him. Another guy, he knocked the teacher down. Then you got guys standing around masturbating while the nurse administers medication. Then you got guards who like to watch that stuff. They like to stand there and watch guys do that. It's a mind-set. A lot of people don't come in here jaded. The prisons make them jaded. Disrespect. 'Bitch this, bitch that. Suck my dick.' All that stuff. Every time you come around, you're naked in front of them. They start becoming jaded. It's a mixed bag.

"Look," he said, "you can't oppress a person and expect them to not act like animals. You strip them of their culture and land. Everything. What else do they know? You start calling them savages and beasts. They have to psychologically take that crap. They start acting like that.

"Like Hillary Clinton said, 'Superpredators.' Think about that. *She's* a superpredator. A blonde savage. A war maker.

"Of course," he continued, "like on the outside, you got guys in prison who are gay, wear women's clothing. They pick someone to be their daddy—their husband in prison—for protection. Or they might have a real relationship going on. I attended a wedding in Trenton State Prison. A prisoner who called himself Dionne and a man got married in the mess hall."

"How many people were there?" I asked.

"Maybe fifty. There was the reception. Cut the cake and everything. I wanted to see it, so I went. Kuwasi Balagoon. He was a BLA member. His girlfriend was a transvestite. Kuwasi was cool. All you had to say was 'Let's go,' and Kuwasi was gone. Gun in hand. Killing the police. He escaped from prison twice. Rahway and Trenton. Kuwasi, that was his preference. A lot of people thought, since me and Kuwasi were comrades, I had a homosexual relationship too. I said that's not the case. You're stereotyping."

Sundiata Acoli, also a former member of the Black Panther Party and the Black Liberation Army, was sentenced to life in prison in 1974 for the alleged murder of a New Jersey state trooper, Werner Foerster. Acoli was one of the first revolutionaries to be placed in the newly created MCU in Trenton. He had been in a car that was stopped by state troopers. Zayd Malik Shakur, in the car with him, was killed by state troopers, and Assata Shakur, also in the car, was wounded and arrested. Shakur escaped from prison on November 2, 1979, when, as Ojore told me, "Black and white combat units known as the Revolutionary Armed Task Force, or RATF, under the tutelage of the Black Liberation Army, liberated Assata Shakur from New Jersey's Clinton Prison for Women."[15,16] She spent five years underground and then fled to Cuba, where she was granted political asylum and where she remains. She denies shooting Foerster, insisting that she had been wounded by the police and her hands were up when the trooper was killed.

Acoli was transferred to an isolation unit in a federal prison in Marion, Illinois, in September 1979 after he was accused by New Jersey prison authorities of being involved in an attempted escape from the MCU that resulted in two guards being shot and the death of a prisoner, John Clark. Another prisoner was wounded in the escape attempt. Acoli remains in federal prison, although he has never been charged with a federal crime. He was granted parole in 2014, but the state challenged the court decision, and the appellate court upheld the state's challenge.[17]

I asked Ojore, who is a voracious reader and has an encyclopedic knowledge of political and especially revolutionary theory, as well as African American history and culture, if he and the other armed members of the Black Liberation Army realized at the time that fomenting armed conflict not only meant inevitable defeat but also would be used by the ruling elites to further demonize Black people and expand police power, police funding, and mass incarceration.

"What choice did you have?" he answered rhetorically. "At some point, you have to stand up. You can't wait for mass involvement. The police took note. They started patrolling differently. They started curtailing their activities. Nobody wants to die. If you got someone out there hunting you because of what your uniform does, think about it. It's psychological. If you don't respect me or fear me, you can do anything you want to me. One cop could arrest ten gang members because of his uniform. It's the fear of authority. If I come along, and I have a badge on, they won't challenge me. They don't shoot up on the police. They don't do that. But if they know you will respond in kind, their attitude and approach will be different. They'll wait until they get a thousand police to confront you. There was a brother in Texas who killed five police. They respected that. A guy in Louisiana killed police. They respected that. That's what it takes. Our freedom is our responsibility. It's not the responsibility of white people. I don't want nobody fighting for me if I'm not going to fight for myself. I would feel cheated. Then they can dictate how it's going to be."

I handed out the transcript of my interview with Ojore, whom all of the class had heard of and a few had known in Trenton. When I told the class that he didn't seem to trust white people, they laughed. "Don't worry," said a student in his early fifties who knew Ojore. "He doesn't trust anybody."

In our play, the character of Ojore would be an old head: a prisoner serving one or two life sentences with no prospect of release. He would articulate the revolutionary past of Black radicals, as well as impart institutional memory. Ojore identifies as an atheist, but the class made the character based on him a Muslim, for in prison, Muslims are usually the most politically conscious and the best organized. Ojore's words were written into the play largely unaltered. It was the Ojore-inspired character who greeted Omar when he first arrived in his prison cell.

OMAR. What'd you in here for, Brother Ojore?
OJORE. Don't be askin' brothas what dey in for. If a
   brotha want you to know what he here for, he'll tell
   you on his own. People take stuff like that another
   way, like you lookin' for information or something.
   Be careful what you ask. But in my case, it's cool. I ex-
   propriated monies in Newark in 1977 from a capitalist bank. I was in the movement. On the way out the
   door, I got into a gunfight with the political police.
OMAR. Movement? Political police?
OJORE. Black Liberation Army. And, yeah, all police
   are political. All police everywhere serve a political system. Here it's called capitalism and white supremacy. I was already on parole for expropriating
   monies from drug dealers to finance the movement
   and stop the sale of drugs in oppressed communities. Got life. I was arrested with New Afrikan[18]
   POW Kojo Bomani Sababu. I was in the struggle

at the time with comrade Andaliwa Clark, who was killed in action inside these walls after he smuggled in a pistol and shot two of the guards in the MCU. I've been involved in the war against the fascist state waged by the New Afrikans since 1970. We targeted members of the state security forces who were murdering our brothers and sisters. The state only speaks one language: violence. And we speak back in the one language they get. An' that was when this whole prison thing got real. I spent twenty-two years in the MCU.

OMAR. Twenty-two years . . .

OJORE. The state created the hole for us revolutionaries back in the day. They had to keep us from the rest of the population, an' they had to break us. They couldn't let us preach resistance. They refined all their torture techniques in the sixties on the Panthers, the Black Liberation Army, the Puerto Rican independence movement, and the American Indian Movement. Today they add Islamic militants, jailhouse lawyers, gangbangers, and political prisoners to the list. But they hate us the most. We know what they don't want you to know. We know the control of Black bodies been seamless, from slavery, to the Black Codes, to convict leasing, to the Jim Crow laws, to the so-called war on drugs. We know promotions, quotas, money from the feds, the money they take off of us is what makes prisons a business. A body ain't worth nothin' on the street, but once inside, once you locked in a cage, you worth fifty thousand a year to all dem prison contractors, food service companies, phone companies, medical companies, an' prison construction companies. An' they got to keep them cages full if they gonna make their money.

And once you get out, once you done yer time, they make sure you got no job, no food stamps, no public housin', so you end up right back in, where you can make dem some more money. People say da system don't work. That's 'cause they don't get it. The system works just the way it designed to work. Inside, you meant to be a slave. You forced to work for a dollar a day. You call the New Jersey Bureau of Tourism, you are talkin' to a prisoner at the Edna Mahan Correctional Institution for Women who is makin' twenty-three cents an hour, no ability to negotiate wages, working hours, or working conditions. An' the state don't want that kind of consciousness. The state knows the power of ideas. But I don't ask 'em what is fair or not fair. They want to destroy us. We want to destroy them. Fair has nothin' to do with it. We still got hundreds of Black revolutionaries, our prisoners of war, our political prisoners in cages all across North America: Mumia Abu-Jamal, Sundiata Acoli, Mutulu Shakur, Imam Jamil Al-Amin, Jalil Abdul Muntaqim, Sekou Odinga, Abdul Majid, Tom Manning, Bill Dunne, and Leonard Peltier. Almost no one remembers we exist. The state done erased our memory. But we survive, even in here, because we have a purpose. We know our history, which means the history and persecution of our people. We got a community, even inside these walls. We got the spiritual and physical strength to face captivity and death. An' that means we always free.

(*Pause.*)

OJORE. You read George Jackson, Julius Lester?
OMAR. I don't do books.

OJORE. Brother, in this cell, we do books. We ain't goin' sit with our mouths half open all day lookin' at *Basketball Wives*. Take this.

(*Ojore hands him the book* Revolutionary Notes *by Julius Lester.*)

OJORE. Consider this the college you never had. An' when you finish with Brother Julius Lester, you can read Brother George Jackson and start on those law books, 'cause *you* the only lawyer goin' help you ever get out of here.

(*Lights down.*)

Steph, who like most of my students said he was bullied in school and on the street as a child, spoke of an older man in Newark nicknamed Hooterville, a rebel outlaw who protected him and taught him how to defend himself.

"Some guy tried to rob him, he actually took the gun from him," Steph said of Hooterville. "He was a different type. He was a guy who had nothing to live for. He rode in stolen cars from time to time. He went away down south for a couple of weeks with his cousins from the projects. While they were down there, they broke into a gun store. They came back with a whole bunch of guns. One day, when we were in the house, he handed me this .44 Magnum with a scope on it. A very big, heavy gun. I want to say I'm sixteen, maybe seventeen. I'm just feeling it. Wow, this gun is so heavy. Powerful gun. This is crazy.

"He was known for being very efficient with guns, to the point where he would shoot a shotgun with one hand, put the shell back in it with one hand—I think Arnold Schwarzenegger did that in *The Terminator*—he would do that," Steph said. "He would always tell us, 'I'm never going back to jail. I'm never going back to prison.' He was in a youth facility. And he may have gone to Bordentown. He did small stints. He never did a lot of time. Maybe two years there. Three years at the most. He'd always say, 'They'd have to kill me before I go back to prison.'

"One night, we're out selling drugs. It's a summer night. A car pulls up. A Mazda. He jumps out the hatchback, and the car pulls off. He comes into a lot where we are selling drugs, hanging out. Summertime, weekend. I think it's a Friday. He hands me that same gun and says, 'Put this up.' He asks me to box the bullets. He said, 'I just shot a cop.' Everybody was like, 'Knock it off. You ain't shoot no cop!' He's like, 'I'm serious, I just shot a cop.' We ran out of drugs. So, I ran home to get some drugs. He literally told me this, and I ran home within that five minutes. When I went into the house to get some drugs, his picture was already on the news. That quick. His picture and his two cousins' pictures. Man, such and such from Newark shot two police officers. His cousins were all in the car. They were parked on the side of a telephone booth. His cousin got out to make a phone call. The police pulled up on the side of the car. It was county cops or state trooper. I think it was county cops. They pulled over, I guess just to see what was going on. He started shooting into the police car—shot both cops. He was on the run. The police were coming into our neighborhood every single day, harassing us. Basically, try to force people to tell them where he was. They would come and literally tell everybody to get on the ground. It was very rough. Guns pointed in your face. Very scary situation. Very loud, authoritative. Menacing. Cursing. 'Get on the fucking ground. We'll kill you. Y'all like to shoot cops?' They would come in kicking people's mother's house doors. 'Where is he? This is going to keep happening until we find out where he is. Y'all are not going to be able to make any money out here. It won't be no drugs sold out here until we find out where is Hooterville.'"

Hooterville, whose legal name was Philip James, went underground. He robbed drug dealers to get money. Steph saw him a few times and always handed him some cash to help him survive.

"The last phone call I got from him, from a pay phone we used to sell drugs at, he said, 'Make sure you take care of my sister for me,'" Steph recalled. "I said, 'Definitely.' Back then, people could call the pay phone. So, we used to always get phone calls from the pay phone. The next day, we seen in the news, while driving to Florida in a stolen car, he got into a chase by an auxiliary cop. Went into the marsh in Florida. Ended up getting into a shoot-out with the cops. The cops shot and killed him.

"This was personal. I cared a lot about him. It was really painful. We mourned him. We did a lot of drinking that day. When I look back, that was the turning point, where I started drinking a lot. Being in that type of situation, happening to see his body in the casket. He was a very caring person. He forced me to learn how to fight so I could care for myself. I wasn't his family. He never hung around me. He just didn't like to see people get bullied. He was a very caring person. From what I understand, he had been through a lot. Certain things, people just don't talk about in the neighborhood. But they said he had a real rough upbringing."

I announced to the class, "The next play we will read is August Wilson's masterpiece *Fences*, which, solely as a piece of writing, is probably flawless. Look closely at the relationship between the father, Troy, and his son, Cory; at what Wilson says about the nature and effects of racism; at why Troy is so dismissive of Cory's dreams to play football; and that of his older son, Lyons, from a previous marriage, to be a musician. What does the play say about marriage, love, and, finally, forgiveness? Why is the play called *Fences*?"

I gathered up my books.

"I can't believe you assigned the parts of homosexuals to some of the toughest guys in the prison, and they read them," Lawrence said laughing on the way out.

Waiting for me at the door stood two older prisoners, recently transferred from Trenton, who were not in the college program. They had gotten permission to come in the school area by getting a pass to the law library, located at the end of the hall. The two had appeared the week before with a pitch for me to join them in a fundraising scheme for "troubled youth," and I had brushed them off. They knew that such a scheme would mean that, as a civilian worker in the prison, I would be jeopardizing my position. If caught, I would be instantly expelled. I was annoyed that they had returned.

"We only need a minute of your time, sir," one of the men, his hair flecked with gray, said.

"Please," said the other. "Can we just have a minute?"

I foolishly agreed, hoping to put an end to the requests.

They opened a door to a small office next to the classroom. I stepped inside. They immediately closed the door. I realized this was a mistake, not because they presented any physical danger, but because it would be harder to cut them off.

"This is my CEO," said the second man about his gray-haired partner. "We want to start a program to help troubled youth, teach them not to make the mistakes we made. We need you to help us get some money."

"I can't raise funds like this and teach in the prison," I said.

"Oh, no one has to know," the man doing all the talking said.

"It's not worth the risk," I said. "I can't do it."

I opened the door and ran into Steph in the hall, who had been watching the encounter.

"You have con artists everywhere," I said.

"You'll never see those guys again," he said tersely.

I never did.

seven

Family

> The most valuable blacks are those in prison, those who
> have the warrior spirit, who had a sense of being Afri-
> can. They got for their women and children what they
> needed when all other avenues were closed to them.
>
> —August Wilson[1]

No other play we read that semester elicited the outpouring of emotions triggered by *Fences*. The play is set in Pittsburgh in the 1950s. The father, Troy Maxson, who is fifty-three, was once a talented baseball player in Negro leagues. He spent time in prison for an accidental murder he committed during a robbery. He works as a trash collector and challenges the color line to become the first Black garbage truck driver in Pittsburgh. He lives with his wife, Rose, and their teenage son Cory, as well as his younger brother, Gabe, who suffered a severe head wound and was disabled as a soldier in World War II. Gabe received $3,000 from the government for his brain injury, which Troy used to purchase their small home. Troy also has an adult son, Lyons, from a previous marriage. The play explores the troubled relationship between Troy and his two sons, damaged manhood, the meaning of love and commitment, racism, infidelity, and how the white-dominated world crushes the dreams and aspirations of Black men and women.

"That was my father, only he beat me more," laughed Boris, speaking of Troy. "My father. My brother. What they said was gospel. My father was a tough street guy. My brother, Tommy Jr., he was modeled after my father. And I went right behind them. It was like ducks imprinting. You ever play house when you're a kid? And you imitate your parents. If there's a little girl yelling at the baby dolls or whatever, she's yelling at the baby dolls because her mother yells at the kids. You understand what I'm saying?

"I was Tommy's son, for real. My father was tough; I was tough. My father didn't give no apologies; I didn't give no apologies. It started out in the house. He'd make sure I was tough. Might was right. I might have had a broom broke over my arm before I was in the fifth grade. Talk about misplaced aggression. I could get a beating in the house. If I walk outside on the porch, some kids are riding by on a bike, I would start fights, like, 'What the fuck is *you* looking at?' So, I started hurting people. A lot of violence goes on in the house. My father was a drug addict. You see what I'm saying? And I had, what you would call, a calm life. Some people, they'd drag their kids into the streets. Everything was so turned up. When you got to the school, the kids were wild, but, I mean, this is how they came up.

"I'm selling drugs, and I'm in this house," he went on. "And the mother has these girl kids. It might be about two in the morning. And the kids were hungry. What she did was, she took one of them little chicken pot pie things and sat it on the floor. She gave it to the kids. And their . . . their little hands . . . I remember their little hands. They were pulling in each direction to try to gain an advantage. And that's how they were eating. That's how she was feeding them. Like, puppies. Like, pit bulls. What do you think you're going to produce with that? Who do you blame? See, at that age right there, you could clearly say it's not that kid's fault.

"I had my mother. We had Bible studies. We did certain

things. We used to read all the time. My mother tried to provide some structure. I know guys who had nothing. They are fundamentally different. They, at their best, is, 'I won't bother you, you don't bother me.' That's the best you're going to get. At their *best*. This is all they're capable of. This is all they know. Between these streets and jail, since they were juveniles, they've been going back and forth to jail since they was twelve years old. My nephew been going to jail since he was twelve. He been going to jail since *I* was going to jail. He in jail right now. All my brothers, every last one of them, all of them have been to jail. My son. My nephew."

The brilliance of Wilson's play is that Troy is conflicted, torn between this toxic need to express the autonomy and power the world denies him, and a deep love for his son, which is nearly impossible for him to express.

Troy believes he was denied a chance to be a professional baseball player because he was Black, although, Wilson adds later in the play, he may also have been too old to compete once he was released from prison. He is not going to allow Cory, who is being recruited by a college football coach, to be victimized also. His hurt will not become his son's hurt, and from that deep well of protectiveness, Troy fails to see that times have changed, that college football teams are now accepting Black players, and that he is, in fact, crushing his son's dreams. The final rupture he has with Cory, which descends to a physical confrontation, replicates the rupture he had with his own father. The trauma of damaged manhood is passed from generation to generation.

Troy says his father, a poor Alabama sharecropper with eleven children and a wife who left him, was "just as evil as he could be."[2]

"Sometimes I wish I hadn't known my daddy," Troy says. "He ain't cared nothing about no kids. A kid to him wasn't nothing. All he wanted was for you to learn how to walk so he could start you working. When it come time for eating . . . he ate first.

If there was anything left over, that's what you got. Man would sit down and eat two chickens and give you the wing."[3]

But his father had two qualities Troy seeks to instill in his own children. He worked hard, and he "felt a responsibility toward us. Maybe he ain't treated us the way I felt he should have . . . but without that responsibility, he could have walked off and left us . . . made his own way."[4]

Cory asks his father why he has never liked him.

Troy answers:

Like you? I go out here every morning . . . bust my butt . . . putting up with them crackers every day . . . 'cause I like you? You about the biggest fool I ever saw. (*Pause*) It's my job. It's my responsibility! You understand that? A man got to take care of his family. You live in my house . . . sleep you behind on my bedclothes . . . fill you belly up with my food . . . 'cause you my son. You my flesh and blood. Not 'cause I like you! 'Cause it's my duty to take care of you. I owe a responsibility to you!

Let's get this straight right here . . . before it go along any further . . . I ain't got to like you. Mr. Rand don't give me my money come payday 'cause he likes me. He gives me 'cause he owe me. I done give you everything I had to give you. I gave you your life! Me and your mama worked that out between us. And liking your black ass wasn't part of the bargain. Don't you try and go through life worrying about if somebody like you or not. You best be making sure they doing right by you. You understand what I'm saying, boy?[5]

One time, Troy's father found him in the fields with a neighborhood girl when he should have been working. His father beat him with the leather harnesses from a mule. "When he commenced to whupping on me . . . quite naturally I run to get out of the way. (*Pause*). Now, I thought he was mad 'cause I ain't done my work. But I see where he was chasing me off so he could have the gal for himself. When I see what the matter of it was, I lost all fear of my daddy," Troy tells his older son, Lyons. "Right there is where I become a man . . . at fourteen years of age."[6]

Troy grabbed the leather straps and began to whip his father, who then beat his son senseless. He woke up with his dog Blue licking his face, his eyes swollen shut. "I laid there and cried. I didn't know what I was gonna do. The only thing I knew was the time had come for me to leave my daddy's house. And right there, the world suddenly got big. And it was a long time before I could cut it down to where I could handle it. Part of that cutting down was when I got to the place where I could feel him kicking in my blood and knew that the only thing that separated us was the matter of a few years."[7]

A student who had been locked up for twenty-three years lamented, "I spent my whole life trying not to be my father. And when I got to Trenton, I was put in his old cell."

Troy walked two hundred miles along the roads to Mobile, Alabama, and joined some men looking for work up north. He got to Pittsburgh and "found out . . . not only couldn't you get a job . . . you couldn't find no place to live. I thought I was in freedom. Shhh. Colored folks living down there on the riverbanks in whatever kind of shelter they could find for themselves."[8]

He stole in order to buy food and basic necessities such as a pair of shoes. "One thing led to another," he tells his older son, Lyons. "Met your mama. I was young and anxious to be a man. Met your mama and had you. What I do that for? Now I got to worry about feeding you and her. Got to steal three times as much. Went out one day looking for somebody to rob . . . that's what I was, a robber. I'll tell you the truth: I'm ashamed of it today. But it's the truth. Went to rob this fellow . . . pulled out my knife . . . and he pulled out a gun. Shot me in the chest. It felt like somebody had taken a hot branding iron and laid it on me. When he shot me, I jumped at him with my knife. They told me I killed him, and they put me in the penitentiary and locked me up for fifteen years."[9]

The rupture between father and son sees Cory join the Marine Corps and sever relations with Troy, returning at the end of the play for his funeral. Cory's mother tells him, "Your daddy wanted you to be everything he wasn't . . . and at the same time, he tried to make you into everything he was. I don't know if he was right or wrong . . . but I do know he meant to do more good than he meant to do harm."[10]

My student James Leak's father had died recently. "My father worked in a factory that used to manufacture plastics," he told the class. "He was an iron-fist, very authoritarian type of guy, y'know? Always pulling me over to teach me lessons or give me wisdom about life. I didn't listen to a lot of it, being a kid. I also have a sister, but she had run away when I was seven years old. Parents weren't trying to be our friends. They laid out the rules and put food on the table. Parents were to be treated as authority figures. So, I wasn't friends with him, but I always wanted to make my father proud. I still, today, wish I could show him how I've grown on the inside—spiritually, I mean—and with how I act toward others."

James, too, left home and his dominating father for the military, becoming an Army Ranger and a member of the US Army boxing team. He fought for three years in arenas across the United States, in Panama and Canada.

"The army was probably the best time of my life," he reflected. "I remember going into the recruitment office—a friend of mine was a marine—and asking about the service. I knew that the army had the best collegiate boxing team. I wanted in on it. After the recruiter saw my Golden Gloves necklace, he knew why I was there. He showed me a brochure, and in it were pictures of paratroopers jumping out of planes, stuff like that. After asking him about it, I knew one hundred percent that I wanted to be in the US Airborne. The army gave me something to be proud of."

I had heard repeatedly around Elizabeth that Leak had been framed by the police for a murder he did not commit. That so many people insisted James was innocent led me to borrow the boxes of his trial transcripts from his mother. The trial was, from start to finish, a farce, lacking in material evidence and reliant on contradictory and confusing testimony from a few drug addicts who appeared to have been badly coached by the police. The tactic of using pliable addicts as witnesses is a common police tactic. It was the way Omar is convicted in *Caged*. Two Newark police officers pressure a junkie named Jackie to say she saw Omar commit the murder.

> OFFICER ONE. He's gonna walk if you don't help us, an' we know he did it.
>
> JACKIE. It don't seem right. I done lied for those other ones 'cause I knowed they was bad. But Omar, Omar is different. I know his mother.
>
> OFFICER TWO. Jackie, you owe us. We watch out for you. Don't we? Besides, you help us on this one, or you goin' back inside. An' you don't want to be dope sick all weekend in the County [jail].
>
> OFFICER ONE. There's that, and this time the judge might keep you.
>
> (*Jackie lowers her head. She is clearly anguished.*)
>
> JACKIE. You write it up. I'll sign it. But you got to give me more than one hundred dollars this time. This one ain't right. It ain't right . . .

To my surprise, it turned out many students had deep roots in the South. Boris's parents, for example, were born in Georgia. His father, like Troy, was pulled out of school at a young age to work the fields. After a confrontation with a white sheriff, his family feared for his life, so he came north and worked a series of menial, low-paying jobs. The doors of opportunity were as tightly shut to a barely literate Black man in the North as they were in the South. Boris's father started selling drugs. Then he started taking drugs and became a heroin addict. By the time Boris was thirteen, he had to provide for himself if he wanted clothes and often meals. His mother, who worked as a phone operator at Piscataway High School, covered the rent. And then one day Boris, who sold drugs but did not use them, came home and couldn't find the stash of drugs he had hidden and intended to sell. He wrote this scene between Quan, Omar's younger brother, and Jimmy, their father, based on a confrontation with his own father:

QUAN. Yo, you seen some stuff in Sharonda's room?
JIMMY, *frowning.* What stuff?
QUAN. My drugs.
JIMMY. I know you ain't bring no drugs in this house.
QUAN. I jus' want to know if you touch my stuff.

(*Jimmy walks into his bedroom. He starts looking through the closet. Chimene wakes up.*)

CHIMENE. Jimmy, what you doing?

(*Jimmy does not answer. Chimene goes into her daughter Sharonda's room, where she sees Quan.*)

CHIMENE. What's goin' on with you and your father?
QUAN. Nothin'. Why?
CHIMENE. I think your Daddy jus' went outside to get his gun.
QUAN. What? . . . 'iight.

(*Chimene shuts the door to Sharonda's room. Quan pulls a .9-millimeter from under the mattress. He puts the gun into his waist under his shirt. He walks out of the room. Jimmy walks in with a shotgun wrapped in a white towel. The two pause.*)

QUAN. What's up?

(*Jimmy looks at him briefly and walks past him. He sits. He puts the shotgun, still wrapped in the towel, behind his legs on the floor. Quan goes back into Sharonda's room, closes the door and begins pacing. Chimene goes into Sharonda's room and closes the door.*)

CHIMENE. What are you going to do?
QUAN. I'm going to talk to him.
CHIMENE. Okay.

(*Chimene leaves Sharonda's room. Quan follows her out. She sits and picks up her Bible. Quan sits across from Jimmy.*)

QUAN. We're family. We can't be livin' like this.
JIMMY. Nigga, you don't say shit to me, and I don't say shit to you.
QUAN, *as he stands up.* Youse a fag.

(*Chimene begins to cry. Jimmy stands up.*)

CHIMENE, *to Quan.* Just go . . . just go . . . just go.

(*Quan begins to walk slowly toward the door and then leaves. Sharonda enters the apartment. Chimene is crying.*)

SHARONDA, *to her mother.* What happened, Mommy? What's wrong? Where's Quan?

(*Chimene does not answer.*)

SHARONDA. Daddy, what happened?

(*Jimmy does not answer. He is now seated again, and his head is down. The gun is still on the floor. Quan walks back into the apartment. Everyone is quiet.*)

QUAN, *to Chimene.* Ma, I'm gonna grab some stuff and go.

(*Jimmy is still looking at the floor.*)

QUAN. I know what you got in the towel . . . but I got somethin' for you.

(*Jimmy jumps up, and Quan pulls out the handgun. Chimene and Sharonda run out of the room. Jimmy grabs a dish off the table and throws it at Quan. Quan ducks. It smashes against the wall.*)

JIMMY. Shoot, nigga.

(*Jimmy runs to the backroom to join Chimene and Sharonda, hitting the glass table and breaking it. Quan points the gun and tries to shoot his father. The gun will not fire.*)

QUAN, *muttering in relief.* Safety's on.

(*Quan is alone in the living room. He leaves the house.*)

And yet, family, however dysfunctional, is all they have. They struggle together against crippling poverty, endemic violence, societal indifference, and hostility. Boris, whose mother was a devout Christian and the glue that held the family together, was quick to add that his father, like Troy, worked hard to shatter any illusions about fairness or justice; that illusions would only cause his children pain and hurt. He, too, in his own way, loved his children and wanted to protect them from the hurt he had endured. And, like Troy, Jimmy tried to equip them with the emotional armor to survive.

"He wanted to make me hard because that was the only way to prepare me for what was coming; that I shouldn't ever expect anything because I was never going to get anything," Boris said. "This was a white man's world. 'You're dark,' he would tell me. 'You're going to have to play hard behind the eight ball. Anything you get won't come easy. And if you do get anything, people are going to say you don't deserve it and you got lucky.'"

The lengthy prison terms see families drift away, no longer coming for their weekly visits, then monthly visits, then at all. The phone conversations often become awkward, stilted, and brief. Children, filled with resentment, grow tired of powerless and absentee fathers or of mothers seeking to impose authority while locked away. Prisoners are often placed, at some point, in isolated confinement after being charged with violating prison rules, cutting them off from visits until they return to the general population. The long waits outside the prison, where visitors, including children, can stand for hours in the rain or the winter cold without shelter or access to a bathroom, the body searches, and the verbal abuse guards inflict on families once they enter the prison, grind everyone down. Many, like Boris, tell their mothers to stop coming.

"It became too painful to see her go through all that," he said of his mother. "The guards can't wait for that moment when they can say, 'The visit is over. You have five minutes. If you're not out of there in five minutes, we're terminating your visits for the next month.' That's when they really get aggressive. And your family is there. You know, as a man, you want to be a man. You don't want people talking to you like a child in front of your own children. An officer and a guy got into it. They jumped the guy in the visiting hall in front of his family. That set off a chain of events. They had a riot, guys jumping the officers. We were in the yard. We could see the guy getting dragged back. He was yelling over the gate, 'They jumped me in front of my family!' And when we got back to the units, the guys jumped on the officers. It was random attacks. They just jumped on whatever officers were going to the tier. The visiting hall is a very tense place because your family is there. You're vulnerable because you want to protect your family.

"I didn't tell any of my children what I was actually arrested for or the fact that I was going to go away," he continued. "We didn't have the conversation. My son, Keyon, he was ten, just knew I never came back around. So, I guess eventually he knew I had been arrested. He didn't want to come up to that county jail to visit. And so I would send different letters or whatever. I remember there was a teacher that worked at his school that I was connected with. I sent her a letter to take to him, with a photo. In the letter, I let him know that I'm always going to come for you. And, you know, just to let him know that no matter what, I'm thinking of you.

"He had started to get in trouble in school. So eventually his mother reached out, after maybe a year or so of me being arrested. She was like, 'Well, I want to bring him up and see you because he's having some difficulties.' It's just weird. Every time it gets to a boiling point, they'll say, 'Okay, maybe we could talk to his father now.' And we were visiting through a glass. We're talking. I'm asking him a few questions. I asked him, 'Do you want to be like me? Do you know who I am? Do you think I'm a thug?' He shrugged, like, 'Kinda.' The thing I remember the most is that he cried the whole time while we talked through that glass. He cried. I remember the last time I cried when I was a young man. I'm looking at him. I'm thinking, like, 'Wow, like, this is it, right?' There was nothing I could do at that point. He has to harden up to deal with the world. I knew he wouldn't cry again. We finished our visit. It was cut short. I just looked at him. He walked away. He looked at me. We looked at each other through the glass. I walked back knowing that's the day I lost him. He never came back to see me in prison.

"I was moving through the system," Boris said. "I'm listening to what's happening with him, and I'm thinking to myself, 'I've got to get out of here. I've gotta get out of this jail in time, for the sake of him and my nephew Zaire.'"

Not long after Boris was released, Keyon was incarcerated with a seven-year sentence for unlawful possession of a weapon. Zaire was also in prison. Keyon's life without his father, who had taken him to the public library after school to do his homework and attended his football games, disintegrated at the age of eleven when Boris was locked up. Boris, wracked by guilt, began planning immediately for Keyon's release. He bought an old truck and on weekends did moving jobs. He wanted to hand the truck over to Keyon when he got out so he could make a living. He sent his son a picture of him in a coat and tie and talked on the phone to him about his job as a community organizer, hoping that when Keyon got out he would not go back to the streets. Keyon, who had repeatedly asked prison authorities to be moved because of violent threats and psychotic episodes by the prisoner who shared his cell, however, was beaten to death in his cell by his cellmate in December 2019.

This process of disengagement, students said, normally takes five years. By then, the exhaustion, humiliation, alienation, and stress defeat even the most determined. Prisoners are largely on their own. But while the presence of families diminishes, and in some cases even disappears, the idea that there is a family on the outside that cares for you is important.

A student who had spent over two decades in prison said quietly, "Just because your family doesn't visit, doesn't mean they don't love you."

Those with life sentences, such as Sincere, often tell their girlfriends or wives to think of them as dead—to forget about them and get on with their lives. Sincere wrote up his side of that conversation, one that many in the room had also delivered from the county jail on the eve of being sent to prison. He had been involved with a woman whose boyfriend frequently called her collect from prison.

> TERRANCE. Hey, baby. It's Terrance. How you doin'?
>
> (*Pause.*)
>
> TERRANCE. I miss you too. I'm going to be shipped out of here soon. Yeah, baby. Yeah.
>
> (*Pause.*)
>
> TERRANCE. Look, this ain't one of them things I can fix with slick talk and money. I know what I signed up for. I can't promise you I'm coming home.
>
> (*Pause.*)
>
> TERRANCE. You with me, Sharon? You with me now?
>
> (*Pause.*)
>
> TERRANCE. Like you was with Kevin?
>
> (*Pause.*)
>
> TERRANCE. You knew *what* was comin'? Sharon, don't forget, I had to make you accept dem phone calls from Kevin. Remember dat?
>
> (*Pause.*)
>
> TERRANCE. I was the one layin' next to you when you was on the phone wit' ole boy. An' you remember what we was doin'?
>
> (*Pause.*)
>
> TERRANCE. Hold up. Slow down. I ain't throwin' this in yer face. I know it was different. It was different 'cause I wasn't the one makin' the collect calls.

(*Pause.*)

TERRANCE. Dat's the point, baby. I ain't him. I ain't
tryin' to be him.

(*Pause.*)

TERRANCE. Look, baby, I ain't gonna be callin' you an'
listenin' to no funny noises in da background. I ain't
goin' through that. An' I ain't sayin' you'd do that
to me, I'm jus' tellin' you I can't stop myself from
thinkin' like that. It ain't got nothin' to do with you.
I got to go now.
Peace, Sharon. I love you!

After reading his scene, Sincere said, "I was sent to Trenton
State Prison in September of 1999. I was housed on Six Left
in Trenton for two weeks until my quarantine period was complete. The room was so small that I could touch all four walls
when I stretched out my arms. In the room was a hole in the wall
that functioned as a toilet. I sat on the bunk. I looked around
the filthy cell. I asked myself, 'How in the hell did you get here?'
I called home and told my mother that you don't have to die in
order to get to hell. I knew that to be absolutely true because I
was in it on Six Left in Trenton State."

The class, many of whom had also been in Trenton State,
now called New Jersey State Prison, nodded and murmured in
agreement.

"I've been incarcerated for nearly sixteen years for a murder that I absolutely did not commit," Sincere went on passionately. "After sixteen years, I still cannot get used to being here.
I still cannot understand how this reality came to be mine. This
is my first time in prison. I received a life sentence for a crime
I didn't commit. I've screamed my innocence in appeals to the
courts and have been sabotaged by court-appointed attorneys

each time. I'm poor, I can't afford a private attorney. I am still as innocent today as I was on July 15, 1996.

"My mom, sister, niece, daughter, nephew, and cousin have stood with me for the last sixteen years. So, they are suffering with me. I'm not in here alone. My family is with me, and they are suffering with me. Neither me nor my family deserve this, but this is nonetheless happening; nonetheless still happening to Black men in America. I'm still fighting for my rightful liberty through appeals to the courts. Think about it: I'm a poor Black male convicted of first-degree murder. Who gives a damn about me besides my family? That's exactly why I refuse to give up, because of my family."

"That's not everyone's experience," Lawrence interjected softly. He wore his usual dark-framed glasses and spoke in his usual staccato voice pattern, inflected with a slight stutter.

"I lost family before I came in," he said with evident pain. "No mother. No father. I got into a cell and, as horrible as jail is, was happy to have a bed, hot food. I was still a child when I got locked up. I didn't have what a lot of other prisoners had."

"How young?" I asked him.

"My father died when I was about two," he replied. "My mother died when I was nine. I was living in an abandoned house by the time I was twelve. And then I got arrested."

"At twelve?" I asked.

"At fourteen. I've been locked up since I was fourteen. I can't apply for parole until I'm seventy."

This was, it turned out, the first time he had spoken publicly in the prison about his arrest and incarceration as a child.

"There are a lot of negative associations with coming in that young to prison," he told me later. "Prison culture is all about the wild things you did, the girls you had, the fast life you led, all your adventures—and you didn't have any of that when you come in as a child. I came to Rahway when I was twenty-six. No one had to know I had been put in jail at fourteen. So, no one did."

Lawrence, whose mother was white and whose father was Black, had been living in an abandoned house in Camden, New Jersey, when he was arrested. He was barely literate. He weighed ninety pounds. Three Camden police detectives pressured him into signing a confession for a murder and rape he insisted at his trial he did not commit, although he admitted he was in the car of the man who dragged a young mother into the bushes, where she was sexually assaulted and then strangled to death. It made no difference. The confession condemned him, although there was no scientific evidence or any independent witnesses tying him to the crime. Lawrence would not be eligible to go before a parole board for fifty-six years. It was a de facto life sentence without parole.

I would meet him seven years later when he was released into the parking lot of the prison. Lawrence and I walked the two blocks to the QuickChek, a ritual for most prisoners released from East Jersey State Prison. The convenience store, which can be seen from the barred windows, has a mythic status in the prison: a symbol of the outside world for those locked inside.

"I feel a mixture of excitement and trepidation," he said as we walked. "It feels so strange right now to be walking outside without handcuffs and shackles."

"How long has it been since you walked outside as a free man?" I asked.

"Thirty years and one day," he said. "June 27, 1990, I came into prison at fourteen years old. I'm now going on forty-five years old. It's amazing. It's scary. But it's here."

Lawrence had woken up at four in the morning to wait by his cell door. He was released at eight thirty.

"It's bittersweet," he said of his release. "A lot of these guys, I grew up with. They're my brothers; they're not just my friends. As happy as I am to be leaving, I won't ever forget the fact that I'm leaving people I love and care for behind. But this is just a chance to help 'em, man, to come back for 'em, just like every-body came back for me. We got to go back for them, too. As I say, it's bittersweet, but somebody got to go at some point to start bringing other people home. And that's just the way I try and keep it in focus; keep myself from having, like, survivor's guilt.

"The hardest thing about getting out is the unknown: not knowing what I'm gonna face, not knowing what's gonna be there, what's not gonna be there, who's gonna be there, particularly for me coming in as a kid—as literally a child," he said. "These are my first steps in the free world as a grown man. I don't know how to pay a bill. I don't know how to open a bank account. I don't know how to apply for insurance. There are so many things I don't know, and I think that is probably the scariest thing for me, trying to figure out how to exist as a grown man in a free world after thirty years."

"When you thought about getting out," I asked him, "was there one thing you wanted to do in particular?"

"As crazy as this sounds, I want to ride a bike and go swimming," he said. "I don't know why. I think that might be a reflection of the fact that I got locked up as a child. I kind of think about the things that I left off doing as a child. I also look forward to getting up that first morning and sitting outside and having myself a cup of coffee on the steps—just quiet, just enjoying freedom."

Lawrence entered the QuickChek, clutching some cash friends had handed him, and came out with a bouquet of flowers for his public attorney, Jennifer Sellitti, who'd spent two and a half years working to get him the resentencing hearing that would reduce his original sentence.

Before going to prison, Lawrence had lived at fourteen different addresses, a common experience for the poor, who are repeatedly evicted from their homes. They often suffer from the same perimigration trauma I saw among refugees and the

displaced in war zones. Perimigration is the phase between initial displacement and eventual resettlement.

Like orphaned children buffeted by war, Lawrence endured
extreme poverty, chronic instability, physical abuse, and the
early death of his parents. He lived in constant fear, even terror, amid street violence—Camden often ranked as the most
dangerous city per capita in America—was exploited by drug
dealers, deprived of his most basic needs, and was rejected and
outcast by the wider society. He had never had an adequate income or sufficient food.

His forlorn efforts at his trial to recant the confession, to
insist he did not commit the rape and murder and did not understand what was in the signed confession or its consequences,
were brushed aside by Judge Isaiah Steinberg. Lawrence was
charged with murder, aggravated sexual assault, kidnapping,
and related offenses in the 1990 rape and murder. Steinberg,
when he announced the aggregate sentence of life plus fifty
years with fifty-five years to be served without parole, sneeringly
called Lawrence in the courtroom a "despicable coward."

Lawrence's life, like that of so many students in the class,
was a train wreck of abuse and neglect. He was terrorized by his
mother's boyfriend Reggie.

"My earliest memory is of coming home from kindergar-
ten," Lawrence said. "My mom and I would watch TV shows
together in the afternoons. That day, I came in through the door
and saw my mom sitting on the couch with Reggie holding a
shotgun to her head. And she said in a very calm voice, 'Go
upstairs.' And so, I did. Something didn't feel right, but I didn't
understand what was going on. At that age, you believe your
mom, so I thought everything must be okay.

"I had a couple of guinea pigs that I would take care of, and
they can be dirty and will, you know, make a mess everywhere,"
he said. "One day, Reggie told me to clean up after them, and
I said, 'Yeah, Okay,' but I didn't clean up the mess right away.

So, later on, without saying anything, he brought his dog up to the second floor where the guinea pigs were kept. He let his dog behind the gate at the top of the stairs, and the dog went in and ate the guinea pigs. He would do things like that. Just sadistic. Another time, we had some small dogs—like, poodles—that were outside one night—and this was winter—and he took some water and threw it all over them and closed the door with them still outside. They froze to death.

"It was like walking on eggshells all the time," he recalled numbly. "Everyone would have to be quiet whenever he was home. My mom would try to keep us all quiet by having us play board games or do other quiet things. The door was set up with a lock on the inside and the outside, so you would need a key to get out of the house. And we couldn't go into the basement or their bedroom. They were off-limits. I don't think I saw into my mom and Reggie's bedroom until I was maybe seven or eight years old. I can remember hearing fights going on upstairs. Like, you would hear things being thrown around and breaking, or, like, my mom being thrown around. And then, after a few minutes, there would just be silence. He would come downstairs like nothing had happened and leave. Then we would go find my mom, and she would have a swollen face and bruises, putting ice on her face in front of the mirror.

"And I just remember wanting to get bigger so I could beat him up. I wanted to kill him for doing that to my mom. The saddest thing was that even when he wasn't home, we would still act like he was. Because he drove a tow truck for work, we didn't know when he was going to show up, so we always acted like he was home."

Lawrence's oldest brother, Gary, was about twenty. He was in and out of prison. Gary was "everybody's hero because he would stand up to Reggie." By the time Lawrence was seven or eight, the only children left in the house were his sister, whom Reggie sexually molested, and himself. His sister once jumped from the attic window trying to escape from Reggie and broke her ankles.

Reggie's fury and violence intensified. His mother tried to leave, but Reggie would take Lawrence or his sister hostage until his mother returned. When Lawrence was about seven or eight, Reggie once picked him up from school and took the boy to a stranger's apartment. Then Reggie called Lawrence's mother and said he was going to give him pills, which he told Lawrence were candy. Lawrence's mother shouted over the phone for him not to swallow the pills. She agreed to return to Reggie if he brought her son home unharmed.

"For a long time, I was angry with her for not leaving," he said. "I blamed her for allowing us to be abused by him. But later on, as I thought more about it, I could see how she couldn't leave. I learned about battered woman syndrome and how people can be manipulated, and I know that's what happened to her. After being angry with her for years, I was able to let go of blaming her. I forgave her. And then I also had to forgive myself for ever blaming her."

On June 22, 1985, his mother collapsed in the kitchen.

"We called 911," he said. "I held her head in my lap while we waited for the ambulance to come. It was a blood clot in her lung; a pulmonary embolism. She was dead there on the floor, but I think they revived her at the hospital. Then she died on the operating table, if I remember correctly."

Reggie came home that night from the hospital.

"Your mother died, and I don't want to hear anything out of you," he told the children.

"He forbade us from crying about it," Lawrence said. "I remember the exact song that was playing when he told us she died. My sister and I just sat there in the living room for what must have been a long time. For months after she died, I wouldn't speak to anyone. Sometimes I would whisper to my sister, but I stopped talking to other people for a while. Before she died, I didn't smoke weed. Before she died, I was a good student. I started getting into trouble at school after that. I got into my first fight that year in school; my first physical fight. A kid said something about my mom, some joke about her being stupid. I grabbed a chair and hit him with it. I think there was a rage inside of me that wasn't there before. No school counselor or anyone else talked to me. I am the epitome of systemic failures. If you want to talk about how systems fail, just look at my life. There isn't anyone available to help you in that situation. I never remember the police coming around the house except for maybe once when my brothers were brought home for playing hooky. So, after the police left, we all watched as they got beaten. But no one ever intervened. No school counselor or anyone else talked to me."

His mother's death deeply affected Lawrence's other older brother, Troy, who was manic-depressive and an alcoholic. He tried to kill himself by cutting his arm from his wrist almost to his elbow with a hunting knife.

"I was sitting on the porch with my sister when Troy called once," Lawrence remembered. "He was crying and drunk. He told her that he was going to kill himself. So, I got in my car—I had been driving since I was twelve. I drove over to the cemetery where my mom was buried. He was sitting at her grave. He was drunk and crying and said he wanted to die. I went over to talk to him. And I'm not sure if it was a moment of clarity or a moment of acceptance, but I went back to my car and got my gun. I loaded it and handed it to him and said, 'Here. If you want to die, put it in your mouth. You won't miss.' He looked at me for a moment, then he got up and walked to my car and got in."

Troy later tried to commit suicide by stabbing himself in the stomach.

"He died a few years ago from heart complications, tuberculosis, alcoholism—you pick the reason," Lawrence said of his brother, who used to visit him in prison.

Six months after Lawrence's mother died, Reggie was arrested and sent to prison. Lawrence moved in with an older woman, a friend of his mother's, who lived across the street. He used to call her Grandma. But she soon left for New York City and passed Lawrence into the care of her daughter Debbie, who was bipolar and physically abusive.

"Debbie was sort of like my guardian, if you can call her that, but she wasn't officially my guardian," he said. "That's now an issue in my case: to this day, the state of New Jersey doesn't know who my legal guardian was after my mom died. Debbie wasn't legally responsible for me, so she wasn't able to give the police permission to interrogate me, like they claimed. I got left with Debbie because I guess Grandma thought it would be good for Debbie to have the responsibility of taking care of me. She thought it would calm her down and give her more stability.

"Reggie's abuse was sometimes physical but mostly psychological, but Debbie's was just physical," he said. "It would get to the point where it was a preemptive beating. When I'd come home from school, she'd say, 'I know you did something,' and beat me. And she was smoking and selling weed. The house was raided by police multiple times when I was staying there. She got me to sell weed for her. She'd say that if I wanted new sneakers, I would need to earn them. I'd see other boys I knew selling drugs and making money. One day Debbie asked me where my friends were getting their money from, and I said drugs. She said, 'Well, why don't you go out there with them?' So, I started selling for her. I'd sell dime bags. One package was thirty-five bags, so I'd give three hundred dollars to Debbie and keep fifty for myself. That was a standard cut at the time. After that, I always had money. I saved a lot of what I made. I was the kind of kid who would keep at least twenty dollars in my shoe at all times. I would take my money, go buy an ounce of weed, pack it up into bags, and sell it myself. I was making more that way. That was the end of depending on her."

He still had a key to his old house on Twenty-Fifth Street, although it was abandoned. He started sleeping there at night. He carried a gun, a .32 special, fearful of being robbed.

"Before I went to sleep, I'd spread some gravel over the porch so that I could hear if anyone came up to the house during the night," said Lawrence. "I could sell drugs and take care of myself without her. My sister was still around. She would argue with me and tell me I needed to stop selling, but at the same time, she was accepting my help. She had little kids by now, and she was struggling financially. So, even though she didn't want me to sell drugs, she needed Pampers for her kids, and she accepted my money."

He got a girl pregnant when he was thirteen. She had an abortion.

"It felt like another loss," he recalled. "I never had suicidal thoughts or a desire to die like Troy, but I will say that I was sort of numb. I didn't care about living. One night I was sitting on my porch smoking weed and taking pain pills. I was drinking beer, too. I had been given a prescription for the pills because I was hit by a car and broke both of my knees. I also had head trauma from the car accident. I was sitting in a chair on my porch with my legs propped up because they were in a soft cast, and taking these pills, but they weren't helping. I took another one, and nothing. I took a few more, still nothing—no help with the pain. A friend of mine had some Xanax, so he gave me some, and I took one or two. Not long after that, my sister came over and saw me on the porch with the pills. And she said, 'What are you doing mixing those pills with all of that? You're gonna kill yourself.' And my response was just, so? That was my attitude toward life then: I didn't care if I died.

"Imagine that you are fourteen, still a kid, and you are brought into a courtroom," he said. "You have these adults around that you've never met before, and they are saying things you don't understand. You catch a few words, like 'murder' and 'rape,' but you still don't know what they are talking about. It happens really fast, and then they take you away, back to the youth house: the correctional facility. That's what it was like. That whole hearing was like a blur. Next thing I know, I'm in the youth house, I was meeting with a lawyer, then going to see a psychiatrist for an evaluation. But I don't fully understand what's going on. That's why I never want to be in a situation where I can't follow what the people around me are saying. Part of what drives me to learn and be ready for anything, any conversation, is wanting to prevent that from ever happening again."

Lawrence spent twenty-two months in jail before going to trial.

"The judge decided to charge me as an adult because of the seriousness of the crime," he explained. "He said I didn't seem remorseful. But what they didn't think about was the effect that being in jail had on me. I saw two people get killed when I was there. During the trial, my mind was partially focused on that, keeping myself prepared for going back into that situation. They interpreted that as indifference and a lack of remorse. One thing that the judge said has stuck with me. He called me 'irredeemable.' I've been working hard and working on myself all this time to prove him wrong. I want him to be able to look at me and admit that he was wrong about that. If I saw him again, I'd tell him, 'You were wrong about me. But that's okay; it's okay as long as other kids—babies—don't end up being locked up like I was.'

"After the trial, they took me away, stripped me down, and put me in a jail uniform," he said. "That's when it became real and I knew what was happening. I went to the jail that night, but the people at the jail didn't want to admit me at first. I was so small and looked young. They were calling their supervisors to find out what to do with me. That first night, I was put in a holding cell with other guys. And one of the guys was staring at me; looking at me funny. I started a fight with him—I felt like I had to. I was taken away, and I ended up being placed in protective custody. It's a block for anyone who can't be in the general population. I was in isolation. It's called 'twenty-three and one': twenty-three hours in isolation and one hour outside of your cell each day. I would count all the bricks in my cell, all the lines on the walls. I still do that. I will count all of the photos in a magazine or every time a word or phrase shows up in a book. I learned that habit while in isolation. The hardest part, probably, is being alone with your thoughts. They were concerned for my safety because I was so small and skinny. But there were, I think, six pedophiles on that block. I wanted out. So, I signed a waiver so that I could join the general population."

Lawrence's brother Gary was known within the prison population. His friends watched out for Lawrence, who was now seventeen years old and at Garden State prison.

"A man named Salaam, who was like a father figure to me; really took care of me," he said. "Whenever I was getting into trouble or fights, he'd come and talk to me. Reverend Du Bois was another person who helped me a lot. He was the head chaplain at Garden State. He showed me respect and really cared about me even though I was Muslim, and he was Christian.

"There was a time when members of the Bloods tried to take over the chapel," he said. "Some guys, including me, intervened on behalf of Reverend Du Bois. He was really well liked and respected by everyone. In the end, the Bloods backed off. I bring up this story because not all Christians were as accepting of me as a Muslim as Reverend Du Bois was. Years ago, I wrote to Centurion Ministries[11] asking for help with my case. They said they wanted to help but that they were focused on helping Christians, not Muslims. They might have felt differently about taking on my case if they had known how I'd put my neck on the line to help Christians like Reverend Du Bois.

"When I was young, people didn't give me chance," Lawrence reflected. "Nobody intervened, nobody tried to help or took me aside and said that they believed in me. But once I got to prison, I encountered people who cared about me and really wanted to help. As soon as I was given a chance, I took to it like a fish to water. So many teachers and classes have had an impact on me over the years. My teachers have been mentors. They stand as examples of what I want to be and show me what is possible. Every day, I am trying to make progress and be a little better than I was yesterday. I'm always learning, growing. It may be that today I learn a new word or work through a puzzle—anything that challenges me. Something in me pushes me to keep getting better.

"My most prized possessions are my books. I have nice, hardbound editions of *The Iliad, The Odyssey, The Aeneid,* and others. I love reading Homer and Ovid and the classics. I've read everything that Shakespeare has written. I actually have a one-volume edition of Shakespeare's works. I like his sonnets and comedies the most. My favorite book is probably *Manchild in the Promised Land* by Claude Brown. I read that one a long time ago and still like it. You've read Dante's *Divine Comedy,* right? Right now, I am writing a book that follows my life as a journey through the different stages in the *Divine Comedy.* It sees my own experiences as part of a journey that leads to the discovery of self. I remember thinking when I first read the *Divine Comedy* that his idea of purgatory is sort of what it feels like being in prison."

It is hard not to internalize the sense of being inferior, worthless. It is hard to break free from the stereotypes imposed by popular culture on Black men, especially when the society offers them little more than life on the streets. This battle between who they are, and who society forces them to be, creates tremendous internal conflicts. My students were intellectuals. They had turned their cells into libraries. They saved, often for months, to be able to buy books. They were passionate about going to school. They were sensitive, erudite, and thoughtful, but these qualities were unrecognized by a society that had branded them as criminals and ex-felons.

The illegal economy is often the only way to survive. Drug dealers have a cachet in the neighborhood. They carry guns. They are feared and, in some cases, even respected. They live precarious, dangerous lives, which usually leads to long prison terms or early death. They rule the streets. Almost everyone in the class had sold drugs, although most, such as Kabir and Lawrence, sold tiny amounts, usually weed, to get a little cash.

Kabir, Lawrence, and others who were imprisoned as teenagers retained some of the mannerisms and characteristics of their adolescence—as if once inside the prison, a part of the teenage boy was trapped in time. Those imprisoned as juveniles often, for this reason, have the hardest time upon release, crippled by their arrested development.

Kabir found himself in the wrong car with the wrong people. He would pay for that misjudgment with sixteen years and fifty-four days of his life, locked away for a crime he did not participate in and did not know was going to take place.

Released from prison six years after the class, he would be tossed onto the streets, without financial resources and, because of fines and fees imposed on him by the court system, $7,000 in debt. He would end up broke in a homeless shelter in Newark, populated with others who could not afford a place to live, addicts, and the mentally ill. The shelter was filthy, infested with lice and bedbugs.

"You have to chain your food up in the refrigerator," he said, wearing a worn, ripped sweatshirt, when I met him at the Newark train station after his release. "There's a chain on the door. There's no stove. There's one microwave that is on its way out. It stinks. I'm trying to stay positive."

Kabir's sweet and gentle disposition and self-deprecating, infectious sense of humor made him beloved in the prison. Nothing seemed capable of denting his good nature, empathy,

and compassion. He loved animals. One of his saddest childhood experiences, he told me, came when he was not allowed to
visit a farm with his class because he had ringworm. He dreamed
of becoming a veterinarian.

But the social hell of urban America is the great destroyer
of dreams. It batters and assaults the children of the poor. It
teaches them that their dreams, and, finally, they themselves, are
worthless. They go to bed hungry. They live with fear. They lose
their fathers, brothers, and sisters to mass incarceration—and,
at times, their mothers. They see friends and relatives killed.
They are repeatedly evicted from their dwellings. The sociologist Matthew Desmond estimates that 2.3 million evictions were
filed in 2016: a rate of four every minute. One in four families
spend 70 percent of their income on rent. A medical emergency,
the loss of a job or a reduction in hours, car repairs, funeral
expenses, fines and tickets—and there is financial catastrophe.
Poor families are hounded by creditors, payday lenders, and collection agencies, and often forced to declare bankruptcy.

This social hell is relentless. It wears them down. It makes
them angry and bitter. It drives them to hopelessness and despair. The message sent to them by the dysfunctional schools,
the decrepit housing projects, the mercenary financial institutions, gang violence, instability, and ever-present police abuse
is that they are human refuse. That Kabir and my students retained their integrity, empathy, and humanity under this assault,
that they defied this hell to make something of their lives, that
they were often the first to reach out to others with compassion
and concern, made them some of the most remarkable and ad-
mirable people I have ever known.

Kabir, the middle of three children, was raised by his mother
in Newark. He met his father, who was from Haiti and spoke
little English, only three times. Kabir does not speak Creole, so
they could barely communicate. His father died in Haiti while
Kabir was in prison. Kabir's family lived on the first floor of a

house at Peabody Place, a few blocks from the Passaic River. His great-aunt, who had adopted his mother, and whom he refers to as his grandmother, lived on the second floor with her husband. His great-uncle's pension and savings provided for the family. But by the time of his mother's generation in the 1980s, well-paying jobs that came with benefits and pensions—and, with them, stability and dignity—were gone.

"That was one of my gripes against my mother," Kabir said sadly. "Damn, if you can't save me, and my father's not around, who the hell gonna save me?"

There were difficulties. His mother, who often left him in the care of his grandmother, cycled through boyfriends, some of whom were abusive.

Like many of my students, Kabir was teased and bullied when he was small because of his tattered secondhand clothes. He was sensitive and introspective; the bullying shattered his childhood. It made it hard to pay attention. He would grow up to be big and strong, aided by his dedicated weight lifting, but the awkward silences that punctuate his stories of bullying show that the pain is still there.

Catastrophe struck in fifth grade, when his great-uncle, who had assumed the role of his grandfather, died. Stability evaporated. They lost their home. They moved to a dilapidated house on Hudson Street. On the night they moved in, it caught fire. They lost everything and moved back to squat in their old house with nothing. The family eventually moved to North Park Street in East Orange, New Jersey. From then on, life became a series of sudden evictions and moves, with Kabir shipped from school to school. The family squatted in abandoned houses without electricity that were used by drug dealers and addicts.

Kabir wrote a scene for the play about a family being evicted.

"It killed my spirit to live," he said. "I used to contemplate suicide. I felt I had no haven. Everywhere I go, there was some type of abuse. Even at home, there was no peace. Why be here?

What's the point of being here? My family life is in disarray. No father. My mother is ignoring me. The other family members we do have, they're not really present. Our structure was so damaged, there's no help from my aunt or uncle. We were all mixed up, living in our own world."

One day, when Kabir was eight or nine, a man was speaking to his mother on the porch. Another man pulled up in a car and started shooting at the man talking to his mom. Then the gunman jumped out of the car and chased his victim into the house.

"My little brother is in the tub naked," Kabir said. "I'm in the living room next to the hallway. My grandmother is upstairs. He starts shooting. I run, get my little brother. He gets out of the tub naked. We haul out the back and run next door. My mother was in the hallway pleading for them to stop. I can't feel safe in my own dwelling."

His schooling effectively ended in the eighth grade. Kabir began smoking weed, "being disruptive, being a clown." He was "very depressed." He drank most of the night and slept most of the day.

"I hustled a little bit, selling drugs," he said. "I was never good at that. I was not patient. I'm idle minded. I'm more of a philosopher. I have a heart for people. I'm not a street person, even though I was in the streets."

Three months after he turned eighteen, Kabir was arrested for the first time. He was in a car with three older men. The older men decided to rob "Ol' Man Charlie," who ran a convenience store. The trio went into the store, while he remained behind in the car, listening to the song "Wanksta" by the rapper 50 Cent.

"They come back to the car," he remembered. "They got this spooked face. They said, 'Man, I had to kill Charlie. He was reaching. Mu told me to hit him.' In my head, it didn't even seem real. I didn't witness it. It was like they were telling me a story. I couldn't fathom it. Even though I knew they were going into the store to rob him. I'm in a daze. We continue to ride around in this car. They hoppin' out robbing people. They don't stop. At the same time, I feel like I'm stuck. If I leave, there could be repercussions."

The police brought him in for questioning. Kabir was taken to a room that had contents from the crime scene, including the gun used to kill Charlie. He tried to be as vague as possible, but he didn't want to lie.

"Now there's a room full of these motherfuckers," he said. "There had to be seven of them. This old, fat white dude. He had blotches on his skin. Like he smoked too much. As soon as he walks in, he just smacked the shit out of me. He's fat and tall. He slapped me good time. *Pow!* He said, 'This shit don't make no sense. You need to tell us what the fuck is going on.' In my head, I felt so guilty about the whole ordeal. He slaps the shit out of me. *Pow!* It was the first time I was arrested for anything. I just come out and tell them what happened. They do the ballistics; eventually it comes back a match. The gun was used for that crime that killed Charlie. They start collecting people. One of the last people were my two [codefendants].

"I felt guilty as hell," he said. "Someone's life was taken behind this shit. If I were intelligent, I would have known this was the cost of robbing somebody. You got the power of life or death in your hands. I snitched, rolled over. The guilt was more than anything. They eventually started grabbing people. I got charged with felony murder. A homicide in the act of committing a robbery. Even though I never left the car. I never had a weapon discharged. But the law charges everyone there equally."

Kabir spent three and a half years in the county jail before being sentenced and going to prison.

"My strongest asset is that I have a connection to people," he told me in Newark after he got out. "At times, I can be a little depressed because it's overwhelming. I felt like I never got out of poverty. You know what I mean? If it wasn't my upbringing, it was prison. Now I'm spit back out as an adult. I never really achieved anything I feel a grown man should have. I can't drive. I was never taught to drive. I went away at eighteen. I don't have my own place. I'm thirty-five. If it ain't a room, it's the shelter. When you meet people of affluence, some people with money, how they look at you. You can almost pierce their eyes and read their mind. You know, when people feel like they're above you. You know when you're treated wrong, whether it's in school, whether it's in a store, or in a certain neighborhood where they feel like you don't belong. And then, you're constantly fed these lily-white dreams on TV, knowing this is the farthest thing from our reality. Then we look at Black reality—it's like they make mockery out of it. It's either overly funny so it's desensitized. Or it's not even true."

In 2020 the Covid-19 pandemic would create an urgent need for frontline workers: those desperate enough to work for low wages and accept being expendable without sick pay or health insurance. Kabir was able to get a job at a Whole Foods supermarket. On the days he had to be there at six in the morning, he walked more than a mile of the 2.3 miles from where he lives to the supermarket because of the erratic bus service at that hour in Newark. It was dark when he set out. He walked past the unhoused, which sometimes include children, sleeping on the street; the handful of prostituted women trying to scare up a few clients; and the junkies passed out, propped up against buildings. He was a model employee, but when the manager received Kabir's background check Kabir lost his job. My calls and letters to the manager on Kabir's behalf had no effect.

Prisoners, once released, have to navigate the netherworld of America's criminal caste system. They are branded for life as felons, although many were locked away for crimes that in most other countries would have warranted a short sentence or none at all. They are denied public assistance, food stamps, public housing, the right to vote, the right to serve on a jury, the ability to collect Social Security for the forty-hour-a-week jobs they had in prison; barred from obtaining hundreds of professional licenses; and burdened with old fees, fines, and court costs they often could not pay. And, in the ultimate catch-22, their criminal records preclude their being protected from employment discrimination. They become part of America's tens of millions of second-class citizens, most of whom are poor people of color, who are stripped of basic civil and human rights and are subject to legal discrimination for life. One-third of all Black men in America are classified as ex-felons.[12] Kabir, through no fault of his own, unless being poor and Black is a fault, would leave prison and live trapped in a social hell from which there is almost no escape.

There were a few people in the class, including Boris and Steph, who had dominated the streets. They earned significant sums dealing drugs. They were adept at using intimidation, and sometimes violence, to prevent anyone from cutting into their business or challenging them.

"My mother sold marijuana," Steph recounted from the back of the room. "She had a third-grade education. She wasn't good with numbers. I used to have to count her money for her. Her profits and proceeds. I used to go to New York with her sometimes to pick up drugs. I understood mathematics very well; it was my favorite subject. Because I knew how to work a scale, I was a benefit, which she really needed at the time. I was pretty much encultured into selling drugs, on many levels.

"After a while, she understood," he went on. "It is what it is. People look at it from a social contract standpoint. You don't do certain things because it's against the law; laws that usually benefit the establishment. We're supposed to follow all these rules because the government is here to protect you. In my neighborhood, where there is an extreme lack of opportunities, literally sixteen people living in a two-bedroom apartment, six of them adults. When you come from this kind of poverty, I won't say that there are no options, but sometimes you *feel* like there are no options. Scarcity brings forth panic. People panic. They think, 'I have to do something right now.' That was pretty much my circumstance. I wasn't thinking of selling drugs. But it kept coming to me. I'm counting the money I could have made. I stayed in a park all day, picking up leaves, picking up dirt for twenty, thirty dollars that day. My mother doesn't have a lot. I don't have a lot. This is a viable option. I think people sometimes don't understand—yes, we should live by the laws of whichever country is governing us. However, when you feel like that country is letting you down, you're less likely to abide by those rules. It's all about strain. Strain brings forth circumstances that people might normally not do.

"One day," Steph recalled, "I was sitting with a friend out on my block. We were fourteen. People kept coming asking if we had drugs. But we weren't into that. I was into numbers, though. So, I said to him, 'We been here for about thirty minutes, and that was over three hundred dollars we could have made.' That was the day I decided to sell drugs. I never agreed to the social contract."

Selling drugs is often the only way for some people to earn an adequate income. But people go to prison in the United States for many years for selling or possessing drugs. The ability to charge whole groups of people with one crime—even a crime the majority did not participate in carrying out—railroads young men and women into prison in groups. Boris was imprisoned because he was involved in a drug deal that went bad, where one of the buyers shot and killed one of the sellers. Boris did not have a weapon. He had nothing to do with the dispute or the shooting. But he and everyone else involved in the drug deal were charged with felony murder. He was forced to plead out when prosecutors piled on so many charges that, should he demand a jury trial and lose, he would have served a life sentence. He spent eleven years in prison.

"There was usually drugs in the homes," Boris said. "I had friends whose homes were raided when they were children. Most of the parents were getting high, including my father. I did not know any child who did not have a drug addict in the home. And if a person was not a drug addict, he or she was often suffering from some form of mental illness. It seemed everyone was dealing with something. Those who were left with their grandparents were in the best situation. Kids would say they were living with their grandmother. They would never mention their mother or father. I never saw the fathers of most of my friends. They had disappeared or were in jail.

"I remember when my friend Carl Anderson's father came home from jail," he went on. "We were in the seventh grade. We were sitting in the classroom. Somebody said, 'Carl, that's your father outside.' We all turned around. Carl was my best friend. I had never seen his father. He looked like the boxer Marvin Hagler. He had a leather jacket, a bald head, and a goatee. Carl was excited because his dad was home.

"That same year, we were walking home from school, and this lady who was getting high ran up to him and said, 'Little Carl, they just locked your father up. He cut somebody's throat down in the projects.' You could see everything drain out of his face. He shut everything down. How do you learn to deal with that? You learn not to care. We were using a lot of misplaced aggression. That night, we were probably fighting somebody. I could feel his pain. You want to get it out? We will get it out. That's how you dealt with it. That's how everybody dealt with it. Take it out on somebody else. When I would get hit in the house, I would come outside, and the first person lookin' at me,

I would say, 'What you lookin' at?' I would jump them or chase them or something. My mother told my father, 'You can't hit him anymore. You are making him violent.'

"There is a stigma that comes with being poor," Boris said. "If you are poor, you are bad. You are worthless. You are ridiculed. You are picked on. Markets are built on this. This is how you can sell a kid from the inner city a pair of two-hundred-dollar sneakers. He is buying his identity. He is buying his self-esteem. And that's why poor people hustle. That's why I started hustling drugs: to buy things. The gratification is immediate. You wear that stuff, and it is like you are magically not poor anymore. It is a trigger to go back to selling drugs. I remember when I was struggling. I had grits one night for dinner because that was all that was in the cabinet. I panicked. By the next day, I'd decided I would do something criminal to change my situation.

"What's the best that can happen to you, even if you don't go to jail?" he asked. "Check out bags at Walmart? A warehouse job? That's as far as you can go in this world if you are poor. The only education the poor are given is one where they get to a place where they learn enough to take orders. They are taught to remember what is said. They are taught to repeat the instructions. There is no thinking involved. We are not taught to think. We are educated just enough to occupy the lowest rung on the social ladder.

"No one in prison wanted to admit they were poor. A friend of mine in prison told all these big drug-dealer stories. He has been in and out of jail for twenty years. But one day we were walking on the basketball court. He got honest. He told me he had been sleepin' in his car. Sometimes motel rooms. Basically homeless. No education. No connections. The only people he knows are inmates. He does not know anyone in the working world who can help him put in an application and say a word for him. When he got out, he went to the guys he knew from jail still in the streets. That was his network. That's most people's network. 'Can you get me some dope? What's the price? Who's moving it?' That's your economy. That's the one you go back to. That's how you survive. His brother is doing thirty years. His nephew is doing sixteen years.

"One of my four children went to school in New Brunswick," Boris went on. "And he is in jail. The other three, who did not go to school in New Brunswick, have college degrees or are in college. You go to schools like the one I went to, and you enter a pipeline straight to jail. When I walked into the mess hall in prison, it looked like my old school lunchroom, including the fights. When I walked into the yard in prison, it looked like my old playground, including the fights. When I was in the projects, it looked like prison. When guys get to prison, the scenery is familiar. If you grow up poor, then prison is not a culture shock. You have been conditioned your whole life for prison."

His voice softened. "Look at the faces of the young kids when they first start out," Boris said wistfully. "They have wide, bright eyes. Then look at the pictures of the faces of people in prison. Their eyes are low, slanted, shifty, beaten. They are worn out. How do you get from that child to that man? Look at the community. Look at the schools. Look at what is done to the poor."

It was Steph and Boris who wrote the scenes about big drug deals, devoid of the allure and glamour that often color Hollywood depictions of street life. The character Stacks—his street name comes from money stacks—is the neighborhood drug dealer. Stacks wants to get out of the game and off the streets. Stacks was based on Steph, who left Newark and drug dealing to start a new life in South Carolina. When Steph ran out of money, however, he returned to Newark, drug dealing, and eventually prison. Stacks teaches Quan how to sell drugs after his brother, Omar, is sent to prison. By now, Quan's mother has died, and Quan, like Lawrence, is a child living on his own.

(*Quan opens the door and lets Stacks into his apartment. Stacks is carrying a plastic bag with one hand and a black duffel bag in the other.*)

STACKS. We gunna need somewhere to set up.
QUAN. The kitchen right through here.
STACKS. Yo, where the fuck is your furniture?
QUAN. I told you I had to sell everything to bury my moms.
STACKS. Oh, iight . . . My bad.
QUAN. That's cool.

(*Quan clears off the small kitchen table. Stacks reaches in the black duffel bag and takes out a small ziplock bag filled with cocaine, a box of razors, two boxes of plastic sandwich bags, and a pair of scissors.*)

STACKS. I need a plate.

(*Quan hands Stacks a plate.*)

QUAN. What's all this for?
STACKS. I'm goin' show you how to bag up the work. This way, when I ain't around, you know what to do.
QUAN, *pointing to the plastic bag.* And what's that?
STACKS. That's lunch.

(*Quan watches as Stacks uses the razor to cut small pieces of cocaine from the larger rock. Stacks shows Quan the size of the rock he's cutting off.*)

STACKS. See that? That's a twenty-cent piece. You don't put no more in the bag than that.

(*Stacks cuts the cocaine into small pieces. He places the small rocks in the corners of the sandwich bags. He hands the bags to Quan, who also starts cutting.*)

STACKS. Tie the tops of the bags. Cut off the extra plastic so we have a neatly packaged product.

QUAN. Yo, why'd you come back?

STACKS. What?

QUAN. Omar told me you got out of the game. Said you was doin' good. Said you moved down south.

STACKS. Yeah, little homey, you right. I was out. Four years out. I moved down south 'cause I wanted to get as far away from this shit as I could.

QUAN. I thought you liked the hood.

STACKS, *laughs.* Me too. Yo, I was younger than you when I started this shit. But this shit gets old. The money, the cars, the girls—all that shit gets old.

QUAN. I don't know 'bout that . . .

STACKS, *chuckling.* I know one thing, little nigga, you gonna get old; then let me hear you talk that shit. You know. The streets stay fast. We get slow. I mean, look at me. I here baggin' up coke wit' you, and you're what, sixteen? I got kids. Little niggas running 'round in one-piece pajamas right now. I got a wifey. She wants me to take her to Beds Bath and Beyond later.

QUAN. What's that?

STACKS. It's where you take your wifey. (*He laughs quietly.*) Real talk. She wants me to be a man and help with the kids, you know?

QUAN. What she say about you gettin' back in the game?

STACKS. She flipped! But she da one who spent all the money. (*Stacks laughs loudly.*) Naw . . . we both fucked the money up. (*Stacks pauses and begins to speak in a serious tone.*)

You know, when I first got out I ain't think I was coming back. I got a construction job down in South Carolina. Minimum wage. I wore old, scruffy boots. I walked to work in hundred-degree heat. I couldn't get any job up here. When I copped those five years of probation, I didn't realize it was a trap. I apply for a job, I got to check the box saying I have a record. That snake-ass prosecutor knew exactly what he was doin'. I thought no jail time, that's what's up. But I didn't know it meant the end of jobs. I can't even get welfare. I didn't know it meant stayin' in the streets.

QUAN. I know you was mad bored out there in the country.

STACKS. Nah, I loved it.

QUAN. Word?

STACKS. It was the first time since I was a kid I didn't have to look over my shoulder. Strangers would say hi to you. There's another world out there. But that shit ain't easy . . . You got to grow up fast, ya know? Shift into mode. An' in the end, I was out of the game, but the game wasn't out of me.

QUAN. What you mean?

STACKS. When I stopped hustling, I was living like I was still sellin' drugs, you know? Once you stop this shit, you can't keep living like you're in a rap video. You got to live like white people, you know? Dirty sneakers and all that shit. No more two-hundred-dollar Jordans, gold chains, and shit, even though that wasn't my twist. I used to spend weekends in Vegas. Gambling was my shit. In the end, the drug money was gone. I was tryin' to feed six little niggas on a job that pays seven twenty-five an hour. An' you can't feed and clothe six kids on that. Anyway, all that shit brings you back. (*Misquoting a rap verse.*) "An' coming back at thirty, give a nigga the chills."

QUAN. So you gonna get out again?

STACKS. That's the plan, you know. Take my kids and blow. (*Pause.*) Okay, Quan. I'm startin' you as a runner.

QUAN. Runner?

STACKS. Yeah. Here. You startin' with a G pack. That's ten dollars a rock. How's your math? My cut is eight hundred; yours is two hundred. Losses are on you. Police catch you, keep your mouth shut. Post up. I'll send the custies to you. And be on point for *la hara*.

QUAN. *La hara?*

STACKS. It's Spanish. It means the cops are comin'.

(*Lights down.*)

(*Quan is standing awkwardly on a street corner.*)

(*A voice from offstage shouts, "Give him three!" There is a pause. "Give her four!" Another pause. "Give him a bundle!" Another pause. "Give them two!" Quan goes back and retrieves vials from a backpack hidden under a dumpster.*)

(*Stacks appears.*)

JUNKY. Say, Stacks, can I get two twenties for thirty-five?

STACKS. What that sign above me say?

JUNKY. Academy Spires.

STACKS. That's right, nigga. You want discounts, you got to get to T. J. Maxx or Marshalls. Thems the only places where slashing prices is good business.

JUNKY. Ah, come on, Stacks. I'm good for it.

STACKS. You have forty dollars or you don't.

JUNKY. That's hard, Stacks. I always come to you . . .

STACKS. Yeah, an' you always short.

(*The junky pulls two $20 bills out of his front shirt pocket and hands them to Stacks.*)

STACKS. Why you make me treat you like dat? Go
down the block and see Shorty in the hallway.

QUAN, *laughing.* Stacks, man, you crazy.

STACKS. Nah, he's the crazy nigga. Damn Uncs will walk
all over you if you let 'em. That's it Quan. We out.

QUAN. You gunna get more?

STACKS. No, that's it. (*Stacks pulls out a wad of bills.*)
Here, this is for you.

QUAN. So you bringin' me in?

STACKS. Yeah, come holla at me later.

QUAN. When you want me to come back?

STACKS. You come back tomorrow. I'll be here.

(*They peace each other out. Quan unfolds the money
and slowly counts out the $200 in small bills in excite-
ment.*)

The play was almost done. There were twenty-eight voices.
Everyone had a role, often playing a version of himself. The
students stood in the classroom as we ran through repeated
readings of the play. The prison authorities would never allow
a full production of the play—not only because they would
find some of the content offensive but also because they would
not allow me in for several weeks of daily visits to direct and
mount a production. But a staged reading was possible. I
asked Cornel West and James Cone if they would be our audience, and both agreed. I requested the forms for their security
clearances.

The promise by these two towering intellectuals to visit East
Jersey State Prison and hear the play electrified the class. That
promise, that visit, validated the work and the lives of my students. Any last vestiges of reserve were shattered. There were
no prisoners anymore in my class. There were only students,
playwrights, and actors. It did not matter how the world looked

at them. It mattered only how they looked at themselves. The walls and bars of the prison were still there, but the four hours a week in that classroom, along with the hours spent writing and practicing scenes, had given my students self-worth, dignity, and, as Boris said, "a taste of freedom."

eight

The Code

Faced with the spectral imminence of slow death, it is not unusual that for some, prison becomes a place of spiritual renewal. Often it is men who fled religion in society at large who seek its solace in the secular hell of society behind bars. Sometimes their searches for spiritual meaning are lauded as evidence of personal progress; sometimes they are discounted as nothing but jailhouse conversions. Some may be. Others are surely not. Who can peer into the well of another's spirit?[1]

—Mumia Abu Jamal, *Death Blossoms:*
Reflections from a Prisoner of Conscience

There is no single, fixed term for the inmate who endures the rigors of imprisonment with dignity, but the label of real man is applied, I think, as frequently as any other. The real man is a prisoner who "pulls his own time," in the phrasing of the inmate population, and he confronts his captors with neither subservience nor aggression. Somewhat aloof, seldom complaining, he embodies the inmates' version of decorum. And if the real man's efforts to maintain his integrity in the face of privation have an important psychological utility—for the real man regains his autonomy, in a sense, by denying the custodians' power to strip him of his ability to control himself—it is also true that his role is of vital functional significance for the social system of imprisoned criminals. In the emphasis on endurance with dignity, the inmates have robbed the rebel of their support; it is the man who can stop himself from striking back at the custodians that wins their admiration and thus their image of the hero functions wittingly or unwittingly to maintain the status quo.[2]

—Gresham M. Sykes, *The Society of Captives:*
A Study of a Maximum Security Prison

In prison, there is an unwritten code with inviolate rules. Do not be a snitch, ratting out other prisoners to prison administrators. Do not ask other prisoners personal questions, especially about why they were incarcerated. Do not touch another prisoner, and if you bump into someone by accident, apologize profusely, unless you want a fight. Stay away from brawls. Mind your own business. Do your time. Keep your promises. Do not lie. Do not steal from other prisoners. Do not sell favors. Pay your debts. Do not be weak. Do not show emotion. Do not whine or complain. Never trust or become friendly with the guards. Stand up for those in your tribe, usually defined by race, gang affiliation, or religion. When someone hurts or murders a family member or a friend, exact revenge. When insulted or attacked, fight back, even if it is certain you will lose.

If you don't defend yourself, you will often be "turned out"—slang for being turned into a "woman"—and become the "property" of a man who will protect you in exchange for service as a slave; service that includes sexual favors, cleaning his cell, and cooking meals in his cell from food bought at the commissary. While these predators, or booty bandits, are looked at with disdain, they nevertheless have an established place in prison culture, especially among men doing a lot of time.

The code, at its core, is about loyalty and solidarity. It is this loyalty and solidarity that prison administrators must crush to maintain control. This is why prison authorities tolerate booty bandits, bullies, and extortionists who dehumanize other prisoners, along with cultivating informants, or rats, to sow mistrust within the prison population. A unified prison population is, by its very nature, a threat to the power of the ruling minority. Prisons are modern-day plantations. They are not concerned, any more than plantations were, with rehabilitation and self-empowerment. They exploit cheap or unpaid prison labor to maintain the institution and toil in state-run industries or private corporations that run prison sweatshops.

The manuals written for slaveholders in the antebellum South on the management of slaves, as Kenneth Stampp details in his 1956 book on the organization of slavery, *The Peculiar Institution: Slavery in the Ante-Bellum South,* differ little from the manuals and tactics used by prison administrators. Strict discipline. The fostering of prejudices, hierarchies of social status, and biases to keep captives divided. Unconditional and humiliating submission to authority to crush pride and self-confidence. The constant implanting within the bonded population of a sense of personal inferiority and worthlessness through verbal abuse and degrading rituals—including forcing captives to be naked—keeps them broken and passive. The isolation of leaders or potential leaders from the general population. Instilling fear and helplessness into the captive population through periodic, and often capricious, demonstrations of the master's overwhelming power to remind the captives of their powerlessness. Constant indoctrination of the captives, often through religious teaching and educational programs, so that they invest themselves in their assigned work and adopt the master's code of good behavior. Destroy their capacity to form personal, independent convictions. Reward those who betray fellow captives and exemplify the abject subservience that marks the model prisoner or the model slave.

Snitches are especially despised. They are usually the first to be attacked and often killed in prison uprisings. There is a constant effort by prisoners to expose informants. Prisoners, for example, will give slightly different stories to those suspected of being snitches. They will tell one suspected snitch they are burying shanks along the wall by the weight pile, tell another they are burying shanks by the water fountain, and tell yet another that they are securing shanks under a table in the mess hall. Then they wait to see where the corrections officers search, which usually exposes the snitch.

In the Trenton prison, the highest-paid prisoner for many years was known as Ol' Mr. Charlie, who shined the guards' boots. He made $150 a month, more than five times what the average prisoner earned. The prisoners called him "the boot Black nigga." The door of his cell was often left open. He roamed the halls while the rest of the prisoners were locked in their cages. He reported any illegal activity he saw or heard about to the guards. He was the broken and abject figure every prisoner was supposed to become. While Ol' Mr. Charlie was feted by the prison administration, members of the African National Ujamaa (ANU) were being isolated in the Management Control Unit (MCU) in Trenton, where they remained for almost a decade. The ANU was a radical Black nationalist group that taught Black history and preached solidarity and resistance.

The philosopher Hannah Arendt, in *The Origins of Totalitarianism*, highlighted the importance to all tyrannies of isolating a population to ensure its "inability to act."[3]

"It has frequently been observed that terror can rule absolutely only over men who are isolated against each other and that, therefore, one of the primary concerns of all tyrannical government is to bring this isolation about," Arendt writes.

"Isolation may be the beginning of terror; it certainly is its most fertile ground; it always is its result. This isolation is, as it were, pretotalitarian; its hallmark is impotence insofar as power always comes from men acting together, 'acting in concert' (Burke); isolated men are powerless by definition."[4]

I taught a history class in the prison a few years later, in which Lawrence and some of my other students from the drama course were enrolled. Prison authorities had banned stingers, the small, homemade electric water heating coils that prisoners use to warm everything from coffee to ramen noodles, a staple commissary item. The prisoners, some from my class, organized a sit-down strike to protest. They first emptied their cells of any item that could get them in trouble, including reading material the prison authorities might find objectionable. The strikers, as they all expected, were seized and interrogated individually by the guards, who were determined to find out who organized the strike. The strikers were threatened with losing the few privileges they had, including their prison jobs and the right to take classes, if they did not disclose the names of the leaders. Their cells were searched and ripped apart. Even I, as their teacher, had my prison credentials revoked temporarily and was called in for five hours of questioning, although I knew nothing about the planning behind the strike or that it would take place.

Eventually the men who led the strike were identified, one of whom was a former corrections officer. They were sent to other prisons and put in indefinite solitary confinement. Many in the class suspected that the former corrections officer was the informant who gave the names of the strike leaders to the prison authorities, although there did not appear to be any evidence for the accusation.

Ol' Mr. Charlie makes his appearance in the play on the first night Omar is in his cell. Omar is listening nervously to the threats shouted out between prisoners. Frightened, he gets out of his bunk and scrapes his toothbrush back and forth across the cement floor to sharpen the end into a point so he can use it as a weapon to defend himself.

> **PRISONER,** *offstage.* You know what? I'm goin' to sharpen my shit tomorrow morning. When the doors bust, that's the bell. Ding! Ding!
>
> **MR. CHARLIE,** *standing outside the cell.* Young 'en, why you sleepin' on the floor?
>
> *Omar grabs his toothbrush and jumps up.*
>
> **MR. CHARLIE.** Easy young 'en. It's jus' ol' Mr. Charlie.
>
> **OMAR.** Who you? Why you out there?
>
> **MR. CHARLIE.** They don't lock my cell. I been here too long. Now, get in yer bunk and go to sleep. Hey, let me see yer face?
>
> *Mr. Charlie examines Omar's face closely.* What's yer name?
>
> **OMAR.** Omar Moore.
>
> **MR. CHARLIE.** Where you from, Omar?
>
> **OMAR.** Newark.
>
> **MR. CHARLIE.** You're not Jimmy Moore's son?
>
> **OMAR.** I didn't really know my daddy. He was a phantom, a floater.
>
> **MR. CHARLIE.** I knew him back in the day. An' I don't know if it is good or bad luck, but when he first come into Trenton, he was in this same cell.
>
> **OMAR.** That's weird shit.
>
> **MR. CHARLIE.** Go to sleep, young 'en. Yer in yer daddy's bed.

Later in the play, Omar and Ojore are in their cell. They hear prisoners making a whooping sound that rises and falls in pitch like a siren. It is the signal that something in the unit is wrong.

Suddenly the prison alarm system goes off. The sound of a siren soon resonates above the alarm. The prison is on lockdown. No one can leave his cell. Omar, confused, looks up at Ojore, who is still lying in his bunk.

OJORE. Probably a fight.

PRISONER, *shouting from offstage*. Some nigga on Four Wing hung himself! Appeal come back denied.

OJORE, *sighing*. I seen a lot of that. Ain't much to life without hope.

OMAR. Who is Mr. Charlie?

OJORE, *laughing*. He a ghost now. You seen Mr. Charlie?

OMAR. Last night. He woke me up.

OJORE. Mr. Charlie . . . Mr. Charlie . . . the prison house nigga . . . spits, polishes, an' shines the boots of the pigs in the barbershop, grinnin' and shufflin' like Stepin Fetchit for a hundred fifty dollars a month. He's what we all supposed to become. Broken. Empty. No will of his own. Ain't nothing left inside the man. He see you makin' hooch, and that afternoon your cell be raided and you be off to the hole.

OMAR. The hole?

OJORE. Jus' another lock-up unit. . . jus' another wing of the prison, but you don't get to take any possessions with you. Ol' Mr. Charlie done snitched once too often . . . was takin' a stroll two days ago on the wing and see a kid pass a bag to another for cigarettes. Two hours later, that kid's cell get raided . . . found a brick of dope . . . kid in the hole. Any day now, Mr. Charlie goin' get his. An' I think Ol' Mr. Charlie knows it. He may not even care.

The class read Tarell Alvin McCraney's play *The Brothers Size*, part of his trilogy *The Brother/Sister Plays*. The play is set in

San Pere, Louisiana. It centers around Ogun Size, his younger brother, Oshoosi Size, and Oshoosi's friend Elegba. Oshoosi has just been released after two years in jail. He is struggling to get his life back together and is staying with Ogun, who employs him at his car repair shop. Ogun never visited his brother in jail. He distrusts Elegba. Ogun is terrified his younger brother will be sent back to jail and admonishes him constantly to get his life in order.

"'Ey, man, you want to go to jail, Og?" Oshoosi asks his brother. "'Cause you mention that shit 'bout every five fucking minutes . . . I swear you ain't let me forget once that I, at one time, was not free."[5]

There is an unbridgeable divide between those who have been incarcerated and those who have not. Prison is its own culture. The stereotypes of prison life, as well as stereotypes of prisoners, are not easily dispelled.

"He ask what we do in the pen," Oshoosi tells Elegba of his brother. "I say, 'Wait, mutha. That's what we do. Man, sometimes he ask dumb-ass questions. He ask me what we do in the pen. 'Wait. Cry. Wait.'"[6]

Elegba, who, it is implied, may have had a sexual relationship with Oshoosi in jail, gets Oshoosi what he longs for most: a car. It is not clear where the car came from. The two men go on a road trip. They get pulled over by the police. The car is searched. Elegba has cocaine in his bag. Oshoosi, who is on parole and will be sent back to jail if he is arrested, flees. He returns to Ogun. It is only a matter of time before the police appear. Ogun, frantic, gives Oshoosi his truck and all his money so he can flee Louisiana. McCraney's moving celebration of love, brotherhood, and loyalty weaves in poetry, music, and Yoruban mythology. (Ogun is the Yoruba god of hard work.) He explores the innate yearning for freedom and the need to belong to something greater than ourselves to give our lives meaning.

Elegba tells Ogun that he remembers when Oshoosi broke

down and hollered from his jail cell one night for his older brother.

> ELEGBA. Yeah, didn't know that; wouldn't know that.
> He had just got in there good.
> He hadn't been in there that long 't all
> But he was strong.
> Quiet to hisself.
> To hisself always, but everyone break somewhere.
> And one night, one night, he . . . call for you . . .
> One night he just say, "I want my brother.
> Somebody call my brother . . ."
> This grown man this man,
> Crying for his brother . . .
> Sobbing into the night,
> "Og, come for Shoosi now . . ."
> At first I thought they gon' get him for that
> They gon' hurt him for being so soft
> But nah, there was a wail in that call,
> And he just singing your name. Growling it
> Like from somewhere I can't see, but I can feel it
> 'Cause it's killing me. You hear dat? Killing me.
> Calling for his brother. Crying for his brother.
> Can't do nothing but grieve for a man who miss his
> brother like that
> Sound like a bear trapped, sanging
> Can't mock no man in that much earthly pain.
> He make us all miss our brothers,
> The ones we ain't neva even have
> All the jailhouse quiet,
> The guards stop like a funeral coming down the
> halls
> In respect, respect of this man mourning the loss of
> his brother

And you just hear the clanging of that voice, like a
trumpet shot
Out o God's Heaven
Bouncing on the cement and the steel . . . chiming
like a bell
Tell he calm down . . . tell he just whispering your
name
Now
My brother . . . my brother . . . where my brother . . .
Gurgling it up from under the tears . . .
My brother . . .[7]

Grief is a solitary burden in prison. Ron Pierce, whom I would
teach in later classes, helped with rewriting *Caged* when he was
released after thirty years, eight months, and fourteen days in
prison. "You got to do your grieving alone," he reflected. "Can't
put any more grief on the brothers. This is a house of grief."
Ron, a Marine Corps veteran whom I met early in the morning
when he was released in 2016 from a halfway house in Newark,
went on to finish his bachelor of arts degree at Rutgers, graduating summa cum laude.

Caged was, at its core, about the bonds of loyalty and love.
This loyalty and love do not save the characters in the play. The
forces arrayed against them are overpowering and lethal. But
the repeated acts of self-sacrifice required by loyalty and love
keep them human.

An older prisoner in the play named Shakur appears at
Omar's cell door on Omar's first day. He is carrying a laundry
bag filled with commissary items for Omar from another "old
head" nicknamed Slash.

(*There is a sudden tap on the door.*)

SHAKUR. As Salammu Alaikim Saleem. What's happening?

OJORE. Wa Alaikum Salaam Shakur. I'll get wit' you
    in a minute. Let me finish holla'n at my man here.

SHAKUR. Yo, I come to holla at him real quick, tho.

OJORE. About what?

SHAKUR. His name Omar Moore?

OMAR. Yeah, dat's me. Who asking?

SHAKUR. Yo, my man Slash on da West compound sent
    some stuff over for you. He asked me to make sure
    you get it.

OMAR. Slash? I don't know no Slash.

SHAKUR. He said him an' ya pops was partners back in
    the day.

OJORE. I know Slash. He an old-timer. Real name is
    Daryl Moore. Ring a bell?

OMAR. No.

OJORE. Brother Shakur, what they used to call Slash
    'fore he cut dude up?

SHAKUR. Uhmmm . . . Boop or, uh, uh, Bip. That's
    right. Bip is what they used to call 'im.

OMAR. Oh shit. Uncle Bip! I ain't seen him since I was
    a kid.

OJORE. So you know him?

OMAR. Yeah, yeah, for sure. Him and my pop was in
    real heavy before Pops got pushed. He was like my
    godfather or some shit like that. Where he at?

SHAKUR. He over on da West Compound. You might
    be able to see 'im tomorrow. I'll get this cop to bust
    so you can get this stuff. Hold on.

(Shakur waves to a guard. The electric whine of the
locking system sounds as the lock is disengaged. Ojore
reaches up to his shelf and grabs a candy bar. He tosses
it to Shakur, who is holding a large laundry bag filled
with commissary items.)

OMAR. Good looking, yo!

SHAKUR. No prob, li'l bro, I'm holla at cha later. I gotta bounce. As Salaamu Alaikum, Ojore.

OJORE. Wa Alaikum As Salaam, Akhi! I'll git wit' ya later.

(*Omar dumps the bag onto his bed. Out tumbles soap, toothpaste, deodorant, shampoo, underclothes, packets of noodle soup, pouched beans, assorted packages of seafood, rice, a Walkman, earbuds, a stinger, and a handwritten note.*)

OMAR, *reading.* "I'll git with ya in the mess in the morning. Slash."

OJORE. Slash hit you off nice.

OMAR. He ain't have to do all that.

OJORE. Yeah, he did.

OMAR. Whatchu mean?

OJORE. If he was like that with ya pops, and he yer godfather or whatever, he goin' look out for ya. He got to, out of respect for yer pop. It ain't got nothin' to do with you. Slash from the old school. He live by the old code. Loyalty everything to dudes like Slash.

Quan's killer is eventually transferred to the prison. The prison code says that Omar, as Quan's brother, has to kill him—something usually done in the mess hall or the yard. Most of those in the class felt that the code demanded that Omar avenge his brother's murder. But a few others, especially those who were most respected, insisted that the code in prison was often more honored in the breach than the observance.

"This *is* the code," Boris said, "but this is not usually the *reality*. Most guys look the other way, pretend they don't know the dude is there. They don't speak about it. The two go about their business. They steer clear. This is why no one in prison uses their legal name, only their street name; you don't give up your legal name to many people. You don't want to be identified. The less dudes know about you, the better. Both dudes stay silent, avoid each other. That's what usually happens."

Revenge, Boris insisted, was the exception, in spite of the prison code.

"We're not animals, although a lot of people on the outside think we're animals," Sincere said passionately. "That's what Piñero gets in his play. Look, the guard in *Short Eyes* is begging the prisoners to kill the pedophile. They do it. But what does the murder do to the killers? Who is the real hero in the play? Juan, 'cause he keeps his humanity, 'cause he tries to stop the murder. He stops people from raping Cupcakes. He doesn't let the fear of prison steal his spirit, 'cause this ain't no pawnshop. 'Cause once you lose your spirit, you don't get it back. Ice in the Piñero play says the only free man in the prison is Juan 'cause he's the only one who stands up. Everybody else is guilty 'cause they let it happen. And we gotta remember that. We can't write for what people think we are, or even who we think we are, but about who we really are, who we try to be, who we know we should be. We can't become victims of the prison code."

It was this kind of insight that made me insist Sincere write solely about prison rather than life on the streets. He may have grown up in a rough section of Paterson, New Jersey, but he was never part of the thug life.

Most prisoners will not stop a murder, although they may assist if the person being attacked fights back. Prisoners will not fight for you, but many will fight alongside you. Not standing up for yourself is fatal in prison. Students cited the case of a prisoner who knew the identity of another prisoner who was stealing items from his cell but did not confront the thief. The thefts, open knowledge on the tier, continued until the victim asked to be moved to voluntary protective custody. Protective custody isolates prisoners from the general population and cuts them off from most programs, including jobs and education.

It is designed for those who believe their lives are in danger. Many gay or transgender prisoners request voluntary protective custody. Former police, former corrections officers, and former judges will also often request voluntary protective custody. The former officials in voluntary protective custody usually get the best equipped and most spacious cells.

The conflict between what the code demands—that Omar avenge his brother's death—and the older prisoners' determination to stop the killing became the focus of the end of the play. Omar tells Ojore that the name of his brother's killer has been posted on the prison transfer board. He will arrive soon.

OJORE. Peace, brother. You a'iight?

OMAR. It come up.

OJORE. How you know?

OMAR. The transfer log . . . name on the list . . . on his way. Push be in this prison soon . . . an' he got my brother's blood on his hands.

OJORE. Ya mind made up?

OMAR. I got my shank. An' I know who it's for . . .

(*Ojore nods gravely.*)

OJORE. Shankin' Push ain't bringin' back Quan. I wish you'd bury that shank and keep your eyes on gettin' out . . . Besides, most of that prison code a fiction. Lot of guys in here look the other way.

OMAR. I decided this a long time ago, Ojore.

OJORE. Well, son, I'll tell you what to prepare for. When they come and get you, 'cause they are gonna get you, have your hands out in front of you with your palms showing. You want them to see you have no weapons. Don't make no sudden moves. Put your hands behind your head. Drop to your knees as soon as they begin barking out commands.

OMAR. My knees?

OJORE. This ain't a debate. I'm telling you how to survive. When you get to the hole, you ain't gonna be allowed to see nobody or have nothing.

OMAR. Why?

OJORE. 'Cause they don't want you sendin' messages to nobody before dey question da brothers on the wing. Internal Affairs gonna come and see you . . . gonna want a statement. The pigs gonna let the cold in . . . gonna mess with ya food . . . gonna wake you up every hour so you can't sleep . . . gonna use the dogs . . . gonna put a spotlight in front of ya cell . . . gonna harass you wit' all kinds of threats . . . gonna send in the turtles[8] . . . give you beat downs . . . maybe a dry cell . . . no water unless they feel like turnin' it on.

OMAR. How long?

OJORE. Till they break you . . . till they don't . . . three days . . . three weeks . . . if you don't think you can take it, then don't start puttin' yerself through this hell . . . tell 'em what they wanna know from the door. You gonna be in MCU for the next two or three years. You lookin' at a life bid. They wait for you to self-destruct . . . self-mutilate . . . paranoia . . . panic attacks . . . hearing voices . . . hallucinations. I seen one man swallow a pack of AA batteries. Then you get restraint hoods, restraint belts, restraint beds, waist and leg chains. I seen a lot of men break.

(*Pause.*)

You ready? You sure this is what you want?

OMAR. I ain't livin' in this prison with Push.

OJORE. I feel you, son. I feel you. But if you think you gonna regret it, don't do it.

OMAR. I may not see you for a while, Ojore.

OJORE. Yeah, quite awhile, you do this.

OMAR. Malcolm, George Jackson, they comin' with me.

OJORE. I had long talks with Brother Jackson. Could almost see him sittin' in the cell. Stay strong, Omar.

(*They shake hands. Lights dim.*)

Ojore and Slash, however, have no intention of allowing the killing to take place. Slash confronts Omar, who has a shank hidden under his prison uniform, outside the mess hall. Boris wrote most of this scene, drawing from an experience where he stopped a prisoner from going into the mess hall to kill someone. Boris had decided that if he failed to talk his friend into turning back, he would start a fight between them so they would both be sent to lockup, and the killing would be prevented.

This was the final scene of the play:

SLASH. What's up, young 'en?

OMAR. What's up?

SLASH. Let me holla at you for a minute.

(*Omar walks over to Slash.*)

OMAR. What's happening?

SLASH, *whispering.* I know you going in there to stab that boy they say killed ya brother . . .

OMAR. Yeah.

SLASH. Yeah, the whole prison know it.

OMAR. Word?

SLASH. You don't think he know what's up?

OMAR. I don't give a fuck what he know!

SLASH. Well, I give a fuck what he know 'cause dem niggas he eating with . . . ain't sitting with him for nothin' . . . They with him 'cause they watching his

back. I watched him put his team together the moment he walked in here . . . 'cause in his mind he got
to kill you 'fore you kill him.

OMAR. He fuckin' right he gotta kill me! That nigga
killed my brother. And I don't give a fuck who wit'
him! They can get it too!

(*The two stare at each other intently.*)

SLASH. Yeah, I can dig it . . . I know you wanna kill that
nigga, and that feeling ain't promise to ever go away
. . . But I know one thing: you gonna wanna get out
of here one day . . . an' if you kill that nigga, you
ain't never leavin' this prison.

OMAR. I don't give a fuck.

SLASH. You don't give a fuck now . . .

OMAR. That's right! How you know I got a shank? Ojore?

SLASH. I'm doin' this fer yer pops, who isn't here to
do it himself. He done lost one son. That's enough.
Slip me the shank. Any shankin' to be done be done
by me. I'm gonna die in here one way or another.
But neither of us shankin' that boy. 'Nough blood
and hate as it is. I ain't sayin' you got to forgive 'im,
but ya got to let him live. He be dyin' in here wit'
me. An' it's Uncle Bip's job to see you get out. One
of us gonna have a life.

(*Pause.*)

OMAR. Quan wasn't cuttin' into his game . . . he could
barely sell anything once I got locked up. Push took
Quan out 'cause of me. Quan's death my fault. This
is the least I can do . . . I don't matter no more.

SLASH. You got yer son. You got yer sister . . .

OMAR. They don't hardly come, and when they do, my
boy sit and sulk. He tired of me preachin' to him

from behind a Plexiglas wall or on the phone. I
wasn't able to be a father to him . . . I tried . . . but he
sees I'm powerless. He do what he want. He angry
. . . an' he got every right to be angry.

SLASH. You do this, you'll never get out . . . you'll never
be a father.

OMAR. Zaire be a man when I get out.

SLASH. That don't mean he don't need you, Omar. I
know the code says you got to shank him. But that's
the public code. There's another code. It says he
stay away from you an' you stay away from him . . .
he a phantom . . . you a phantom . . . and there's
more people than you think playin' by this code.

OMAR. I can't be livin' in here with Push.

SLASH. You know how I got my life sentence?

OMAR, *coldly.* Naw.

(*Omar starts to walk away. Slash blocks him and grabs
his shoulder. It is clear Slash will, if he has to, use force
to stop Omar from going into the mess hall.*)

SLASH. You think I came to jail with a life sentence?
Fuck no! I came in here like you. Doing about a
dime, and I run into a nigga did something to my
family. Yeah, an' I thought I had to do something to
that nigga to make a statement . . . prove I wasn't a
weak motherfucker . . . huh, so I could live freely in
a *goddamn prison.*

OMAR. That ain't why I'm doing it. I don't give a fuck
what these niggas think.

SLASH. It don't matter why you doin' it. The fact is you
gonna do it . . . jus' like I did it . . . Yeah, I stabbed
a nigga in that mess hall twenty years ago, an' he
died. I remember standing there . . . watching him
bleed to death. The shit didn't even feel real . . . like

a dream. All the sound sucked out of the world . . .
silence . . . all I could do was close my eyes and
cry . . . Then I heard this voice screaming, *"What the
fuck did you do? What the fuck did you do?"*

Spent over a year in the Ad Seg 'fore I realized
that voice was mine. When I killed that nigga, it
drove me crazy! Now I'm doing life in this shit hole!
I watched a lot of dumb niggas come and go, but
I've been here ever since . . . listening to the same
sounds, wearing the same clothes, looking at these
same walls, eatin' the same shit in that same mess
hall where I lost my goddamn mind . . . I'm trapped
in time . . . For what? Killing a nigga that was already
dead . . . Push got life! I know what that's like . . .
Give me that shank, young 'en . . . Ya brother dead,
and that nigga dead! Case closed. All I can do now
is try to save yo' life. Give me the shank. Don't go in
that mess hall. I'll send some food over to ya wing,
and we'll figure this shit out tomorrow, but right
now I need you to hand me that shank.

OMAR. Slash, you know I can't walk away from this.

SLASH. Yeah you can . . . Come to Jama'ah⁹ with me
Friday . . . don't matter what you believe . . . When
you line up in a row with the other brothers, you
gonna get their strength . . . feel their spirit! An' you
gonna need it! You gonna need a lot of it, 'cause
you still got awhile 'fore you get outta here. An' I'm
gonna make sure you get outta here . . . hear me?
Give me the shank, Omar.

*(Omar stares at Slash. He slowly reaches up his sleeve
and passes the shank to Slash in what looks like a
handshake and embrace. Lights go down.)*

nine

The Play

We have been buried alive behind these walls for years, often decades. Most of the outside world has abandoned us. But a few friends and family have never forgotten that we are human beings and worthy of life. It is to them, our saints, that we dedicate this play.

—The dedication to *Caged*

The play was finished. The students arrived for the final classes with their scripts. We did repeated readings of the play. The students worked to inhabit and bring to life their characters. All twenty-eight had a part. The impending arrival of Cornel West and James Cone, whose books I had distributed to the class a few weeks earlier, electrified the men; they felt as thrilled as if they were staging a production in New York City. That these two intellectual giants would travel to the prison to hear the play validated and celebrated my students. The students counted down the days. They worked, in and out of class, on their readings. They were nervous. They wanted to be worthy of the visit.

But there was also a deep sadness. Our class was coming to an end. I had stumbled into this blind. I had not originally intended to help my students write a play. I did not know that the process would peel back layers of emotional armor and allow my students to be, many for the first time in prison, vulnerable. I did not imagine that these men, many bulked up by weight lifting and covered with crude prison tattoos, would stand in front of the class, their hands shaking slightly, as they read their scenes, tears welling up in their eyes. Perhaps it worked only because it was organic; because none of it was planned or premeditated. We dreaded the end. There was, amid the excitement, a sense of mourning.

The day for the formal reading came. I stood with Eunice, who had agreed to read the female parts, Cornel, and James in the lobby of the prison, with its plastic chairs and guard booth behind bulletproof glass. We waited to be buzzed through the door and walk the gauntlet to my classroom. I saw the administrator of the prison walking down the corridor with several corrections officers. He came into the lobby.

"We are going to do this in the chapel," he told me curtly. "We will send your class down."

This unexpected development meant that the play could not be read, at least in its entirety, for fear of angering the prison administrator and the corrections officers, who had become our uninvited audience. I gloomily followed the administrator and about a half dozen high-ranking officers—including a few captains, in their distinctive white shirts—and lieutenants down the hall, into the small room with the metal detector and X-ray machine, and out into the rotunda with the arc of iron bars. We turned right instead of going straight to the classrooms and went out a door and down some steps. We passed the yard, surrounded by cyclone fencing. The yard—paved with cracked concrete—had a small area with weights and a blacktop basketball court.

We came to the redbrick chapel. We entered a hallway, with the chaplain's office on the right and the bathroom on the left. The hallway opened into the large main chapel, with off-white walls. The chapel had rows of wooden pews and a lectern at the front, along with a small electric piano and a drum set. The windows overlooking the yard were barred. By now, there were probably a dozen corrections officers, all white, who stood at the back of the hall.

My class was brought into the hall after we arrived. Their prison IDs were collected by corrections officers at the door. They knew something was amiss the moment they were told to go to the chapel rather than the classroom. They looked at us. They looked at the administrator. They looked at the corrections officers. They walked to the front of the room, holding their scripts, along with copies of *Race Matters* by Cornel West and *The Cross and the Lynching Tree* by James Cone, and gathered in a circle. They decided hastily which parts of the play it was safe to read in front of the prison authorities and which parts should be left out. I wanted to hear their discussion, but I moved away. It was their play. They owned it. For months, editing the play had dominated my life, forcing me to set aside the book I was working on. But I let go, with loss but deep pride in my students.

You become fatalistic when you strive against a monolithic evil. You know that whatever you achieve is pyrrhic, that the system will flourish despite your efforts. And yet, what binds you, what keeps you going, are these relationships. How can you walk away? How can you do nothing? If you stand with the marginalized and the oppressed, those whom James Cone calls the "crucified of the earth," and are defeated, have you failed? Or do you succeed by being willing to make that journey; to show them they are not forgotten, not alone? And while the writing of the play was minuscule when set against the vast injustice around us, it was not minuscule to us. The play made human those who had been rendered, often for decades, inhuman. My students were no longer prison numbers.

Aleksandr Solzhenitsyn, in the last volume of *The Gulag Archipelago*, once he was released and sent into internal exile, wrote of a Serb, a teacher, also in forced exile, named Georgi

Stepanovich Mitrovich. He, too, had been recently freed from the gulag. Mitrovich would not give up his dogged battle with local authorities on behalf of his students.

"His battle was utterly hopeless, and he knew it," Solzhenitsyn writes. "No one could unravel that tangled skein. And if he had won hands down, it would have done nothing to improve the *social order*, the system. It would have been no more than a brief, vague gleam of hope in one narrow little spot, quickly swallowed by the clouds. Nothing that victory might bring could balance the risk of rearrest—which was the price he might pay. (Only the Khrushchev era saved Mitrovich.) Yes, his battle was hopeless, but it was human to be outraged by injustice, even to the point of courting destruction! His struggle could only end in defeat—but no one could possibly call it useless. If we had not all been so sensible, not all been forever whining to each other: 'It won't help! It can't do any good!' our land would have been quite different."[1]

The class, in their khaki prison uniforms, assembled in a line on the small, low stage, with Cornel, James, and I sitting in the front row. The students reading the first scene stood up and moved to the front of the platform, scripts in hand. One student, off to the side, read the stage directions. Boris read the part of Omar, and Eunice read Chimene, the mother of Omar in the play. They paused, looking out at the row of corrections officers standing, arms crossed, at the back of the chapel. Then they began.

> (*A warm September morning. The porch of a small row house in Newark, New Jersey. Peeling paint, sagging steps, littered with boxes, an old bike missing a front wheel and the seat, and a large green plastic garbage can. Chimene, wearing a baggy dress, is standing on the porch. She keeps turning to look up and down the street. Finally, she sees who she is looking for.*)

(*Omar enters. He looks exhausted.*)

OMAR. What's up Ma?

CHIMENE. Boy, where you bin?

OMAR. Me and Lucille was at Stacks's house all night.

(*Chimene looks at her son for several seconds.*)

CHIMENE. What's on your face, child? Why you got
that cut over your eye?

OMAR. I got into a scrap, Ma. The other dude looks a
lot worse.

CHIMENE. That's what comes from being out on these
streets at night. There was 'nother shooting down the
block. The way people talked, I thought he was you.

(*Omar hugs his mother.*)

OMAR. Don't worry, Ma. Nobody gonna do nothin' to
me.

CHIMENE. If you don't want me to worry, call me so I
don't be sittin' up all night wonderin' if you layin'
somewhere dead.

(*They walk into the kitchen. It is small and brightly lit
by fluorescent lights. The room is clean. There is a set
of black, cast-iron frying pans on the wall that are lined
up according to size. There is a spice rack. It takes up
nearly half the counter space next to the stove. The floor
is linoleum. There are brown and beige floor mats to
cover holes in the linoleum. There are three matching
chairs at the table. There are green plastic placemats on
the table in front of each chair. The refrigerator is covered with posted memos and bills. The stove is white but
covered with spots of old grease stains. Only the stain-
less steel sink looks to be new. The sink is small and
looks like it should be in a bathroom.*)

OMAR. You losin' weight, Ma?

CHIMENE. It's the medicine. I can't hold nothin' down.

(*She pats the empty chair. There are stacks of pictures Chimene is arranging into albums.*)

CHIMENE. I'm makin' albums for you and Quan for when I'm gone. Remember this?

(*She holds up a photo.*)

OMAR. No.

CHIMENE. That was back home. You was 'bout four. You were always so serious, Mama say you had an old soul.

OMAR. Yeah.

CHIMENE. Look here. This is you and Quan when he was jus' two. That's when we moved here.

(*She pauses, lost in thought.*)

CHIMENE. I wanted so much for you boys. I can't do much now. Worrin' is all I have left.

OMAR. Now, Ma . . . don't be worrin' 'bout us.

CHIMENE, *looking up.* Can you walk Quan to the bus stop?

OMAR. I need a shower, Ma.

CHIMENE. Take him to the bus stop first. It won't be but a minute.

OMAR, *shouting upstairs.* Quan!

(*There is a long pause.*)

OMAR. *shouting again,* Quan!

(*Quan slowly walks into the kitchen. He looks tired.*)

OMAR. You up all night on PlayStation?

QUAN. No.

OMAR, *clearly disbelieving him.* Yeah, right. Let's go.

(*Chimene holds out a bagel. Quan takes it.*)

CHIMENE, *speaking to Quan.* You got money for lunch?

QUAN. Omar give me twenty dollars for the week.

CHIMENE. Okay. Get home as soon as practice ends. We got to have dinner early. Omar's got the night shift.

(*The two brothers hug their mother and begin to walk to school.*)

QUAN. You cut up, Omar. What happened?

OMAR. Mutaqqimi started talkin' shit to Lucille last night. Nigga always lookin' for drama. I told him to chill, leave my girl alone . . . pushes me . . . I had enough . . . popped 'im. He got the bad end of that.

QUAN. Damn. You gettin' bored drivin' that forklift in da warehouse? You always talked 'bout goin' back to school.

OMAR. It's a job. It pays the food and rent. It buys Mama's medicine. We ain't in the street. Can't survive and go to school. Maybe one day . . .

(*Omar halts and then begins in a serious tone.*)

OMAR. I got to take Mama at seven in da morning again for her chemo at Beth Israel. I need you to pick up her medicine at the Rite Aid on the way home from school. Make sure you put it right in the fridge. I got a box in there got all her medicine . . .

There's nobody runnin' that plant makin' less than $50,000 a year. My boss make $125,000 a year. He's the coolest guy you'll ever meet. An' once you finish high school, I'm gonna talk to him about givin' you a job. But then, if you don't get yourself a record, you can get a job anywhere.

QUAN. Lewis's brother work at the post office.
OMAR. Now, that's a state job. That's a lot of money.

(*Omar stops and open his wallet. He hands Quan some money.*)

OMAR. This is for Ma's medicine. I got enough syringes.
I got to git home to sleep. I'm played out . . .
You still seein' that Spanish girl?
QUAN, *smiling*. Yeah.
OMAR. Don't let her daddy find out. And don't be hav-
ing no little *niños,* either. I see you tonight.

Ojore, the revolutionary, with his talk of "shooting pigs" and "expropriating" funds from "capitalist banks" had been largely left out of the reading, as were the scenes of the night raid by the police on the family home, Omar's arrest, his interrogation by police detectives, the detectives' recruiting the woman junkie to be a false witness against Omar in court, and the scene where Officer Watkins strip-searches the prisoners. I looked back at the corrections officers, watching stone-faced as my incarcerated students brought them to life on the stage, and wondered what they were thinking. Most students read what they had written and spoke of experiences they had endured. The reading had an electrifying power. It could never be replicated on a professional stage. The decades of pain and the memories of every man who spoke were palpable behind the words, however unpolished.

Timmy, when he read his monologue about calling his mother from jail, broke down. He stood alone on the stage clutching his script, shaking visibly. He wrenched each word from his gut. This was the monologue in which he took the weapons charge on himself so that his half brother, the son his mother loves the most, would not go to prison. It was the same monologue in which he revealed he was a product of rape. The writing was not always artfully crafted, and Timmy's voice was thin and untrained. His eyes clung to the page. He never looked up or engaged the audience. But, as Eunice said afterward, no professional actor could have replicated what Timmy summoned up in that chapel. His grief reverberated throughout the hall.

Guilt, shame, anger, rage, loss, betrayal, and love poured out of my students. Their voices often became hoarse as they stood on a stage, before the warden and a phalanx of corrections officers, before strangers from the outside, and spoke truths that had never before been uttered in public in the prison.

When the reading was finished, the class stood before us, subdued and stunned. There was no elation, but a palpable sadness. Bonds like these were rarely forged in prison, and almost never among a group.

After our standing ovation, I noticed Timmy had disappeared.

"Where's Timmy?" I asked, worried by his prolonged absence.

"I think he's in the bathroom," someone answered.

I walked to the entrance of the chapel and into the bathroom. Timmy sat hunched over in the corner on the tiled floor, shaking and sobbing. I knelt beside him until he regained his composure.

"Let's go back outside," I said gently, helping him up.

The students had organized a dinner after the reading. Those who worked in the kitchen, like Lawrence, had cooked it. The food was served from a table at the back. We ate off paper plates with plastic utensils. We sat in the pews, ate, and talked. The administrator seemed mollified. He left without commenting on the play. The corrections officers, some of whom I knew, did not appear offended. Cornel and James were surrounded by students, who asked them to sign their books. The prison Imam, who had heard reports of the coarse language in the play and was worried about how it would reflect on Islam, and who had stood at the back of the chapel to hear the reading, told me he was pleased.

The 140 students in the college program, who were not allowed to hear the reading of the play, were escorted into the chapel after the dinner to listen to talks from Cornel and James.

"Remember what Goethe said," Cornel told them. "He or she who has never despaired has never lived. There's nothing wrong with wrestling with despair. The question is not allowing it to have the last word. The vocation of the intellectual is to let suffering speak. Let the victim be visible. Let social misery be placed on the agenda of the powerful.

"August Wilson said that Black people authorize an alternative reality from the nightmarish present reality by performance—performance in a communal context. There is a call and a response. This creates agency. It creates self-confidence and self-respect. You saw this in churches under slavery. You saw this in communal music and art under Jim and Jane Crow. Ma Rainey. Bessie Smith. Sarah Vaughan. Mary Lou Williams. Miles Davis. Duke Ellington. Count Basie. I decided long ago to stay on the love train Curtis Mayfield talked about when he sang 'People get ready,' the love train of the Isley Brothers, the love train of the O'Jays. Those are not just songs. They are existential declarations of a certain way of being in the world. I come from a people who've been Jim and Jane Crowed, enslaved and despised and devalued, who dished out to the world the love supreme of John Coltrane, dished out to the world the love and essays of a James Baldwin. How is it that these particular people, so hated, had the courage and the imagination to dish out love—figures like Martin King and Toni Morrison, and a whole host of others?

"And this is what my dear brothers did with the play *Caged* we heard earlier today. These are the preconditions for the creations of new realities. They create spaces that are decolonized to give us a sense of who we are, that we are human rather than subhuman, that we are not a commodity, that we are not an object, that we are not an entity to be manipulated."

James followed Cornel. He looked out over his audience: prisoners in khaki uniforms packed into church pews. He lifted his eyes to the wall of white guards in the back. His face grew darker, flushed, I could tell, with anger. He knew this world. He had grown up in it. He picked cotton as a barefoot boy and stuffed it in a burlap sack for white farmers for $1 a day. As a boy in the 1940s, he stood trembling by the window of his family's shack when it grew dark, waiting for his father, a woodcutter who had only a sixth-grade education, to come home. He knew instinctively, even as a small child, that Black men in Bearden, Arkansas, found on the roads at night sometimes never made it home.

James was forced to adopt the humiliating code of deference demanded by white people, keeping his eyes lowered before them, being obsequious and excessively polite, never talking back, moving out of their way on the street. He had worn the mask my students wore, the one the poet Paul Laurence Dunbar writes in the mid-1890s, that "grins and lies."[2] He could no more contradict a white person, who always had to be addressed as Mister and Missus, than my students could contradict a corrections officer. He always went to the back door of white homes. He drank water from "colored" fountains. He lived in terror of the police, as well as any armed white man, who humiliated, beat, shot, and killed Black people with impunity; who hauled Blacks in front of white juries for crimes they did not commit and sent them away for life. He saw the chain gangs, Black men toiling in shackles in the sweltering sun on the roads, watched over by white guards cradling shotguns.

Bookish, introspective, and intellectually gifted, James lived in a white-dominated world where the less education given to a Black person, the better. He said he never met a white person who acknowledged his humanity until he got to Philander Smith

College, in Little Rock. His only two sanctuaries were his family and the Macedonia AME Church of Bearden.

"When I was a boy," he addressed the students in his high, distinctive voice, "I remember hearing the blues being played from the juke joints, especially Sam's Place, on the weekends, although my mother, Lucy, never let my brothers or me near the juke. Bo Diddley sang, 'I'm a Man,' and *man* was spelled out 'M-A-N.' He was speaking to all those white people who denied his humanity, his masculinity. Big Bill Broonzy sang, 'When Will I Get to Be Called a Man?' That's because white people treated Black men, and often still treat Black men, like children. Just to say you are a man affirms Black resistance. During Martin Luther King's last march in Memphis, right before he was assassinated, the striking garbage workers carried signs that read: 'I'm a Man.'

"Every time we cried out, through song or in church, in Bearden, Arkansas, against the terror of this world, we said that trouble and sorrow would never defeat us, never be our final meaning. We were, to white society, a scandalized people, the losers, the down-and-out. So, I know something of what you are enduring. I know something about where you come from. I know something about the injustices you have suffered. I know something of your lonesome journey. I know something about your dread and feelings of powerlessness. But I also know who you are. And you are not who they tell you *you* are. No. No.

"Remember, when Jesus was crucified, God took up the existence of a slave, a criminal, and was executed like a criminal. Jesus was victimized by the Roman Empire—the way Blacks and other people of color are victimized by the American Empire. Many white Americans were surprised and shocked at the images from the Abu Ghraib prison in Iraq. But most Blacks were not shocked or surprised. We have been tortured by white Americans for four hundred years. Lynching has not ended. People can be lynched without a rope or a tree. Lynching takes place every day on our streets, in our courts, in our prisons. And every time a Black person is lynched, Jesus is lynched. The lynching tree is the real cross in America. We can only find Jesus among the crucified bodies in our midst."

I watched the students as James spoke, possessed by a prophetic fury. Many were in tears. When he finished speaking, he turned to me and said, slightly shaken, "I saw myself in them. I could have easily ended up where they are. It would not have taken much."

The next night was my final class. The students had somehow located a picture of James and a picture of Cornel and put them up in the hall outside the classrooms. These two intellectuals were who they were studying to become. When I entered the classroom, one of my students immediately stood up.

"You may have seen me crying last night," he said to the class. "I have been on the inside since 1987. I was eleven years on death row. The night Dr. West and Dr. Cone came to speak to us was the only happy night I have ever spent in prison."

We spent the last class remembering the long process, joking about some of the blind alleys we started down in writing the play, celebrating the dramatic readings by individual students, and dreading the final bell.

"This is your song," I said, holding up the script, in the final minutes. "I will do everything in my power to make your song heard. I will take it to every theater director willing to read it. I don't know anything about what it takes to mount a play, but I will learn.

"I admire you so much," I said, my voice beginning to falter with emotion. "I don't know who you were, but I know who you are now, who you have become: students endowed with brilliance, passion, and integrity. It has been the honor of my life to be your teacher. I will never forget you."

The bell would ring momentarily. None of us could speak. The class stood. They walked forward, one by one, and signed the front page of my script. We hugged good-bye. The bell rang. They lined up in the hall. I made my way past them for the last time. I clutched their song in my hands. I carried their song past the lines of corrections officers, through the iron-barred gate in the rotunda, through the twin metal doors in the small room with the metal detector and X-ray machine, down the long corridor, through the last metal door that was buzzed open, through the lobby, and into the darkened parking lot.

———

Boris was the first student from the class to be released, in April 2015. I waited with his mother and sister to meet him as he walked out of prison. His mother, on the car ride there, read Bible verses out loud to her daughter. Boris had spent eleven years incarcerated. We watched him walk down the road from the prison toward the gate where we waited. He was wearing the baggy gray sweatpants, oversized white T-shirt, and white Reebok sneakers that prisoners are required to purchase before their release. Boris had been charged $50 for his new, ill-fitting clothes. A prisoner in New Jersey earns, on average, $28 a month working[3] a forty-hour week in prison.

He clutched a manila envelope containing his medical records, instructions for parole, his birth certificate, his Social Security card, and an ID issued by the Department of Motor Vehicles—his official form of identification. All his prison possessions, including his collection of roughly a hundred books, had to be left behind.

The first words he spoke to me after more than a decade in prison were: "I have to rebuild my library."

Boris and I spent three years revising the script. We merged and cut the twenty-eight roles into a smaller, more manageable cast. We worked with Eunice and the theater director Jeff Wise, who funded and oversaw three workshops of the play in New York City over several weeks, to give the characters depth and complexity. It was excruciating to make cuts. Boris and I could hear the voices of the students in every line. Sometimes we would sit silently in front of my computer for several moments before removing a sentence or a scene, as if it were an execution. That Boris, one of the best writers in the class, was released first was fortuitous. He was able to fill in the holes the script needed, especially the family dynamics, drawn from his own family. James Cone, the film director Marty Brest, Ojore Lutalo, and other formerly incarcerated men and women, including Ron Pierce, the Marine Corps veteran, sat through readings of the revised scripts and offered critiques and suggestions. Then we would take our notes and go back and work on the script again.

By the spring of 2018, the play was ready for the stage. The Passage Theatre in Trenton mounted the production. The script would later be published by Haymarket Books. Jerrell L. Henderson, based in Chicago, directed the play with professional actors, most from New York. Boris played the roles of a social worker, Officer Watkins, and Slash, who was doing two life sentences.

"When I read the script," said Henderson, "it never read to me in any way like a plea or a demand for social change. This is a play about people, about human beings. People make mistakes, and this play does not try to excuse or gloss over those mistakes. If you see this merely as a show about prisoners, then, like much of society, you will have forgotten about them as people. Omar is a man. A person. Once a man has been inside, that man may face obstacles he didn't even dream existed. He may feel stripped of his own humanity.

"I worked on another play in Chicago," said Henderson, "that had as a character a woman who had just been released from prison and who was having a conversation with her son, who remembered her as she had been. She said, 'I am not those mistakes, and I am trying to be with you here and now,' and I thought those were great lines."[4]

We organized one performance exclusively for the families of the students. The theater was filled with the mothers, fathers, grandparents, sisters, brothers, and children of my students. A few minutes into the play, I heard members of the audience begin to weep softly; weeping that grew into moans and sobbing that was sustained for the ninety-minute production. When Omar was strip-searched on stage, the audience gasped. Once the play ended, there was a silence and then thunderous applause.

Ron and I spoke to Ta'nazia, the daughter of my student Marvin Spears, the army veteran who wrote the part of Officer Watkins, and her mother, Cheyonne. "That scene where they only allowed him fifteen minutes in the funeral home to see his brother, that hit me," Ta'nazia, who was in her twenties, said after the play. "They were going to do that to my dad. My cousin was gonna pay for him, but when they figured out it was fifteen minutes and they was gonna charge, like, twenty-five-hundred dollars, my dad was like, 'Don't even worry about it.'"

Cheyonne added, "They said nobody else could be there, and his mom was saying, 'Can't I be there to console him?' They said no. So, when they told him, he said, 'Don't do it.'"

"I went to see my father when he passed," said Ron. "The amount of money we spent wasn't worth it. You gotta have at least two officers. I had to get three. You have to give the officers at least four hours of overtime. You have to pay for the mileage for the car. Everything is charged to you, for them to bring you there. And then, you go through a whole process of getting in and getting out, then getting back in. When they pulled into the funeral parlor, they kept me locked in the car while they looked in cars and bushes. They said, 'If a motorcycle passes by while you're in there, we're pulling you out.'" Ron had been part of a motorcycle gang. "Like, how will I have any control if somebody's driving by the funeral parlor? But they also told my family, if we see anybody come in, we're hauling him out.

I got to spend some time with my father, but a wake is more about sharing with each other than just sitting in a room by yourself, looking at the person that passed. So, it wasn't worth it. It wasn't always like that. When my brother died back in '93, I went to see my brother's viewing. And my immediate family, his daughters, his wife, my mother, my father, my brothers, my sister, were all allowed to be there. The officers stayed in the back. My feet were still shackled, but they let my hands free. I was still allowed to be with my family. That would be worth paying for. But we didn't pay anything for it because, back then, there was the inmate welfare fund. Then they got the 'tough on crime' policy. Everybody wanted to be tough on crime, and, after awhile, you have such an oppressive system that it's not even worth doing it."

"When he comes home, I hope that his mom is still here," Cheyonne said of Marvin. "His mom is eighty. His father died right before the play."

Ron turned to Marvin's daughter.

"Marvin carries himself in a way that commands respect," he told her gently. "He's small in stature, but he is large in the community. It's just that—I can't put my finger on it exactly—but you get the respect that you command yourself to get. And it's not that he's gonna jump anybody or beat anybody up, but if you have an issue, you'll want to talk to Marvin. He's the type of person who can help you through it. There's a lot of people and a lot of different personalities, but when you're speaking about Marvin, he had a presence about himself. And that's just the way you're sizing everybody up. And you're not sizing everybody up by their muscles. Look, I could show you pictures of me, my arms out to here, my chest out to here. People used to laugh, like, 'Oh, you can put a beer bottle on that chest!' That was back in my younger days—much, much younger—but there are people like that nobody respects. But people show him respect.

"When I first got locked up, I didn't know the difference between respect and fear. I operated thinking respect was fear. I tried to make people fear me. I got very few people to respect me. I had a transformation after awhile. I started seeing people getting real respect. I started seeing the difference. Your father, to his credit, knows how to be respectful and how to gain respect."

"You should be very proud of your dad," I told Ta'nazia. "He's a very good man."

"There's nothing easy about the whole situation, but it makes it easier to know that he's good," Cheyonne said.

On the morning of May 10, 2019, I took my black suit and clerical collar out of the closet. I put on my clerical collar because what took place in the prison classrooms was sacred. I had worn the collar only a handful of times after I was ordained: once to attend the funeral of Father Daniel Berrigan; once to attend the funeral of my mentor and professor at Colgate University, the Reverend Coleman Brown, a descendant of the nineteenth-century abolitionist John Brown; once to officiate at the wedding of Ron Pierce and his wife, Karen; and in 2016, when Cornel West and I joined hundreds of unhoused people in a protest march to the Wells Fargo Center in Philadelphia, where the Democratic National Convention was being held.

I reached into the top drawer of the dresser and took out two oval gold cuff links with the initials *THH* engraved upon them. My father's. I slipped them into the cuff link slits on my white shirt.

I drove to the Sonny Werblin Recreation Center at Rutgers University in New Brunswick for the graduation ceremony to honor the twenty-seven formerly incarcerated men and women in the New Jersey Scholarship and Transformative Education in Prisons (NJ-STEP) program. They had started work on their degrees in prison through NJ-STEP and completed them upon release at Rutgers. I had taught many of them, including Boris and Steph, the latter of whom had greeted me the first day with deep suspicion but became, like Kabir, so protective. They had matriculated to Rutgers from prison. They sat with their families at large, round tables. The ceremony, like the play, was emotionally charged. Each of the students spoke, reflecting on how he or she never thought they would be a college graduate and what it meant to their self-esteem to be enrolled in college, even in the prison.

I walked up a few steps onto the stage. I laid my text before me. I looked out at the 250 people who had gathered to celebrate what can only be called a miracle. I began, for my students and the other graduates in the room, what would be my final sermon to them:

"My fellow college graduates: integrity is not an inherited trait. It is not conferred by privilege or status or wealth. It cannot be bequeathed by elite schools or institutions. It is not a product of birth or race or gender. Integrity is not a pedigree or a brand. Integrity is earned. Integrity is determined not by what we do in life, but what we do with what life gives us. It is what we overcome. Integrity is the ability to affirm our dignity even when the world tells us we are worthless. Integrity is forged in pain and suffering, loss and tragedy. It is forged in the courtrooms where you were sentenced. It is forged in the shackles you were forced to wear. It is forged in the cages where you lived, sometimes for decades. It is forged in the cries of your children, those who lost their mothers or their fathers to the monstrosity of mass incarceration. It is forged in the heartache of your parents, your brothers, your sisters, your spouses, and your partners. Integrity is forged by surmounting the hell around you to study in a cramped and claustrophobic cell for the college degree no one, perhaps not even you, thought you would ever earn. Integrity is to refuse to become a statistic. Integrity is to rise up and shout out to an indifferent universe: 'I am somebody!' And today no one can deny who you are, what you have achieved and what you have become: college graduates; men and women of integrity who held on fiercely to your dignity and your capacity to exert your will, and triumphed.

"Several of you are my former students: Boris, Steph, Tone, Hanif, and Ron—although, to be honest, it is hard for me to use the word *former*. To me, you always will be my students. I have spent many hours with you in prison classrooms. I know the scars you bear. You will bear these scars, this trauma, for life. Own your suffering. Do not deny it. And know that healing comes only by reaching out to others who suffer. It is to say to those thrown aside by society: 'I too was despised. I too was where you are. I too felt alone and abandoned. But like me, you can and will endure.' I am not romantic about suffering. I saw a lot of it as a war correspondent.

"Suffering can make some people better. Others, it degrades and destroys. But those who surmount suffering, who hold fast to compassion and empathy, can become what Carl Jung called 'wounded healers.' Thornton Wilder, in his play *The Angel That Troubled the Waters*, writes, 'Without your wounds, where would your power be? . . . The very angels themselves cannot persuade the wretched and blundering children on earth as can one human being broken on the wheels of living. In love's service, only wounded soldiers can serve.'[5] And there was something else I learned as a war correspondent: education is morally neutral. The highly educated can be as cruel and sadistic as the illiterate. This is why so many human predators who profit from the misery of the poor in corporations such as Goldman Sachs have been groomed in Ivy League universities. This is why James Baldwin writes that 'brilliance without passion'—and by this he means moral passion—'is nothing more than sterility.'

"In Tony Kushner's play *Angels in America*, he writes of the suffering and demonization of gay men with AIDS, not unlike the suffering and demonization many of you have felt as members of the criminal caste.

"'In your experience of the world. How do people change?' the character Harper asks.

"'Well, it has something to do with God, so it's not very nice,' the Mormon mother answers. 'God splits the skin with a jagged thumbnail from throat to belly and then plunges a huge filthy hand in, he grabs hold of your bloody tubes and they slip to evade his grasp, but he squeezes hard, he insists, he pulls and pulls till all your innards are yanked out and the pain! We can't even talk about that. And then he stuffs them back, dirty, tangled, and torn. It's up to you to do the stitching.'

"'And then get up,' Harper says. 'And walk around.'

"'Just mangled guts pretending,' the Mormon mother affirms.

"'That's how people change,' says Harper.[6]

"Trauma is not static. It is dynamic. It is written on your flesh. These scars will keep you honest if you use them to see your own face in those who are demonized: women, immigrants, the LGBTQ community, Muslims, poor people of color. If truth is to be heard, as Theodor Adorno writes, suffering must be allowed to speak.

"Flannery O'Connor recognized that the moral life always entails confrontation with the world:

"'St. Cyril of Jerusalem, in instructing catechumens, wrote: "The dragon sits by the side of the road, watching those who pass. Beware lest he devour you. We go to the Father of Souls, but it is necessary to pass by the dragon." No matter what form the dragon may take, it is of this mysterious passage past him, or into his jaws, that stories of any depth will always be concerned to tell, and this being the case, it requires considerable courage at any time, in any country, not to turn away from the storyteller.'[7]

"There are people in this room who committed crimes, but

there are no criminals here today. Not that criminals do not exist. Is it not criminal to allow more than twelve million[8] in the United States to go to bed hungry every night while Amazon, which earned $11 billion in profits last year, paid no federal taxes? In fact, in our system of corporate welfare, Amazon received a $129 million tax rebate from the federal government.[9] Is it not criminal that half of all Americans live in poverty, or near poverty, while the three richest men in America, including the founder of Amazon, Jeff Bezos, have combined fortunes worth more than the total wealth of the poorest half of Americans?[10] Is it not criminal that millions of factory jobs, which once allowed families to earn a living wage with health and retirement benefits, have been shipped to places like Monterrey, Mexico, where Mexican workers in GM plants earn three dollars an hour without benefits?[11] Is it not criminal that our families have been sacrificed to feed the mania for corporate profit, left to rot in violent and postindustrial wastelands such as Newark or Camden? Is it not criminal to harass and terrorize the poor on the streets of our cities for petty activities such as selling loose cigarettes or 'obstructing pedestrian traffic,' which means standing too long on a sidewalk, while Bank of America, Citibank, and Goldman Sachs have never been held accountable for trashing the global economy, wiping out forty percent of US wealth through fraud?[12] Is it not criminal that, as poverty has gone up and crime has actually gone down, our prison population has more than doubled?[13]

"George Bernard Shaw got it right.

"'Poverty,' he writes, 'is the worst of crimes. All the other crimes are virtues beside it; all the other dishonors are chivalry itself by comparison. Poverty blights whole cities, spreads horrible pestilences, strikes dead the very souls of all who come within sight, sound, or smell of it. What you call crime is nothing: a murder here and a theft there, a blow now, and a curse then. What do they matter? They are only the accidents and illnesses of life; there are not fifty genuine professional criminals in London. But there are millions of poor people, abject people, dirty people, ill-fed, ill-clothed people. They poison us morally and physically; they kill the happiness of society; they force us to do away with our own liberties and to organize unnatural cruelties for fear they should rise against us and drag us down into their abyss. Only fools fear crime; we all fear poverty.'[14]

"Rabbi Abraham Joshua Heschel said of society that 'few are guilty, but all are responsible.'[15] The crime of poverty is a communal crime. Our failure, as the richest nation on earth, to provide safe and healthy communities, ones where all children have enough to eat and a future, is a communal crime. Our failure to provide everyone, and especially the poor, with a good education is a communal crime. Our failure to make health care a human right and our forcing parents, burdened with astronomical medical bills, to bankrupt themselves to save their sick sons or daughters are communal crimes. Our failure to provide meaningful work—in short, the possibility of hope—is a communal crime. Our decision to militarize police forces and build prisons, rather than invest in people, is a communal crime. Our misguided belief in charity and philanthropy rather than justice is a communal crime. 'You Christians have a vested interest in unjust structures which produce victims to whom you then can pour out your hearts in charity,' Karl Marx said, chastising a group of church leaders.[16]

"If we do not work to eliminate the causes of poverty, the greatest of all crimes, the institutional structures that keep the poor *poor*, then we are responsible. There are issues of personal morality, and they are important, but they mean nothing without a commitment to social morality. Only those who have been there truly understand. Only those with integrity speak the truth. And this is why I place my faith in you.

"My first student to get out of prison, nearly four years ago, Boris Franklin, is graduating today. I met him with his mother at the gate. He had spent eleven years inside. His first words to me were 'I have to rebuild my library.'

"Boris was part of the class in East Jersey State Prison that wrote the play *Caged*. He and I devoted hundreds of hours over the last four years editing and rewriting it for the stage. It was performed a year ago at the Passage Theatre in Trenton, with Boris taking one of the pivotal roles. It was sold out nearly every night, attended by families who knew too intimately the pain of mass incarceration.

"Boris was as determined as I to make that song, your song, heard outside the prison walls, to lift up that truth, to affirm the integrity of those the world has forgotten and demonized. Your song is vital. It must be heard. I do not know if I could have endured what you have endured and become who you have become. Boris once told our friend the filmmaker Michael Nigro that he did not understand why people like me went into the prison—that in the hood, when somebody did something for you, he or she usually wanted something. But you should know, my students, what you have given me. It cannot be quantified monetarily. It is one of the most precious things I possess. It is your friendship. And that is why today I am the *most* blessed among you."

Acknowledgments

For nearly fifteen years, Eunice has been my most important editor. She dedicated many hours to editing, revising, and critiquing this manuscript. This book, as with previous books, was heavily shaped and formed by her wisdom and insight, as well as her considerable skills as a writer. Every page bears her imprint. I could not have written the book without her.

I am also deeply indebted to several people who worked with me throughout the reporting and writing. I am forbidden from contacting, even by mail, anyone in the prison system because I teach in the prison. I relied heavily on Ron Pierce, who was one of my students and graduated summa cum laude from Rutgers University, Christopher Renshaw, who is a seminarian at Princeton Theological Seminary, and Sylas Pelikan, a student at Middlebury College, to handle all communications with students who remain incarcerated. They collected additional biographical information, checked facts, typed up transcripts, carried out interviews, and double-checked quotes. Christopher and Sylas made numerous trips to East Jersey State Prison and Northern State Prison to speak with students who were in the class.

As usual, I leaned heavily for advice on my former student and good friend Boris Franklin, who devoted hundreds of hours to rewriting the play with me after he was released and took one of the leading roles in the production of the play in Trenton.

Julianna Cook, a kind, gentle and intelligent woman who

we lost as I began the book to the scourge of the opioid crisis, also worked doing research, communicating with students in the prisons and typing transcripts.

I received a generous grant from the Wallace Change Makers Fund to hire Ron to work with me on the book. In addition to communicating with my students in prison by phone and email, Ron accompanied me to interviews I did with family members of my students. Because he spent thirty-one years in prison, and because he is thoughtful and reflective, Ron provided tremendous insights into prison culture. I constantly learn from him. He pushed the interviews we did to depths that would have been impossible without him. He also edited the manuscript and consistently provided invaluable advice.

I was, in addition, very fortunate to rely on the superb editing skills of Naila Kauser, who meticulously proofread the book, correcting and improving it, along with Beth Gianfagna and Philip Bashe, two of the most skilled copy editors in the business. I also relied on the editing prowess of the poet and writer Meghan Marohn.

I am indebted to the great prison rights activists Bonnie Kerness and Ojore Lutalo, who dedicated many hours to this project and are on the front lines of prison reform.

There was some material in the book taken from columns I wrote for the online magazine *Truthdig* before the staff and I were fired in March 2020 for going on strike to protest the publisher's attempt to fire the editor in chief, Robert Scheer, as well as demand the right to form a union and end unfair labor practices. These sections were edited by the gifted Thomas Caswell, who worked for many years as a senior editor at the *Los Angeles Times*. I also drew from two columns published on Scheerpost, which Bob started when we were fired from *Truthdig*. My Scheerpost columns were edited by Bob Scheer, one of the finest journalists and editors in the country, as well as the highly talented editors Chris Scheer and Narda Zacchino.

Bob Bender at Simon & Schuster edited each chapter as it was completed, offering crucial ideas and suggestions not only on the writing but also on the structure and themes in the book. He was vital to the formation of the book. His insight and skill are unrivaled. I am fortunate to have him as an editor. I would also like to thank Philip R. Metcalf and Johanna Li at Simon & Schuster, who carried out the careful fact checking and copyediting.

The Rutgers college program in the New Jersey prison system, known as the New Jersey Scholarship and Transformative Education in Prisons (NJ-STEP) inside the prison, is administered by an amazing group of dedicated people, including Chris Agans, Margaret Atkins, Toby Sanders, Gerardine Phillipe, Emily Allen-Hornblower, Haja Kamara, and Don Roden, who founded the prison college program and is beloved by all the students whose lives he has transformed. It is an honor to be part of their degree program. Celia Chazelle, who recruited me to teach in prisons a decade ago, is a cherished colleague and friend.

All of us who teach in the prisons are in debt to several Department of Corrections officials who make the college degree program possible, including Marcus Hicks, Patrick Nogan, William Anderson, Jecrois Jean-Baptiste, Al Kandell, James Jones, Diane Patrick, Christian Porrovecchio, Gary Lanigan, Darcella Sessomes, and Jesus S. Reyes, who is assigned to the classrooms at East Jersey State Prison and is unfailingly respectful and considerate to professors and students. The college degree program has enriched and changed many lives. The facilitating of the classes by these DOC officials, which is logistically difficult and time consuming, makes this possible.

The Passage Theatre in Trenton mounted the play *Caged* on May 3, 2018, where it ran for a month. It was sold out nearly every night. This was the culmination of my students' work. The production of the play was made possible by June

Ballinger, C. Ryanne Domingues, and Damion A. Parran. It
was directed by Jerrell L. Henderson. The set was designed by
Germán Cárdenas-Alaminos. The lighting design was by Daniel
Schreckengost. The sound design was by Beth Lake. The cos-
tume design was by An-lin Dauber. The production design was
by Miranda Kelley. The stage manager was Laura Marsh. The
production coordinator was Dan Viola. The actors in the cast,
who brought our play to life on the stage, were Will Badgett,
Andrew Binger, Boris Franklin, Ural Grant, Nicolette Lynch,
Brandon Rubin, and Monah Yancy. The director Jeff Wise gen-
erously workshopped the play over several weeks in New York,
crafting and revising it for the stage. The production would not
have been possible without Jeff's commitment, keen insight, financial support, and dedication. Jeff also organized the special
performance for the families of my students.

I would like to thank the film director Marty Brest for sitting in on workshops of *Caged* and offering his critiques. Naomi
Murakawa, Anthony Arnove, at Haymarket Books and who
published *Caged*, Omar McNeil, who was in the class that wrote
Caged and was released in 2016, Nafeesah Goldsmith, and
James Cone also attended dramatic readings of the play and
offered important advice and feedback. Dwayne Booth, aka
Mr. Fish, the finest political cartoonist in the country, who il-
lustrates my columns, drew a powerful illustration for the cover
of the published version of the play. Cornel West, and my close
friend James Cone, whom we lost in 2018 and who was the most
important American theologian since Reinhold Niebuhr, have
long been the torchbearers for the Black Prophetic tradition,
our most important intellectual tradition. They are moral and
intellectual inspirations to my students and to myself. Their visit
to the prison was a momentous day for my students. They also
officiated at my ordination. Cornel, despite commitments that
would slay lesser mortals, returned to East Jersey State Prison
after his visit to teach an introduction to philosophy course to

the 140 students in the college degree program, a course the students still speak about with awe and reverence. I sat in on his class, learning, as I always do, from Cornel's erudition and brilliance.

I would like to thank my close friend the cartoonist Joe Sacco, who provided invaluable advice as we revised the play, along with Sharonda Weatherspoon, whose critiques and suggestions proved vital to the final formation of the play.

Others to whom I owe debts of friendship and assistance are Mumia Abu Jamal, Ralph Nader, Kevin Zeese (who, sadly, we lost as the book was being completed), Dr. Margaret Flowers, Alice and Staughton Lynd (who have worked for many years defending the rights of prisoners in Ohio), Jennifer Sellitti, the Director of Training and Communications at New Jersey Office of the Public Defender, who devoted over two years to getting Lawrence Bell a resentencing hearing and released from prison, Joe Mazraani, Steve Kinzer, Kasia Anderson, Ann and Walter Pincus, Jennifer and Peter Buffett, Randall Wallace, and Matt Taibbi. Matt taught a course with me in East Jersey State Prison in the spring of 2020 where the Department of Corrections prohibited us from teaching two books on our reading list, Matt's very fine book *I Can't Breathe: A Killing on Bay Street*, which uses the police killing of Eric Garner to examine systemic racism and police violence, and the book I did with the cartoonist Joe Sacco, *Days of Destruction, Days of Revolt*. I would also like to thank Richard Wolff, Michael Goldstein, Tom Artin, the Reverend Michael Granzen, the Reverend Karen Hernandez, the Reverend Mel White, Joe and Heidi Hough, Lee Lakeman, Alice Lee, Sheik Hamza Yusuf, one of the country's most important religious scholars, my former Shakespeare professor, Margaret Maurer, the attorneys Bruce Afran and Carl Mayer, Ajamu Baraka, Kshama Sawant, Rebecca Myles, the producer of my show *On Contact*, Misha Solodovnikov, who runs RT America and hired me to do my weekly show, John Richard,

Irene Brown, Russell Banks, Walter Fortson, Serena Green, Larry Hamm, Derrick Jensen, Lola Mozes, Abby Martin, Gary Francione, and John Ralston Saul. Dorothea von Molke and Cliff Simms, who donated more than seven hundred books to the prison library at East Jersey State Prison, run Labyrinth in Princeton, one of the finest bookstores in the country, where I spend many hours and buy many books.

I would also like to thank my agent Kristine Dahl at ICM Partners for her help and advice in preparing the manuscript and promoting this book as well as my previous book.

Eunice, my four children Thomas, Noëlle, Konrad, and Marina, along with our rescued greyhounds Marlow and Olive, are the fulcrum of my life. The healing power of family, after years of living amid war and conflict, are what keep the demons at bay.

Bibliography

Alexander, Michelle. *The New Jim Crow: Mass Incarceration in the Age of Colorblindness*. New York: New Press, 2010.

Arendt, Hannah. *The Origin of Totalitarianism*. New York: Harcourt, 1976.

Baldwin, James. *The Fire Next Time*. In *Collected Essays*. Edited by Toni Morrison. New York: Library of America, 1998.

_____. *I Am Not Your Negro*. New York: Vintage International, 2017.

_____. *No Name in the Street*. In *Collected Essays*. Edited by Toni Morrison. New York: Library of America, 1998.

Bauer, Shane. *American Prison: A Reporter's Undercover Journey into the Business of Punishment*. New York: Penguin Press, 2018.

Bettelheim, Bruno. *Surviving and Other Essays*. New York: Alfred A. Knopf, 1979.

Blackman, Douglas A. *Slavery by Another Name: The Re-Enslavement of Black Americans from the Civil War to World War II*. New York: Anchor Books, 2009.

Bruno, Anthony. *The Iceman: The True Story of a Cold-Blooded Killer*. New York: Bantam Books Trade Paperbacks, 2013.

Burrough, Brian. *Days of Rage: America's Radical Underground, the FBI, and the Forgotten Age of Revolutionary Violence*. New York: Penguin Books, 2015.

Camisa, Harry. *Inside Out: Fifty Years Behind the Walls of New Jersey's Trenton State Prison*. Windsor, NJ: Windsor Press, 2003.

Carlo, Philip. *The Butcher: Anatomy of a Mafia Psychopath*. New York: HarperCollins, 2009.

Carter, Rubin "Hurricane." *The Sixteenth Round: From Number 1 Contender to Number 45472.* New York: Penguin, 1974.

Coffin, William Sloan. *The Heart Is a Little to the Left: Essays on Public Morality.* Hanover, NH: Dartmouth College Press, 1999.

Cone, James. *The Cross and the Lynching Tree.* Maryknoll, NY: Orbis Books, 2011.

———. *Martin & Malcolm & America: A Dream or a Nightmare.* Maryknoll, NY: Orbis Books, 2006.

———. *Said I Wasn't Gonna Tell Nobody.* Maryknoll, NY: Orbis Books, 2018.

Davis, Angela. *Are Prisons Obsolete?* New York: Seven Stories Press, 2003.

Desmond, Matthew. *Evicted: Poverty and Profit in the American City.* New York: Crown, 2016.

Dostoyevsky, Fyodor. *The House of the Dead.* Digireads.com, 2020.

Forman, James. *Locking Up Our Own: Crime and Punishment in Black America.* New York: Farrar, Straus and Giroux, 2017.

Foucault, Michel. *Discipline & Punish.* New York: Vintage Books, 1995.

Genovese, Eugene D. *Roll Jordan Roll: The World the Slaves Made.* New York: Vintage Books, 1976.

Gottschalk, Marie. *Caught: The Prison State and the Lockdown of American Politics.* Princeton, NJ: Princeton University Press, 2015.

Hall, Stuart, Charles Critcher, and Tony Jefferson. *Policing the Crisis: Mugging the State and Law and Order.* New York: Palgrave Macmillan, 2013.

Herbert, John. *Fortune and Men's Eyes.* New York: Grove Press, 1967.

Heschel, Abraham. *The Prophets.* New York: Harper Perennial, 2001.

Jamal, Mumia Abu. *Death Blossoms: Reflections from a Prisoner of Conscience.* New York: Litmus Press, 1996.

Jackson, George. *Soledad Brother: The Prison Letters of George Jackson.* Brooklyn, NY: Lawrence Hill Books, 1970.

Jones, Le Roi. *Dutchman.* New York: Harper Perennial, 1964.

Kurashige, Scott. *The Fifty-Year Rebellion: How the U.S. Political Crisis Began in Detroit.* Oakland: University of California Press, 2017.

Kushner, Tony. *Angels in America.* New York: Theatre Communications Group, 1995.

Lester, Julius. *Revolutionary Notes*. New York: Grove Press, 1970.

Litwack, Leon F. *Trouble in Mind: Black Southerners in the Age of Jim Crow*. New York: Vintage Books, 1999.

Lynd, Staughton. *Lucasville: The Untold Story of a Prison Uprising*. Oakland: PM Press, 2011.

McCraney, Tarell Alvin. *The Brother/Sister Plays*. New York: Theatre Communications Group, 2010.

Murakawa, Naomi. *The First Civil Right*. New York: Oxford University Press, 2014.

New Jersey Prison Theater Cooperative, Chris Hedges, and Boris Franklin. *Caged*. Chicago: Haymarket Books, 2020.

O'Connor, Flannery. *Mystery and Manners*. Edited by Sally Fitzgerald and Robert Fitzgerald. New York: Farrar, Straus & Giroux, 1969.

Orwell, George. *An Age Like This, 1920–1940: Collected Essays*. Edited by Sonia Orwell and Ian Angus. New York: Harcourt, Brace, & World, 1968.

_____. *Animal Farm*. Harmondsworth, UK: Penguin Books, 1981.

_____. *The Complete Works of George Orwell: I Belong to the Left: 1945*. Edited by Peter Davison. London: Secker & Warburg, 1998.

_____. *The Complete Works of George Orwell: Smothered Under Journalism, 1946*. London: Secker & Warburg, 1998.

Oshinsky, David M. *Worse Than Slavery: Parchman Farm and the Ordeal of Jim Crow Justice*. New York: Free Press, 1997.

Parenti. Christian. *Lockdown America: Police and the Prisons in the Age of Crisis*. Brooklyn, NY: Verso, 2008.

Piñero, Miguel. *Short Eyes*. New York: Hill and Wang, 1993.

Rhodes, Richard. *Why They Kill: The Discoveries of a Maverick Criminologist*. New York: Vintage Books, 1999.

Richie, Beth E. *Arrested Justice: Black Women, Violence, and America's Prison Nation*. New York: NYU Press, 2012.

Shakespeare, William. *The Merchant of Venice*. In *The Riverside Shakespeare*. Textually edited by G. Blakemore Evans. Boston: Houghton Mifflin, 1974.

_____. "Sonnet 29." In *The Riverside Shakespeare*. Textually edited by G. Blakemore Evans. Boston: Houghton Mifflin, 1974.

Shaw, Bernard. *Major Barbara*. New York: Penguin Classics, 2000.

Simon, Jonathan. *Governing Through Crime: How the War on Crime Transformed American Democracy and Created a Culture of Fear.* Oxford: Oxford University Press, 2009.

Solzhenitsyn, Aleksandr. *The Gulag Archipelago.* Vols. 1 and 3. New York: Harper Perennial, 2007.

Stamp, Kenneth M. *The Peculiar Institution: Slavery in the Ante-Bellum South.* New York: Vintage Books, 1989.

Stevenson, Bryan. *Just Mercy: A Story of Justice and Redemption.* New York: Spiegel & Grau, 2015.

Sykes, Gresham M. *The Society of Captives: A Study of a Maximum Security Prison.* Princeton, NJ: Princeton University Press, 2007.

Thompson, Heather Ann. *Blood in the Water: The Attica Prison Uprising of 1971 and Its Legacy.* New York: Pantheon Books, 2016.

Toller, Ernst. *I Was a German: The Autobiography of a Revolutionary.* New York: Paragon House, 1991.

Vitale, Alex S. *The End of Policing.* New York: Verso, 2017.

West, Cornel. *Black Prophetic Fire.* Boston: Beacon Press, 2014.

———. *The Cornel West Reader.* New York: Basic Books, 1999.

———. *Race Matters.* New York: Vintage, 1994.

Wilder, Thornton. *Thornton Wilder: Collected Plays & Writings on Theater.* New York: Library of America, 2007.

Wilson, August. *Fences.* New York: Theater Communications Group, 2007.

———. *Joe Turner's Come and Gone.* New York: Theater Communications Group, 2007.

———. *The Piano Lesson.* New York: Theater Communications Group, 2007.

Zinn, Howard. *A People's History of the United States.* New York: Harper Perennial Modern Classics, 2015.

Notes

Epigraphs

1 William Shakespeare, *Hamlet, Prince of Denmark,* act 2, scene 2, lines 604–5, in *The Riverside Shakespeare,* textual ed. G. Blakemore Evans (Boston: Houghton Mifflin, 1974), 1159.

2. Michelle Alexander, *The New Jim Crow: Mass Incarceration in the Age of Colorblindness* (New York: New Press, 2010), 138.

3. Heather Ann Thompson, *Blood in the Water: The Attica Prison Uprising of 1971 and Its Legacy* (New York: Pantheon Books, 2016), 564–65.

one. The Call

1. James Baldwin, *I Am Not Your Negro* (New York: Vintage International, 2017), 49.

2. Rubin "Hurricane" Carter, *The Sixteenth Round: From Number 1 Contender to Number 45472* (New York: Penguin, 1974), 317.

3. Ibid., 323.

4. Ibid., 328.

5 Pruno, prison wine, is made by fermenting pilfered cut fruit, sugar cubes, and ketchup from the kitchen and mess hall. Pruno, in its most virulent form, can cause alcohol poisoning. It also produces a vicious hangover.

6. Eric Boettlert, "Dylan's 'Hurricane': A Look Back," *Rolling Stone,* June 21, 2000.

7. "BoxRec: James Scott," accessed May 6, 2020, https://boxrec.com /en/proboxer/2347.

8. Celia Chazelle first became interested in prisons after researching the treatment of those accused of crimes in the early medieval period. In early medieval society there was a premium placed on maintaining the integrity of the community and keeping the manpower in the community. Early medieval criminal justice centered, she found, around negotiations that provided restitution between opposing parties and peacemaking, rather than abstract notions of criminal law. The primary goal was not retribution, but to restrain violence, end feuds and punish offenders while maintaining social cohesion. Chazelle originally offered in 2008 to work as a teacher's aide at the Albert C. Wagner facility, but the prison administrator, Alfred Kandell, encouraged her to teach one of her college classes to students on the inside. She said when she first went to the white rural community of Bordentown, where the prison is located, she saw white children playing in a little league game across from the prison. She looked into the fenced-in yard of the prison and saw only Black and brown faces. "This is apartheid," she thought.

9. James Baldwin, *The Fire Next Time,* in *Collected Essays,* ed. Toni Morrison (New York: Library of America, 1998), 309–310.

10. Ibid., 314.

11. James Baldwin, *No Name in the Street*, in *Collected Essays*, ed. Toni Morrison (New York: Library of America, 1998), 460.

12. George Orwell, "Why I Write," in *An Age Like This, 1920–1940: The Collected Essays, Journalism, and Letters of George Orwell,* ed. Sonia Orwell and Ian Angus (New York: Harcourt, Brace & World, 1968), 6.

13. George Orwell, *Animal Farm* (Harmondsworth, UK: Penguin Books, 1981), 17.

14. George Orwell, *The Complete Works of George Orwell: I Belong to the Left: 1945,* ed. Peter Davison (London: Secker & Warburg, 1998), 227.

15. George Orwell, *The Complete Works of George Orwell: Smothered Under Journalism, 1946,* ed. Peter Davison (London: Secker & Warburg, 1998), 66.

16. James Baldwin, *The Fire Next Time*, in *Collected Essays*, ed. Toni Morrison (New York: The Library of America, 1998), 339.
17. James Baldwin, *The Creative Process*, in *Collected Essays*, ed. Toni Morrison (New York: Library of America, 1998), 670.
18. Ibid., 669.
19. "BOSS chair (Body Orifice Security Scanner)," Xeku Corp online, accessed May 7, 2020, https://bodyorificescanner.com/b-o-s -s-press/).
20. Nearly every prison has a small, dedicated group of writers who share books and critique, edit, and discuss the essays, poems, articles and manuscripts they write, as well as what they read. When the boxer Hurricane Carter was in Trenton State Prison and later Rahway, he gravitated to the writers. In his book *Eye of the Hurricane: My Path from Darkness to Freedom*, written with Ken Klonsky (Chicago: Lawrence Hill Books, 2011), 98, he writes:

    "I only had an eighth-grade education. Trenton State Prison and Rahway had other aspiring writers, there being an underground book industry growing in American prisons at the time, and we would help one another. Tommy Trantino, reputed to be a cop killer, wrote a group of short stories called *Lock the Lock* that was published four years after *The Sixteenth Round*. [Trantino was released on February 11, 2002, after spending thirty-eight years in the New Jersey prison system.] Frank Andrews, Al Dickens, I, and a few others wrote a prison short-story anthology, *Voices from the Big House*, that we published ourselves with help from David Rothenberg of the Fortune Society. Andrews was also writing his own book. Most of these guys had gone the same matriculation route from Jamesburg [State Home for Boys] that I had, so we were basically self-taught. If I had writer's block, I would send the pages down to Andrews, and he would get me straightened out. He also sent things to me, and I would provide him with a fresh perspective on his material. It also helped that I had read a lot as a child. Cowboy writers such as Louis L'Amour impressed me by the way they could keep a story fresh and interesting through powerful metaphor. I tried to imitate his writing style. I found out recently that he was also a former boxer."

21. New Jersey Prison Theater Cooperative, Chris Hedges, and Boris Franklin, *Caged* (Chicago: Haymarket Books, 2020), 21–22.
22. Ibid., 22.

two. The Antenna

1. Aleksandr Solzhenitsyn, *The Gulag Archipelago*, vol. 1 (New York: Harper Perennial Modern Classics, 2007), 186.
2. Duran Banks, Paul Ruddle, Erin Kennedy, and Michael G. Planty, *Arrest-Related Deaths Program Redesign Study, 2015–16: Preliminary Findings* (Washington, DC: Bureau of Justice Statistics, December 15, 2016), https://www.bjs.gov/content/pub/pdf/ardprs1516pf.pdf.
3. Mark Berman, John Sullivan, Julie Tate, and Jennifer Jenkins. "Protests Spread over Police Shootings. Police Promised Reforms. Every Year, They Still Shoot and Kill Nearly 1,000 People," *Washington Post* online, June 8, 2020, https://www.washingtonpost.com/investigations/protests-spread-over-police-shootings-police-promised-reforms-every-year-they-still-shoot-nearly-1000-people/2020/06/08/5c204f0c-a67c-11ea-b473-04905b1af82b_story.html.
4. Alexander, *The New Jim Crow*, 197.
5 Erica Goode, "Stronger Hand for Judges in the 'Bazaar' of Plea Deals," *The New York Times*, March 22, 2012, https://www.nytimes.com/2012/03/23/us/stronger-hand-for-judges-after-rulings-on-plea-deals.html.
6. Bureau of Justice Statistics, *Capital Punishments 1979*, 66, https://www.bjs.gov/content/pub/pdf/cp79.pdf.
7. Naomi Murakawa, *The First Civil Right* (New York: Oxford University Press, 2014), table A.5.
8. Ibid., 131.
9. Ibid.
10. *Congressional Record*, August 22, 1994, S12258, https://www.congress.gov/103/crecb/1994/08/22/GPO-CRECB-1994-pt17-4.pdf.
11. Murakawa, *First Civil Right*, 113, 142–43.
12. "Prisoners 1925–81," *Bureau of Justice Statistics Bulletin*, December 1982, table 1, https://www.bjs.gov/content/pub/pdf/p2581.pdf.

13. Jeff Stein, "The Clinton Dynasty's Horrific Legacy: How 'Tough-on-Crime' Politics Built the World's Largest Prison System," *Salon*, last modified April 13, 2015, https://www.salon.com/2015/04/13/the_clinton_dynastys_horrific_legacy_how_tough_on_crime_politics_built_the_worlds_largest_prison/.

14. Alexander, *New Jim Crow*, 195.

15. August Wilson, *The Piano Lesson* (New York: Theater Communications Group, 2007), 37–38.

three. **Mama Herc**

1. John Herbert, *Fortune and Men's Eyes* (New York: Grove Press, 1967), 23.

2. "Aramark, Get the Facts," https://www.aramark.com/landing-pages/corrections-facts, accessed May 17, 2020.

3. Aramark was acquired in 2007 for $8.3 billion by a group that included the giant investment firm Goldman Sachs and in 2018 brought in a reported $14 billion in revenues. Once a corporation such as Aramark takes over the prison food service, the old civilian kitchen staff, often unionized, are fired, and poorly paid temp workers take their places. In California, Aramark and Alameda County sheriff Gregory Ahern were sued in 2019 for using inmates to prepare and package more than sixteen thousand meals a day for jails in the state and not compensating the prisoner workers. Aramark is contracted to provide food to prisoners for as low as $1.20 a meal. Corrections officers, who once ate at the prison in mess halls staffed by prisoners, started bringing their own food to the prison—not only because the food doled out by Aramark is meager, of poor quality, and often spoiled, but also because prisoners began to have periodic bouts of diarrhea and vomiting. The food service at Union County Jail, a few blocks from St. Joseph, was run by Aramark.

4. Aramark has been plagued by scandal in jails and prisons across the country. The *Detroit Free Press* documented a range of abuses in 2015 by Aramark in Michigan prisons, including serving prisoners

maggot-ridden potatoes, drug smuggling by Aramark employees into the prison, and sexual relations with prisoners, incidents that led the state to cancel its contract with Aramark.

In April 2008 more than 270 prisoners at Florida's Santa Rosa Correctional Institution became ill after eating Aramark chili, while two months earlier, its chili had sickened some fifty inmates at Colorado's Larimer County Detention Center. Prisoners in Clayton County, Georgia, were not served hot food from October 2009 until January 2010 because the pressure cookers in the jail kitchen were inoperable. In February 2009 a health report commissioned by Camden County, New Jersey, found that the Aramark-run kitchen in the county jail had "mice throughout kitchen and storage area." Mouse droppings were discovered in butter. Several food items, including grits, chicken, rice, and beef, were not stored at temperatures low enough to protect against contamination. Prisoners at the county jail in Santa Barbara, California, went on a hunger strike to protest the Aramark food, and prisoners at Bayside State Prison in New Jersey did the same. Prisoners in Macomb County, Michigan, were reduced to eating only cold food because of a mold problem in the jail kitchen. In addition, auditors at Florida's Department of Corrections found that Aramark billed the state for $5 million worth of "phantom" meals.

When Eric J. Foss, the president and chief executive officer and president of Aramark Corporation, stepped down in 2019, he received nearly $17 million in total compensation: $1.7 million in salary, a $2.9 million bonus, $3.6 million in stock options, $8.4 million in stock, and $317,391 from other types of compensation.

I met later with Crystal Jordan, who had spent twenty-three years as a corrections officer in New Jersey and who worked at the Burlington County Jail, and another corrections officer at the jail, who did not want to be named. They told me that the food doled out by Aramark is not only substandard but often spoiled. For nearly a decade, Jordan filed complaints about the conditions in the jail, including persistent mold on walls and elsewhere, with the federal Occupational Safety and Health Administration (OSHA) and state and county officials. Her complaints brought negligible results.

"The big shift came in 2004 when the state got rid of the employees who worked in the kitchen and gave the food service contract to Aramark," she explained. Before then, "The food was not great, but the officers ate it along with the prisoners. Once Aramark came in, that changed. The bread was stale. I saw food in the kitchen with mold on it. The refrigerator broke down, and the food was left outside in the cold or trucked in from another facility. Those who ate the food began to get sick. The officers demanded the right to bring in their own food or order out, which the jail authorities granted. But the prisoners had no choice. Diarrhea and vomiting are common among the prisoners. A few weeks ago, one of the officers got a bowl of the prisoners' chili. We all told him not to eat it. He ended up with diarrhea.

"The kitchen where the food for the inmates is prepared in Burlington is a disaster," Jordan went on. "The walk-in freezer is corroded. You can't open it because of the stench inside. Stagnant water, mold, and mildew are everywhere. The food vans that bring food from Mount Holly, New Jersey, have maggots and no refrigeration. I have seen inmates served bread that has hair on it, luncheon meat that has mold on it, spoiled fruit and food on the trays that have bugs in it. But this is part of the deep cuts throughout the prison system. We have had periods in the jail when the inmates had no toilet paper, no sanitary napkins, no soap, and no surgical gloves for the officers, and there has been no bleach or Lysol available to disinfect the jail. Officers bring in their own personal supplies. We buy toilet paper and hand it out to the inmates ourselves."

Jordan showed me a copy of a complaint she had submitted to the Burlington County Department of Health, contending that Aramark employees had hidden a food van during a health inspector's visit to the jail so it could not be checked.

5. Charles P. Norman, "Fighting the Ninja," Pen America online, last modified June 24, 2008, https://pen.org/fighting-the-ninja/.
6. S. P. Sullivan, "Sexual Abuse of Inmates at N.J. Women's Prison Is

an 'Open Secret,' Federal Inquiry Finds," NJ Advance Media for NJ.com, last modified April 14, 2020, https://www.nj.com/corona virus/2020/04/sexual-abuse-of-inmates-at-nj-womens-prison-is-an -open-secret-federal-inquiry-finds.html.

7. Carter, *Sixteenth Round*, 170.
8. William Shakespeare, *The Merchant of Venice*, act 4, scene 1, lines 184–197, in *The Riverside Shakespeare*, textual ed. G. Blakemore Evans (Boston: Houghton Mifflin, 1974), 276–77.
9. Herbert, *Fortune and Men's Eyes*, 85–86.
10. William Shakespeare, "Sonnet 29," in *The Riverside Shakespeare*, textual ed. G. Blakemore Evans (Boston: Houghton Mifflin, 1974), 1754.

four. Rage and Terror

1. Baldwin, *I Am Not Your Negro*, 60.
2. Kuklinski's string of brutal killings were the subject of two documentaries on HBO called *The Iceman Tapes: Conversations with a Killer* and *The Iceman Confesses: Secrets of a Mafia Hitman*. Philip Carlo wrote *The Iceman: Confessions of a Mafia Hitman* in 2006 about Kuklinski (New York: St. Martin's Press, 2006).
3. Bruno Bettelheim, "Individual and Mass Behavior in Extreme Situations," in *Surviving and Other Essays* (New York: Alfred A. Knopf, 1979), 49.

In the essay, Bettelheim lists the goals of the gestapo administrators of the concentration camps—goals that are the same, although not always in this extreme form, for every society that has a large prison population. These goals were: [1] *"to break the prisoners as individuals* and change them into docile masses from which no individual or group act or resistance could arise; [2] *to spread terror among the rest of the population* by using prisoners as hostages for good behavior, and by demonstrating what happened to those who oppose Nazi rulers; [3] *to provide the gestapo members with a training ground* in which they were educated to lose all human emotions and attitudes and learn the most effective ways of breaking resistance in a defenseless civilian population; [4] *to provide the gestapo with an experimental laboratory* in which to study effective means for breaking civilian resistance, as well as the minimum nutritional, hygienic, and medical requirements needed to keep prisoners alive and able to perform hard labor when threat of punishment is the sole incentive, and the influence on performance if no time is allowed for anything but hard labor and the prisoners are separated from their families."

4. Ibid., 79.

5. This prisoner would eventually write letters to the funders of the college education program run by NJ-STEP, making baseless claims of fraud and mismanagement in an attempt to shut down a program he benefited from. He then filed a series of complaints against the prison administration at Rahway that led to him being transferred to the Supermax prison in Trenton, a transfer all prisoners dread.

6. One of the first stories I covered for the *New York Times* in June 1990 was the arrest of Thomas Pitera, a thirty-five-year-old martial arts enthusiast and a member of the Bonanno organized-crime family. Pitera, whose nickname was "Tommy Karate" and who owned a nightclub in Brooklyn, specialized in robbing and killing drug traffickers. Pitera would climb naked into the bathtub to decapitate his victim and sever the limbs from the body. The dismembered corpses were frequently buried in suitcases or plastic garbage bags on the edge of the William R. Davis Wildlife Refuge on Staten Island. When police raided his apartment at 2355 East Twelfth Street in the Gravesend section of Brooklyn, where he lived alone, they found more than sixty weapons, including automatic assault rifles, pistols, and dozens of knives. They also discovered a large collection of literature on torture, execution techniques, and Mafia history, including *The Hitman's Handbook*, *How to Kill*, and *Getting Started in the Illicit Drug Business*. It was estimated that Pitera had carried out dozens of killings, including the 1986 slaying of Wilfred "Willie Boy" Johnson, a former boxer and close associate of John Gotti, the head of the Gambino crime family. Johnson had for several years worked secretly as an informant for the FBI. Pitera's other victims included a woman who

made the "fatal mistake" of allowing Mr. Pitera's wife to die of a drug overdose, two men who insulted him, another suspected informer, and a man who was "in the wrong place at the wrong time," according to Elisa L. Liang, the federal prosecutor in the case.

Pitera recruited a group of young acolytes he called GITs—short for gangsters in training—to assist in the murders, dismemberments, and internments, where severed heads would often be buried apart from the bodies to make identification more difficult. More than a dozen of his young associates were arrested with him. Most pleaded guilty to various drug charges and testified against him. Pitera's operation oversaw the sale of about 220 pounds of cocaine a year, multi-kilos of heroin, and hundreds of pounds of marijuana. He was sentenced to life without parole. Carlo, who wrote the book about Kuklinski, also wrote a book about Pitera in 2009 called *The Butcher: Anatomy of a Mafia Psychopath.*

7. Anthony Bruno, *The Iceman: The True Story of a Cold-Blooded Killer* (New York: Bantam Books, 2013), 230–31.

8. Howard Taubman, "The Theater: *Dutchman,*" *New York Times*, March 25, 1964, 46, https://timesmachine.nytimes.com/timesmachine /1964/05/25/issue.html.

9. LeRoi Jones, *Dutchman* (New York: Harper Perennial, 1964), 16.

10. Ibid., 5–8.

11. Ginia Bellafante, "Why Amy Cooper's Use of 'African-American' Stung," *New York Times* online, May 29, 2020, https://www.nytimes .com/2020/05/29/nyregion/Amy-Cooper-Central-Park-racism .html.

12. Ibid.

13. Jae Jones, "The Ellenton Riot of 1876," Black Then, last modified September 7, 2019, https://blackthen.com/ellenton-riot-1876/.

14. Jasmine Aguilera, "Archeologists Have Located a Possible Mass Grave Associated with the 1921 Tulsa Race Riots. Here's What to Know," *Time* online, December 17, 2019, https://time.com/5751321 /archeologists-possible-mass-grave-1921-tulsa-race-riots/, accessed June 20, 2020.

15. Jessica Glenza, "Rosewood Massacre a Harrowing Tale of Racism

and the Road Toward Reparations," *Guardian* online (US edition), last modified January 3, 2016, https://www.theguardian.com /us-news/2016/jan/03/rosewood-florida-massacre-racial-violence -reparations.

16. Jones, *Dutchman,* 18.
17. Ibid., 19.
18. Ibid., 34.

five. The Song

1. August Wilson, *Joe Turner's Come and Gone* (New York: Theater Communications Group, 2007), 15.
2. Baldwin, *No Name in the Street,* 381.
3. Amiri Baraka, "The Black Artist in America," *Negro Digest*, April 1965, 65, 75–76.
4. Baldwin, *The Creative Process* in *Collected Essays*, ed. Toni Morrison (New York: Library of America, 1998), 670.
5. Leon F. Litwack, *Trouble in Mind: Black Southerners in the Age of Jim Crow* (New York: Vintage Books, 1999), 270.
6. Wilson, *Joe Turner,* 67–68.
7. Ibid., 82.
8. Chris Hedges, "War in the Gulf: The Soldiers; Still Time for Tenderness; G.I. Makes Last Call Home," February 21, 1991, *New York Times*, A1.
9. Ernst Toller, *I Was a German: The Autobiography of a Revolutionary* (New York: Paragon House, 1991), 261.
10. Ibid., 261–62.
11. "Singer Factories—Elizabethport, New Jersey, USA," singerse winginfo.co.uk (vintage Singer sewing machines information site), accessed May 8, 2020, https://www.singersewinginfo.co.uk/eliza bethport/.
12. William E. Geist, "Singer Plant Closing: A Way of Life Ends," *New York Times,* February 23, 1982, 1.
13. "QuickFacts Elizabeth City, New Jersey," US Census Bureau online, accessed May 8, 2020, https://www.census.gov/quickfacts /elizabethcitynewjersey.

six. **Rebels**

1. James Baldwin, "To Be Baptised," pt. 2 of *No Name in the Street,* in *Collected Essays*, ed. Toni Morrison (New York: Library of America, 1998), 472.

2. William Glaberson, "'Megan' Prosecution Rests After Rape Is Described," *New York Times* online, May 23, 1997, https://www.nytimes.com/1997/05/23/nyregion/megan-prosecution-rests-after-rape-is-described.html.

3. Miguel Piñero, *Short Eyes* (New York: Hill and Wang, 1993), 30–31.

4. A quadroon is one-quarter Black.

5. Ibid., 48–50.

6. Gresham M. Sykes, *The Society of Captives: A Study of a Maximum Security Prison* (Princeton, NJ: Princeton University Press, 2007), 100.

7. Harry Camisa, *Inside Out: Fifty Years Behind the Walls of New Jersey's Trenton State Prison* (Windsor, NJ: Windsor Press, 2003), 195.

8. *Hampton v. City of Chicago, Cook County, Illinois,* 339 F. Supp. 695 (N.D. Ill. 1972).

9. William Lee, "In 1969, Charismatic Black Panthers Leader Fred Hampton Was Killed in Hail of Gunfire. 50 Years Later, the Fight Against Police Brutality Continues," *Chicago Tribune* online, December 3, 2019, https://www.chicagotribune.com/news/ct-black-panthers-raid-fred-hampton-50-years-20191203-kbzgztrvtfh7tp7x4ggtvhncpm-story.html, accessed July 16, 2020.

10. Philip Taubman, "U.S. Files Its Rights Suit Charging Philadelphia Police with Brutality," *New York Times*, August 15, 1979, D15.

11. Jake Blumgart, "The Brutal Legacy of Frank Rizzo, the Most Notorious Cop in Philadelphia History," *Vice News* online, last modified October 22, 2015, https://www.vice.com/en_us/article/kwxp3m/remembering-frank-rizzo-the-most-notorious-cop-in-philadelphia-history-1022.

12. David Gambacorta and Barbara Laker, "Frank Rizzo Leaves a Legacy of Unchecked Police Brutality and Division in Philadelphia,"

Philadelphia Inquirer online, June 3, 2020, https://www.inquirer.com/news/philadelphia-frank-rizzo-police-violence-legacy-shootings-20200603.html.

13. In 1976 the Select Committee to Study Governmental Operations with Respect to Intelligence Activities of the United States Senate, known as the Church Committee after its chairman, Senator Frank Church, investigated COINTELPRO. In its final report the committee wrote:

"The Committee finds that the domestic activities of the intelligence community at times violated specific statutory prohibitions and infringed the constitutional rights of American citizens. The legal questions involved in intelligence programs were often not considered. On other occasions, they were intentionally disregarded in the belief that because the programs served the 'national security,' the law did not apply. While intelligence officers on occasion failed to disclose to their superiors programs which were illegal or of questionable legality, the Committee finds that the most serious breaches of duty were those of senior officials, who were responsible for controlling intelligence activities and generally failed to assure compliance with the law. Many of the techniques used would be intolerable in a democratic society even if all of the targets had been involved in violent activity, but COINTELPRO went far beyond that . . .

"[T]he Bureau conducted a sophisticated vigilante operation aimed squarely at preventing the exercise of First Amendment rights of speech and association, on the theory that preventing the growth of dangerous groups and the propagation of dangerous ideas would protect the national security and deter violence." Ward Churchill and Jim Vander Wall, *The COINTELPRO Papers: Documents from the FBI"'s Secret Wars Against Domestic Dissent in the United States* (Boston: South End Press, 1990).

14. Bryan Burrough, *Days of Rage: America's Radical Underground, the FBI, and the Forgotten Age of Revolutionary Violence* (New York: Penguin Books, 2015), 176.

15. Sha Be Allah, "Today in Hip Hop History: Assata Shakur Escapes

from Federal Prison," *Source* online, last modified November 3, 2014, https://thesource.com/2014/11/03/today-in-hip-hop-history -assata-shakur-escapes-from-federal-prison/.

16. Krissah Thompson, "Assata Shakur Was Convicted of Murder. Is She a Terrorist?," *Washington Post* online, May 8, 2013, https://www .washingtonpost.com/lifestyle/style/assata-shakur-was-convicted -of-murder-is-she-a-terrorist/2013/05/08/69acb602-b7e5-11e2-aa9e -a02b765ff0ea_story.html.

17. "Sundiata Acoli," Prisoner Solidarity, accessed July 17, 2020, https://www.prisonersolidarity.com/prisoner/sundiata-acoli.

18 The Republic of New Afrika (RNA) is a Black separatist organization founded in 1968 that was popular among many Black revolutionaries.

seven. **FAMILY**

1. "Playwright August Wilson on Writing About Black America," Moyers on Democracy, last modified February 25, 2017, https:// billmoyers.com/story/august-wilson-on-writing-about-black-america/.

2. August Wilson, *Fences* (New York: Theatre Communications Group, 2007), 49.

3. Ibid., 48.

4. Ibid., 49.

5. Ibid., 39.

6. Ibid., 50.

7. Ibid.

8. Ibid., 51.

9. Ibid., 52.

10. Ibid., 88.

11. A nonprofit organization based in Princeton, New Jersey, that works to exonerate innocent individuals who have been wrongly convicted and sentenced to life sentences or death.

12. "One Third of Black Men Have Felony Convictions," *Race & Justice News* (the Sentencing Project e-newsletter), October 10, 2017, https://www.sentencingproject.org/news/5593/.

eight. THE CODE

1. Mumia Abu Jamal, *Death Blossoms: Reflections from a Prisoner of Conscience* (New York: Litmus Press, 1996), 40.
2. Gresham M. Sykes, *The Society of Captives*, 102.
3. Hannah Arendt, *The Origins of Totalitarianism* (New York: Harcourt, 1976), 474.
4. Ibid.
5. Tarell Alvin McCraney, *The Brother/Sister Plays* (New York: Theatre Communications Group, 2010), 166–67.
6. Ibid., 150.
7. Ibid., 210–11.
8. Turtles, also known as Ninjas, are members of the Prison Special Operations Group (SOG), the prison's version of a SWAT team. The SOG teams, which handle disturbances in the prison, wear black uniforms, body armor, helmets with visors, shin guards, forearm pads, and are equipped with gas masks. They carry batons, shields, and pepper spray.
9. Muslim prayers.

nine. THE PLAY

1. Aleksandr Solzhenitsyn, *The Gulag Archipelago*, vol. 3 (New York: Harper Perennial, 2007), 433.
2. Paul Laurence Dunbar, "We Wear the Mask," in *The Norton Anthology of African American Literature*, ed. Henry Louis Gates and Nellie Y. McKay (New York: W. W. Norton, 1977), 896.
3. "Standard 620: Inmate Wages," State of New Jersey Department of Corrections, February 7, 1998, available at Prison Policy Initiative online, https://www.prisonpolicy.org/scans/New_Jersey_wages_Standard_620.pdf.

   Prisoners are paid from $1.30 up to $10 per day. General job assignments are paid $1.30 to $1.60 per day. Special job assignments are paid $1.40 to $10 per day. These jobs include food service, grounds and garden care, maintenance, sewage treatment and disposal, work release drivers, upholstery production and instruction, paraprofessionals, skilled tradesmen, farm and livestock work, highway detail, community service projects, and commissary. DEPTCOR, run by the New Jersey Department of Corrections, refurbishes furniture; makes baked goods, apparel, shoes, signs, and decals; and runs a print shop that produces letterheads, business cards and provides copy services. It pays at the high end of $10 per day. DEPTCOR products and services are sold outside the prison, severely undercutting local businesses that cannot compete.

4. Ted Otten, "Theater: 'Caged' Presented by Trenton's Passage Theater Company, *Times of Trenton* (New Jersey) online, May 2, 2018, https://www.nj.com/times-entertainment/2018/05/theater_caged _presented_by_tre.html.

5. Thorton Wilder, *Thorton Wilder: Collected Plays & Writings on Theater* (New York: Library of America, 2007), 56.

6. Tony Kushner, *Angels in America* (New York: Theatre Communications Group, 1995), 229–30.

7. Flannery O'Connor, *Mystery and Manners,* ed. Sally Fitzgerald and Robert Fitzgerald (New York: Farrar, Straus & Giroux, 1969), 35.

8. This number, with the Covid-19 crisis, has risen to eighteen million children. "Child Hunger Facts." Feeding America online, https://www.feedingamerica.org/hunger-in-america/child-hunger-facts.

9. Christopher Ingraham, "Amazon Paid No Federal Taxes on $11.2 Billion in Profits Last Year," *Washington Post* online, February 16, 2019, https://www.washingtonpost.com/us-policy/2019/02/16/amazon -paid-no-federal-taxes-billion-profits-last-year/.

10. Chuck Collins and Josh Hoxie, "The Three Wealthiest People in the United States Now Own More Wealth Than the Bottom Half of the Country Combined," Institute for Policy Studies, November 8, 2017.

11. Steven Rattner, "Autoworkers Face a Tough Road Ahead," *New York Times* online, September 23, 2019, https://www.nytimes.com /2019/09/23/opinion/gm-uaw-strike.html?searchResultPosition=1. Rattner points out that auto workers in the United States earn an average of $23.48 an hour, while Mexican auto workers are paid an average of $3.29 an hour—about 14 percent of what US workers make.

12. Ylan Q. Mui, "Americans Saw Wealth Plummet 40 Percent from 2007 to 2010, Federal Reserve Says," *Washington Post* online, June 11, 2012, https://www.washingtonpost.com/business/economy/fed-americans-wealth-dropped-40-percent/2012/06/11/gJQAllsCVV_story.html.

13. Timothy Williams, "Murder Rate Drops Across U.S., but Not in All Large Cities: The Decline in Killings and Property Crimes in 2018 Continues a Decades-Long Trend, According to F.B.I. Data," *New York Times* online, September 30, 2019, https://www.nytimes.com/2019/09/30/us/fbi-crime-data.html?searchResultPosition=1.

14. Bernard Shaw, *Major Barbara* (New York: Penguin Classics, 2000), 142.

15. Abraham Heschel, *The Prophets* (New York: Harper Perennial, 2001), 19.

16. William Sloan Coffin, *The Heart Is a Little to the Left: Essays on Public Morality* (Hanover, NH: Dartmouth College Press, 1999), 6.

Index